50% OFF FTCE General Knowledge

MW00783838

Dear Customer,

We consider it an honor and a privilege that you chose our FTCE General Knowledge Study Guide. As a way of showing our appreciation and to help us better serve you, we have partnered with Mometrix Test Prep to offer you **50% off their online FTCE GK Prep Course.** Many FTCE courses are needlessly expensive and don't deliver enough value. With their course, you get access to the best FTCE General Knowledge prep material, and you only pay half price.

Mometrix has structured their online course to perfectly complement your printed study guide. The FTCE GK Test Prep Course contains **in-depth lessons** that cover all the most important topics, over **500 practice questions** to ensure you feel prepared, more than **700 flashcards** for studying on the go, and over **200 instructional videos**.

Online FTCE General Knowledge Prep Course

Topics Covered:

English Language Skills

- o Foundations of Grammar
- o Clauses and Phrases
- o Style and Form

Reading

- o Prose and Poetry
- o Literary Analysis
- o Theme and Plot

Mathematics

- o Numbers and Operations
- o Classification of Functions
- o Linear Algebra

And More!

Course Features:

FTCE General Knowledge Study Guide

- o Get access to content from the best reviewed study guide available.

Track Your Progress

- o Their customized course allows you to check off content you have studied or feel confident with.

4 Full-Length Practice Tests

- o With 500+ practice questions and lesson reviews, you can test yourself again and again to build confidence.

FTCE General Knowledge Flashcards

- o Their course includes a flashcard mode consisting of over 700 content cards to help you study.

To receive this discount, visit them at www.mometrix.com/university/ftcegk/ or simply scan this QR code with your smartphone. At the checkout page, enter the discount code: **TPBFTCE50**

If you have any questions or concerns, please contact them at universityhelp@mometrix.com.

SCAN ME

FREE Test Taking Tips Video/DVD Offer

To better serve you, we created videos covering test taking tips that we want to give you for FREE. **These videos cover world-class tips that will help you succeed on your test.**

We just ask that you send us feedback about this product. Please let us know what you thought about it—whether good, bad, or indifferent.

To get your **FREE videos**, you can use the QR code below or email freevideos@studyguideteam.com with "Free Videos" in the subject line and the following information in the body of the email:

    a. The title of your product

    b. Your product rating on a scale of 1-5, with 5 being the highest

    c. Your feedback about the product

If you have any questions or concerns, please don't hesitate to contact us at info@studyguideteam.com.

Thank you!

FTCE General Knowledge Test Prep Book

3 Full-Length Practice Exams and FTCE Study Guide [9th Edition]

Joshua Rueda

Interested in buying more than 10 copies of our product? Contact us about bulk discounts:
bulkorders@studyguideteam.com

ISBN 13: 9781637752876
ISBN 10: 1637752873

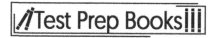

Table of Contents

Quick Overview -- *1*

Test-Taking Strategies --- *2*

FREE Videos/DVD OFFER --- *6*

Introduction to FTCE General Knowledge Test ---------------- *7*

Study Prep Plan for the FTCE General Knowledge Test ------- *9*

English Language Skills --- *11*

Language Structure -- 11

Vocabulary Application -- 20

Standard English Conventions -- 25

Practice Quiz --- 34

Answer Explanations --- 36

Math --- *37*

Number Sense, Concepts, and Operations --------------------------- 37

Geometry and Measurement --- 47

Algebraic Thinking and the Coordinate Plane ------------------------ 63

Probability, Statistics, and Data Interpretation--------------------- 72

Practice Quiz --- 89

Answer Explanations --- 91

Reading -- *92*

Key Ideas Based on Text Selections ---------------------------------- 92

Craft and Structure Based on Text Selections----------------------- 98

Integration of Information and Ideas -------------------------------- 105

Practice Quiz --- 114

//Test Prep Books!!!

Answer Explanations -- 116

Essay --117

Essay Skills-- 117

Practice Test #1 ---121

Answer Explanations #1---148

Practice Test #2 ---166

Answer Explanations #2---191

Practice Test #3 ---211

Answer Explanations #3---236

Quick Overview

As you draw closer to taking your exam, effective preparation becomes more and more important. Thankfully, you have this study guide to help you get ready. Use this guide to help keep your studying on track and refer to it often.

This study guide contains several key sections that will help you be successful on your exam. The guide contains tips for what you should do the night before and the day of the test. Also included are test-taking tips. Knowing the right information is not always enough. Many well-prepared test takers struggle with exams. These tips will help equip you to accurately read, assess, and answer test questions.

A large part of the guide is devoted to showing you what content to expect on the exam and to helping you better understand that content. In this guide are practice test questions so that you can see how well you have grasped the content. Then, answer explanations are provided so that you can understand why you missed certain questions.

Don't try to cram the night before you take your exam. This is not a wise strategy for a few reasons. First, your retention of the information will be low. Your time would be better used by reviewing information you already know rather than trying to learn a lot of new information. Second, you will likely become stressed as you try to gain a large amount of knowledge in a short amount of time. Third, you will be depriving yourself of sleep. So be sure to go to bed at a reasonable time the night before. Being well-rested helps you focus and remain calm.

Be sure to eat a substantial breakfast the morning of the exam. If you are taking the exam in the afternoon, be sure to have a good lunch as well. Being hungry is distracting and can make it difficult to focus. You have hopefully spent lots of time preparing for the exam. Don't let an empty stomach get in the way of success!

When travelling to the testing center, leave earlier than needed. That way, you have a buffer in case you experience any delays. This will help you remain calm and will keep you from missing your appointment time at the testing center.

Be sure to pace yourself during the exam. Don't try to rush through the exam. There is no need to risk performing poorly on the exam just so you can leave the testing center early. Allow yourself to use all of the allotted time if needed.

Remain positive while taking the exam even if you feel like you are performing poorly. Thinking about the content you should have mastered will not help you perform better on the exam.

Once the exam is complete, take some time to relax. Even if you feel that you need to take the exam again, you will be well served by some down time before you begin studying again. It's often easier to convince yourself to study if you know that it will come with a reward!

Test-Taking Strategies

1. Predicting the Answer

When you feel confident in your preparation for a multiple-choice test, try predicting the answer before reading the answer choices. This is especially useful on questions that test objective factual knowledge. By predicting the answer before reading the available choices, you eliminate the possibility that you will be distracted or led astray by an incorrect answer choice. You will feel more confident in your selection if you read the question, predict the answer, and then find your prediction among the answer choices. After using this strategy, be sure to still read all of the answer choices carefully and completely. If you feel unprepared, you should not attempt to predict the answers. This would be a waste of time and an opportunity for your mind to wander in the wrong direction.

2. Reading the Whole Question

Too often, test takers scan a multiple-choice question, recognize a few familiar words, and immediately jump to the answer choices. Test authors are aware of this common impatience, and they will sometimes prey upon it. For instance, a test author might subtly turn the question into a negative, or he or she might redirect the focus of the question right at the end. The only way to avoid falling into these traps is to read the entirety of the question carefully before reading the answer choices.

3. Looking for Wrong Answers

Long and complicated multiple-choice questions can be intimidating. One way to simplify a difficult multiple-choice question is to eliminate all of the answer choices that are clearly wrong. In most sets of answers, there will be at least one selection that can be dismissed right away. If the test is administered on paper, the test taker could draw a line through it to indicate that it may be ignored; otherwise, the test taker will have to perform this operation mentally or on scratch paper. In either case, once the obviously incorrect answers have been eliminated, the remaining choices may be considered. Sometimes identifying the clearly wrong answers will give the test taker some information about the correct answer. For instance, if one of the remaining answer choices is a direct opposite of one of the eliminated answer choices, it may well be the correct answer. The opposite of obviously wrong is obviously right! Of course, this is not always the case. Some answers are obviously incorrect simply because they are irrelevant to the question being asked. Still, identifying and eliminating some incorrect answer choices is a good way to simplify a multiple-choice question.

4. Don't Overanalyze

Anxious test takers often overanalyze questions. When you are nervous, your brain will often run wild, causing you to make associations and discover clues that don't actually exist. If you feel that this may be a problem for you, do whatever you can to slow down during the test. Try taking a deep breath or counting to ten. As you read and consider the question, restrict yourself to the particular words used by the author. Avoid thought tangents about what the author *really* meant, or what he or she was *trying* to say. The only things that matter on a multiple-choice test are the words that are actually in the question. You must avoid reading too much into a multiple-choice question, or supposing that the writer meant something other than what he or she wrote.

5. No Need for Panic

It is wise to learn as many strategies as possible before taking a multiple-choice test, but it is likely that you will come across a few questions for which you simply don't know the answer. In this situation, avoid panicking. Because most multiple-choice tests include dozens of questions, the relative value of a single wrong answer is small. As much as possible, you should compartmentalize each question on a multiple-choice test. In other words, you should not allow your feelings about one question to affect your success on the others. When you find a question that you either don't understand or don't know how to answer, just take a deep breath and do your best. Read the entire question slowly and carefully. Try rephrasing the question a couple of different ways. Then, read all of the answer choices carefully. After eliminating obviously wrong answers, make a selection and move on to the next question.

6. Confusing Answer Choices

When working on a difficult multiple-choice question, there may be a tendency to focus on the answer choices that are the easiest to understand. Many people, whether consciously or not, gravitate to the answer choices that require the least concentration, knowledge, and memory. This is a mistake. When you come across an answer choice that is confusing, you should give it extra attention. A question might be confusing because you do not know the subject matter to which it refers. If this is the case, don't eliminate the answer before you have affirmatively settled on another. When you come across an answer choice of this type, set it aside as you look at the remaining choices. If you can confidently assert that one of the other choices is correct, you can leave the confusing answer aside. Otherwise, you will need to take a moment to try to better understand the confusing answer choice. Rephrasing is one way to tease out the sense of a confusing answer choice.

7. Your First Instinct

Many people struggle with multiple-choice tests because they overthink the questions. If you have studied sufficiently for the test, you should be prepared to trust your first instinct once you have carefully and completely read the question and all of the answer choices. There is a great deal of research suggesting that the mind can come to the correct conclusion very quickly once it has obtained all of the relevant information. At times, it may seem to you as if your intuition is working faster even than your reasoning mind. This may in fact be true. The knowledge you obtain while studying may be retrieved from your subconscious before you have a chance to work out the associations that support it. Verify your instinct by working out the reasons that it should be trusted.

8. Key Words

Many test takers struggle with multiple-choice questions because they have poor reading comprehension skills. Quickly reading and understanding a multiple-choice question requires a mixture of skill and experience. To help with this, try jotting down a few key words and phrases on a piece of scrap paper. Doing this concentrates the process of reading and forces the mind to weigh the relative importance of the question's parts. In selecting words and phrases to write down, the test taker thinks about the question more deeply and carefully. This is especially true for multiple-choice questions that are preceded by a long prompt.

9. Subtle Negatives

One of the oldest tricks in the multiple-choice test writer's book is to subtly reverse the meaning of a question with a word like *not* or *except*. If you are not paying attention to each word in the question, you can easily be led astray by this trick. For instance, a common question format is, "Which of the following is…?" Obviously, if the question instead is, "Which of the following is not…?," then the answer will be quite different. Even worse, the test makers are aware of the potential for this mistake and will include one answer choice that would be correct if the question were not negated or reversed. A test taker who misses the reversal will find what he or she believes to be a correct answer and will be so confident that he or she will fail to reread the question and discover the original error. The only way to avoid this is to practice a wide variety of multiple-choice questions and to pay close attention to each and every word.

10. Reading Every Answer Choice

It may seem obvious, but you should always read every one of the answer choices! Too many test takers fall into the habit of scanning the question and assuming that they understand the question because they recognize a few key words. From there, they pick the first answer choice that answers the question they believe they have read. Test takers who read all of the answer choices might discover that one of the latter answer choices is actually *more* correct. Moreover, reading all of the answer choices can remind you of facts related to the question that can help you arrive at the correct answer. Sometimes, a misstatement or incorrect detail in one of the latter answer choices will trigger your memory of the subject and will enable you to find the right answer. Failing to read all of the answer choices is like not reading all of the items on a restaurant menu: you might miss out on the perfect choice.

11. Spot the Hedges

One of the keys to success on multiple-choice tests is paying close attention to every word. This is never truer than with words like almost, most, some, and sometimes. These words are called "hedges" because they indicate that a statement is not totally true or not true in every place and time. An absolute statement will contain no hedges, but in many subjects, the answers are not always straightforward or absolute. There are always exceptions to the rules in these subjects. For this reason, you should favor those multiple-choice questions that contain hedging language. The presence of qualifying words indicates that the author is taking special care with their words, which is certainly important when composing the right answer. After all, there are many ways to be wrong, but there is only one way to be right! For this reason, it is wise to avoid answers that are absolute when taking a multiple-choice test. An absolute answer is one that says things are either all one way or all another. They often include words like *every*, *always*, *best*, and *never*. If you are taking a multiple-choice test in a subject that doesn't lend itself to absolute answers, be on your guard if you see any of these words.

12. Long Answers

In many subject areas, the answers are not simple. As already mentioned, the right answer often requires hedges. Another common feature of the answers to a complex or subjective question are qualifying clauses, which are groups of words that subtly modify the meaning of the sentence. If the question or answer choice describes a rule to which there are exceptions or the subject matter is complicated, ambiguous, or confusing, the correct answer will require many words in order to be expressed clearly and accurately. In essence, you should not be deterred by answer choices that seem

4

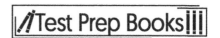

excessively long. Oftentimes, the author of the text will not be able to write the correct answer without offering some qualifications and modifications. Your job is to read the answer choices thoroughly and completely and to select the one that most accurately and precisely answers the question.

13. Restating to Understand

Sometimes, a question on a multiple-choice test is difficult not because of what it asks but because of how it is written. If this is the case, restate the question or answer choice in different words. This process serves a couple of important purposes. First, it forces you to concentrate on the core of the question. In order to rephrase the question accurately, you have to understand it well. Rephrasing the question will concentrate your mind on the key words and ideas. Second, it will present the information to your mind in a fresh way. This process may trigger your memory and render some useful scrap of information picked up while studying.

14. True Statements

Sometimes an answer choice will be true in itself, but it does not answer the question. This is one of the main reasons why it is essential to read the question carefully and completely before proceeding to the answer choices. Too often, test takers skip ahead to the answer choices and look for true statements. Having found one of these, they are content to select it without reference to the question above. Obviously, this provides an easy way for test makers to play tricks. The savvy test taker will always read the entire question before turning to the answer choices. Then, having settled on a correct answer choice, he or she will refer to the original question and ensure that the selected answer is relevant. The mistake of choosing a correct-but-irrelevant answer choice is especially common on questions related to specific pieces of objective knowledge. A prepared test taker will have a wealth of factual knowledge at their disposal, and should not be careless in its application.

15. No Patterns

One of the more dangerous ideas that circulates about multiple-choice tests is that the correct answers tend to fall into patterns. These erroneous ideas range from a belief that B and C are the most common right answers, to the idea that an unprepared test-taker should answer "A-B-A-C-A-D-A-B-A." It cannot be emphasized enough that pattern-seeking of this type is exactly the WRONG way to approach a multiple-choice test. To begin with, it is highly unlikely that the test maker will plot the correct answers according to some predetermined pattern. The questions are scrambled and delivered in a random order. Furthermore, even if the test maker was following a pattern in the assignation of correct answers, there is no reason why the test taker would know which pattern he or she was using. Any attempt to discern a pattern in the answer choices is a waste of time and a distraction from the real work of taking the test. A test taker would be much better served by extra preparation before the test than by reliance on a pattern in the answers.

FREE Videos/DVD OFFER

Doing well on your exam requires both knowing the test content and understanding how to use that knowledge to do well on the test. We offer completely FREE test taking tip videos. **These videos cover world-class tips that you can use to succeed on your test.**

To get your **FREE videos**, you can use the QR code below or email freevideos@studyguideteam.com with "Free Videos" in the subject line and the following information in the body of the email:

      a. The title of your product

      b. Your product rating on a scale of 1-5, with 5 being the highest

      c. Your feedback about the product

If you have any questions or concerns, please don't hesitate to contact us at info@studyguideteam.com.

Thanks again!

Introduction to FTCE General Knowledge Test

Function of the Test

In order to become a certified teacher in the state of Florida, a candidate must pass the Florida Teacher Certification Examinations (FTCE). In 2001, the No Child Left Behind Act began the administration of the FTCE. These exams are part of a teacher's certification process in the state of Florida. The Bureau of Educator Certification (BEC) determines the specific exams that a candidate needs to take to teach and become certified in Florida. The required tests depend on certifications that a candidate holds in other states or countries, their change of career status, and whether the candidate graduated from a teaching institute in Florida. In order to determine which tests to take, a candidate must submit an application to the BEC, who will then determine a candidate's testing requirements.

The FTCE General Knowledge (GK) exam is a computer-based test (CBT) that assesses the general knowledge of prospective teachers in the state of Florida and is designed to verify that teachers of all grades and subjects have the minimum necessary skills and knowledge across the general curricular areas. As such, all teachers seeking licensure in the state of Florida typically need to pass the GK exam. In some cases, sufficient scores on previously taken GRE exams may satisfy the GK requirement. Candidates must contact the BEC for an individual determination of exam requirements. The GK exam consists of four subtests: an Essay, English Language Skills, Reading, and Mathematics. The subtests may be attempted individually or combined in one testing appointment.

Test Administration

After the BEC determines which tests a candidate needs to take, an applicant can then register for a test; this application process is required prior to registering for the GK exam. Admission tickets are sent via email and must be presented at the test appointment along with proper identification. Exam sites are available throughout Florida and the United States.

A candidate must report to the test site 30 minutes before the appointment time on the admission ticket in order to complete pre-administration activities, such as an identity verification procedure, which includes a photo and palm scan. If a candidate wears glasses, a visual inspection is conducted, but the candidate's glasses will not be handled or touched. All personal items are kept in a secure storage area and a candidate receives an erasable notepad and pen. Then, a tutorial is given on how to take a computer-based test, as well as a test agreement and waiver. These processes need to be completed in 5 minutes. If the waiver is not accepted within 5 minutes, the candidate will be required to wait 31 calendar days before a retest, and he or she will not be given a refund. Breaks for the restroom are counted as part of the test time, unless scheduled breaks are given.

Candidates with disabilities need to complete an Alternative Testing Arrangements Request Form. The form must be submitted to FTCE customer service as soon as possible because test appointment cannot be made until approval.

Test Format

The FTCE GK exam is administered via computer and consists of four subtests. As mentioned, the subtests may be taken individually or in combination at a given testing appointment. A reference sheet with formulas and an on-screen calculator are provided for the Mathematics subtest.

The following table shows the breakdown of the subtests

Subtest	Allotted Time	Approximate Format
Essay	50 minutes	1 essay
English Language Skills	40 minutes	40 multiple choice questions
Reading	55 minutes	40 multiple choice questions
Mathematics	100 minutes	40 multiple choice questions

Test takers are permitted to take a 15-minute break if they are attempting all four subtests in one testing appointment.

Scoring

Test takers receive unofficial notification of their passing status for the multiple-choice subtests immediately upon completion. Official score reports are released within a month of the testing date for the multiple-choice subtests and within 6 weeks for the Essay subtest. Candidates must pass all four subtests in order to pass the General Knowledge exam. The Essay subtest is scored on a 12-point scale and test takers must receive at least an 8 to pass the section. The passing scaled score on each of the other three subtests is 200. Scaled scores are converted from raw scores, based on the number of correct responses. Score reports include an analysis of the test taker's performance for sections that he or she does not pass, as well as the numeric score that was achieved. For subtests that are passed, test takers simply receive the passing status notification but no numerical score is reported. Candidates wishing to take a retest must wait 31 calendar days after the most recent attempt before taking a retest.

Study Prep Plan for the FTCE General Knowledge Test

1 **Schedule -** Use one of our study schedules below or come up with one of your own.

2 **Relax -** Test anxiety can hurt even the best students. There are many ways to reduce stress. Find the one that works best for you.

3 **Execute -** Once you have a good plan in place, be sure to stick to it.

One Week Study Schedule		
Day 1	English Language Skills	
Day 2	Math	
Day 3	Algebraic Thinking and the Coordinate Plane	
Day 4	Reading	
Day 5	Practice Test #1 & #2	
Day 6	Practice Test #3	
Day 7	Take Your Exam!	

Two Week Study Schedule			
Day 1	English Language Skills	Day 8	Reading
Day 2	Standard English Conventions	Day 9	Integration of Information and Ideas
Day 3	Practice Quiz	Day 10	Practice Quiz
Day 4	Math	Day 11	Practice Test #1
Day 5	Algebraic Thinking and the Coordinate Plane	Day 12	Practice Test #2
Day 6	Probability, Statistics, and Data Interpretation	Day 13	Practice Test #3
Day 7	Practice Quiz	Day 14	Take Your Exam!

One Month Study Schedule						
Day 1	English Language Skills	Day 11	The Pythagorean Theorem	Day 21	Identifying Literary Contexts
Day 2	Commonly Confused Words	Day 12	Algebraic Thinking and the Coordinate Plane	Day 22	Practice Quiz
Day 3	Vocabulary Application	Day 13	Solving Linear Equations	Day 23	Essay
Day 4	Standard English Conventions	Day 14	Probability, Statistics, and Data Interpretation	Day 24	Practice Test #1
Day 5	Spelling	Day 15	Mean, Median, Mode, and Range	Day 25	Answer Explanations
Day 6	Practice Quiz	Day 16	Conditional Probabilities	Day 26	Practice Test #2
Day 7	Math	Day 17	Practice Quiz	Day 27	Answer Explanations
Day 8	Word Problems and Applications	Day 18	Reading	Day 28	Practice Test #3
Day 9	Geometry and Measurement	Day 19	Craft and Structure Based on Text Selections	Day 29	Answer Explanations
Day 10	Symmetry	Day 20	Integration of Information and Ideas	Day 30	Take Your Exam!

English Language Skills

Language Structure

Dangling and Misplaced Modifiers

Modifiers enhance meaning by clarifying or giving greater detail about another part of a sentence. However, incorrectly-placed modifiers have the opposite effect and can cause confusion. A **misplaced modifier** is a modifier that is not located appropriately in relation to the word or phrase that it modifies:

> Because he was one of the greatest thinkers of Renaissance Italy, John idolized Leonardo da Vinci.

In this sentence, the modifier is "because he was one of the greatest thinkers of Renaissance Italy," and the noun it is intended to modify is "Leonardo da Vinci." However, due to the placement of the modifier next to the subject, John, it seems as if the sentence is stating that John was a Renaissance genius, not Da Vinci.

> John idolized Leonard da Vinci because he was one of the greatest thinkers of Renaissance Italy.

The modifier is now adjacent to the appropriate noun, clarifying which of the two men in this sentence is the greatest thinker.

Dangling modifiers modify a word or phrase that is not readily apparent in the sentence. That is, they "dangle" because they are not clearly attached to anything:

> After getting accepted to college, Amir's parents were proud.

The modifier here, "after getting accepted to college," should modify who got accepted. The noun immediately following the modifier is "Amir's parents"—but they are probably not the ones who are going to college.

> After getting accepted to college, Amir made his parents proud.

The subject of the sentence has been changed to Amir himself, and now the subject and its modifier are appropriately matched.

Parallelism

Parallel structure occurs when phrases or clauses within a sentence contain the same structure. Parallelism increases readability and comprehensibility because it is easy to tell which sentence elements are paired with each other in meaning.

> Jennifer enjoys cooking, knitting, and to spend time with her cat.

This sentence is not parallel because the items in the list appear in two different forms. Some are **gerunds**, which is the verb + ing: *cooking, knitting.* The other item uses the **infinitive** form, which is to + verb: *to spend.* To create parallelism, all items in the list may reflect the same form:

> Jennifer enjoys cooking, knitting, and spending time with her cat.

11

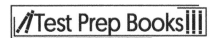

All of the items in the list are now in gerund forms, so this sentence exhibits parallel structure. Here's another example:

> The company is looking for employees who are responsible and with a lot of experience.

Again, the items that are listed in this sentence are not parallel. "Responsible" is an adjective, yet "with a lot of experience" is a prepositional phrase. The sentence elements do not utilize parallel parts of speech.

> The company is looking for employees who are responsible and experienced.

"Responsible" and "experienced" are both adjectives, so this sentence now has parallel structure.

Sentence Fragments

A complete sentence requires a verb and a subject, and it must express a complete thought. Sometimes, the subject is omitted in the case of the implied *you*, used in sentences that are the command or imperative form, like "Look!" or "Give me that." It is understood that the subject of the command is *you*, the listener or reader, so it is possible to have a structure without an explicit subject. Without these elements, though, the sentence is incomplete—it is a **sentence fragment**. While sentence fragments often occur in conversational English or creative writing, they are generally not appropriate in academic writing. Sentence fragments often occur when dependent clauses are not joined to an independent clause:

> *Sentence fragment*: Because the airline overbooked the flight.

The sentence above is a dependent clause that does not express a complete thought. What happened as a result of this cause? With the addition of an independent clause, this now becomes a complete sentence:

> *Complete sentence*: Because the airline overbooked the flight, several passengers were unable to board.

Sentences fragments may also occur through improper use of conjunctions:

> I'm going to the Bahamas for spring break. And to New York City for New Year's Eve.

While the first sentence above is a complete sentence, the second one is not because it is a prepositional phrase that lacks a subject [I] and a verb [am going]. Joining the two together with the coordinating conjunction forms one grammatically-correct sentence:

> I'm going to the Bahamas for spring break and to New York City for New Year's Eve.

Run-ons

A **run-on** is a sentence with too many independent clauses that are improperly connected to each other:

> This winter has been very cold some farmers have suffered damage to their crops.

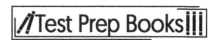

The sentence above has two subject-verb combinations. The first is "this winter has been"; the second is "some farmers have suffered." However, they are simply stuck next to each other without any punctuation or conjunction. Therefore, the sentence is a run-on.

Another type of run-on occurs when writers use inappropriate punctuation:

This winter has been very cold, some farmers have suffered damage to their crops.

Though a comma has been added, this sentence is still not correct. When a comma alone is used to join two independent clauses, it is known as a **comma splice**. Without an appropriate conjunction, a comma cannot join two independent clauses by itself.

Run-on sentences can be corrected by either dividing the independent clauses into two or more separate sentences or inserting appropriate conjunctions and/or punctuation. The run-on sentence can be amended by separating each subject-verb pair into its own sentence:

This winter has been very cold. Some farmers have suffered damage to their crops.

The run-on can also be fixed by adding a comma and conjunction to join the two independent clauses with each other:

This winter has been very cold, so some farmers have suffered damage to their crops.

Inconsistent Verb Tense

Verb tense reflects when an action occurred or a state existed. For example, the tense known as **simple present** expresses something that is happening right now or that happens regularly:

She *works* in a hospital.

Present continuous tense expresses something in progress. It is formed by to be + verb + -ing.

Sorry, I can't go out right now. I *am doing* my homework.

Past tense is used to describe events that previously occurred. However, in conversational English, speakers often use present tense or a mix of past and present tense when relating past events because it gives the narrative a sense of immediacy. In formal written English, though, consistency in verb tense is necessary to avoid reader confusion.

I traveled to Europe last summer. As soon as I stepped off the plane, I feel like I'm in a movie! I'm surrounded by quaint cafes and impressive architecture.

The passage above abruptly switches from past tense—*traveled*, *stepped*—to present tense—*feel*, *am surrounded*.

I *traveled* to Europe last summer. As soon as I *stepped* off the plane, I *felt* like I was in a movie! I *was surrounded* by quaint cafes and impressive architecture.

All verbs are in past tense, so this passage now has consistent verb tense.

13

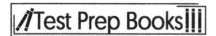

Split Infinitives

The **infinitive form** of a verb consists of "to + base verb"—e.g., to walk, to sleep, to approve. A **split infinitive** occurs when another word, usually an adverb, is placed between *to* and the verb:

I decided *to simply walk* to work to get more exercise every day.

The infinitive *to walk* is split by the adverb *simply*.

It was a mistake *to hastily approve* the project before conducting further preliminary research.

The infinitive *to approve* is split by *hastily*.

Although some grammarians still advise against split infinitives, this syntactic structure is common in both spoken and written English and is widely accepted in standard usage.

Subject-Verb Agreement

In English, verbs must agree with the subject. The form of a verb may change depending on whether the subject is singular or plural, or whether it is first, second, or third person. For example, the verb *to be* has various forms:

I am a student.

You are a student.

She is a student.

We are students.

They are students.

Errors occur when a verb does not agree with its subject. Sometimes, the error is readily apparent:

We is hungry.

Is is not the appropriate form of *to be* when used with the third person plural *we*.

We are hungry.

This sentence now has correct subject-verb agreement.

However, some cases are trickier, particularly when the subject consists of a lengthy noun phrase with many modifiers:

Students who are hoping to accompany the anthropology department on its annual summer trip to Ecuador needs to sign up by March 31st.

The verb in this sentence is *needs*. However, its subject is not the noun adjacent to it—Ecuador. The subject is the noun at the beginning of the sentence—students. Because *students* is plural, *needs* is the incorrect verb form.

> *Students* who are hoping to accompany the anthropology department on its annual summer trip to Ecuador *need* to sign up by March 31st.

This sentence now uses correct agreement between *students* and *need*.

Another case to be aware of is a **collective noun**. A collective noun refers to a group of many things or people but can be singular in itself—e.g., family, committee, army, pair team, council, jury. Whether or not a collective noun uses a singular or plural verb depends on how the noun is being used. If the noun refers to the group performing a collective action as one unit, it should use a singular verb conjugation:

> The family is moving to a new neighborhood.

The whole family is moving together in unison, so the singular verb form *is* is appropriate here.

> The committee has made its decision.

The verb *has* and the possessive pronoun *its* both reflect the word *committee* as a singular noun in the sentence above; however, when a collective noun refers to the group as individuals, it can take a plural verb:

> The newlywed pair spend every moment together.

This sentence emphasizes the love between two people in a pair, so it can use the plural verb *spend*.

> The council are all newly elected members.

The sentence refers to the council in terms of its individual members and uses the plural verb *are*.

Overall, though, American English is more likely to pair a collective noun with a singular verb, while British English is more likely to pair a collective noun with a plural verb.

Colons and Semicolons

In a sentence, **colons** are used before a list, a summary or elaboration, or an explanation related to the preceding information in the sentence:

> There are two ways to reserve tickets for the performance: by phone or in person.

> One thing is clear: students are spending more on tuition than ever before.

As these examples show, a colon must be preceded by an independent clause. However, the information after the colon may be in the form of an independent clause or in the form of a list.

Semicolons can be used in two different ways—to join ideas or to separate them. In some cases, semicolons can be used to connect what would otherwise be stand-alone sentences. Each part of the sentence joined by a semicolon must be an independent clause. The use of a semicolon indicates that these two independent clauses are closely related to each other:

> The rising cost of childcare is one major stressor for parents; healthcare expenses are another source of anxiety.

> Classes have been canceled due to the snowstorm; check the school website for updates.

Semicolons can also be used to divide elements of a sentence in a more distinct way than simply using a comma. This usage is particularly useful when the items in a list are especially long and complex and contain other internal punctuation.

> Retirees have many modes of income: some survive solely off their retirement checks; others supplement their income through part time jobs, like working in a supermarket or substitute teaching; and others are financially dependent on the support of family members, friends, and spouses.

Commonly Confused Words

Its and It's

These pronouns are some of the most confused in the English language as most possessives contain the suffix –'s. However, for *it*, it is the opposite. *Its* is a possessive pronoun:

> The government is reassessing *its* spending plan.

It's is a contraction of the words *it is*:

> *It's* snowing outside.

Saw and Seen

Saw and *seen* are both conjugations of the verb *to see*, but they express different verb tenses. *Saw* is used in the simple past tense. *Seen* is the past participle form of *to see* and can be used in all perfect tenses.

> I seen her yesterday.

This sentence is incorrect. Because it expresses a completed event from a specified point in time in the past, it should use simple past tense:

> I *saw* her yesterday.

This sentence uses the correct verb tense. Here's how the past participle is used correctly:

> I *have seen* her before.

The meaning in this sentence is slightly changed to indicate an event from an unspecific time in the past. In this case, present perfect is the appropriate verb tense to indicate an unspecified past experience. Present perfect conjugation is created by combining *to have* + past participle.

Then and Than

Then is generally used as an adverb indicating something that happened next in a sequence or as the result of a conditional situation:

> We parked the car and *then* walked to the restaurant.

> If enough people register for the event, *then* we can begin planning.

Than is a conjunction indicating comparison:

> This watch is more expensive *than* that one.

> The bus departed later *than* I expected.

They're, Their, and There

They're is a contraction of the words *they are*:

> *They're* moving to Ohio next week.

Their is a possessive pronoun:

> The baseball players are training for *their* upcoming season.

There can function as multiple parts of speech, but it is most commonly used as an adverb indicating a location:

> Let's go to the concert! Some great bands are playing *there*.

Insure and Ensure

These terms are both verbs. *Insure* means to guarantee something against loss, harm, or damage, usually through an insurance policy that offers monetary compensation:

> The robbers made off with her prized diamond necklace, but luckily it was *insured* for one million dollars.

Ensure means to make sure, to confirm, or to be certain:

> *Ensure* that you have your passport before entering the security checkpoint.

Accept and Except

Accept is a verb meaning to take or agree to something:

> I would like to *accept* your offer of employment.

Except is a preposition that indicates exclusion:

> I've been to every state in America *except* Hawaii.

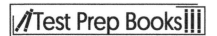

Affect and Effect

Affect is a verb meaning to influence or to have an impact on something:

> The amount of rainfall during the growing season *affects* the flavor of wine produced from these grapes.

Effect can be used as either a noun or a verb. As a noun, *effect* is synonymous with a result:

> If we implement the changes, what will the *effect* be on our profits?

As a verb, *effect* means to bring about or to make happen:

> In just a few short months, the health committee has *effected* real change in school nutrition.

Organization

Good writing is not merely a random collection of sentences. No matter how well written, sentences must relate and coordinate appropriately with one another. If not, the writing seems random, haphazard, and disorganized. Therefore, good writing must be organized, where each sentence fits a larger context and relates to the sentences around it.

Transition Words

The writer should act as a guide, showing the reader how all the sentences fit together. Consider this example concerning seat belts:

> Seat belts save more lives than any other automobile safety feature. Many studies show that airbags save lives as well. Not all cars have airbags. Many older cars don't. Air bags aren't entirely reliable. Studies show that in 15 percent of accidents, airbags don't deploy as designed. Seat belt malfunctions are extremely rare.

There's nothing wrong with any of these sentences individually, but together they're disjointed and difficult to follow. The best way for the writer to communicate information is through the use of transition words. Here are examples of transition words and phrases that tie sentences together, enabling a more natural flow:

- To show causality: as a result, therefore, and consequently
- To compare and contrast: *however*, *but*, and *on the other hand*
- To introduce examples: *for example*, *namely*, and *including*
- To show order of importance: *foremost*, *primarily*, *secondly*, and *lastly*

Note that this is not a complete list of transitions. There are many more that can be used; however, most fit into these or similar categories. The important point is that the words should clearly show the relationship between sentences, supporting information, and the main idea.

18

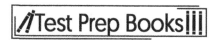

Here is an update to the previous example using transition words. These changes make it easier to read and bring clarity to the writer's points:

> Seat belts save more lives than any other automobile safety feature. Many studies show that airbags save lives as well; however, not all cars have airbags. For example, some older cars don't. Furthermore, air bags aren't entirely reliable. For example, studies show that in 15 percent of accidents, airbags don't deploy as designed, but, on the other hand, seat belt malfunctions are extremely rare.

Also, be prepared to analyze whether the writer is using the best transition word or phrase for the situation. Take this sentence for example: "As a result, seat belt malfunctions are extremely rare." This sentence doesn't make sense in the context above because the writer is trying to show the contrast between seat belts and airbags, not the causality.

Logical Sequence

Even if the writer includes plenty of information to support their point, the writing is only coherent when the information is in a logical order. First, the writer should introduce the main idea, whether for a paragraph, a section, or the entire piece. Second, they should present evidence to support the main idea by using transitional language. This shows the reader how the information relates to the main idea and to the sentences around it. The writer should then take time to interpret the information, making sure necessary connections are obvious to the reader. Finally, the writer can summarize the information in a closing section.

Though most writing follows this pattern, it isn't a set rule. Sometimes writers change the order for effect. For example, the writer can begin with a surprising piece of supporting information to grab the reader's attention, and then transition to the main idea. Thus, if a passage doesn't follow the logical order, don't immediately assume it's wrong. However, most writing usually settles into a logical sequence after a nontraditional beginning.

Introductions and Conclusions

Examining the writer's strategies for introductions and conclusions puts the reader in the right mindset to interpret the rest of the text. Look for methods the writer might use for introductions such as:

- Stating the main point immediately, followed by outlining how the rest of the piece supports this claim.

- Establishing important, smaller pieces of the main idea first, and then grouping these points into a case for the main idea.

- Opening with a quotation, anecdote, question, seeming paradox, or other piece of interesting information, and then using it to lead to the main point.

Whatever method the writer chooses, the introduction should make their intention clear, establish their voice as a credible one, and encourage a person to continue reading.

Conclusions tend to follow a similar pattern. In them, the writer restates their main idea a final time, often after summarizing the smaller pieces of that idea. If the introduction uses a quote or anecdote to grab the reader's attention, the conclusion often makes reference to it again. Whatever way the writer

19

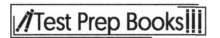

chooses to arrange the conclusion, the final restatement of the main idea should be clear and simple for the reader to interpret. Finally, conclusions shouldn't introduce any new information.

Vocabulary Application

Words and Phrases in Context

There will be many occasions in one's reading career in which an unknown word or a word with multiple meanings will pop up. There are ways of determining what these words or phrases mean that do not require the use of the dictionary, which is especially helpful during a test where one may not be available. Even outside of the exam, knowing how to derive an understanding of a word via context clues will be a critical skill in the real world. The **context** is the circumstances in which a story or a passage is happening and can usually be found in the series of words directly before or directly after the word or phrase in question. The clues are the words that hint towards the meaning of the unknown word or phrase.

There may be questions that ask about the meaning of a particular word or phrase within a passage. There are a couple ways to approach these kinds of questions:

- Define the word or phrase in a way that is easy to comprehend (using context clues).
- Try out each answer choice in place of the word.

To demonstrate, here's an example from *Alice in Wonderland*:

> Alice was beginning to get very tired of sitting by her sister on the bank, and of having nothing to do: once or twice she peeped into the book her sister was reading, but it had no pictures or conversations in it, "and what is the use of a book," thought Alice, "without pictures or conversations?"

> Q: As it is used in the selection, the word peeped means:

Using the first technique, before looking at the answers, define the word "peeped" using context clues and then find the matching answer. Then, analyze the entire passage in order to determine the meaning, not just the surrounding words.

To begin, imagine a blank where the word should be and put a synonym or definition there: "once or twice she _____ into the book her sister was reading." The context clue here is the book. It may be tempting to put "read" where the blank is, but notice the preposition word, "into." One does not read *into* a book, one simply reads a book, and since reading a book requires that it is seen with a pair of eyes, then "look" would make the most sense to put into the blank: "once or twice she looked into the book her sister was reading."

Once an easy-to-understand word or synonym has been supplanted, readers should check to make sure it makes sense with the rest of the passage. What happened after she looked into the book? She thought to herself how a book without pictures or conversations is useless. This situation in its entirety makes sense.

This material is provided for exam preparation purposes only and does not indicate an endorsement of any specific scientific, political, or religious point of view. © TPB Publishing. You have been licensed one copy of this document for personal use only. Any other reproduction or redistribution is strictly prohibited. All rights reserved.

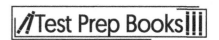

Now check the answer choices for a match:
   a. To make a high-pitched cry
   b. To smack
   c. To look curiously
   d. To pout

Since the word was already defined, Choice C is the best option.

Using the second technique, replace the figurative blank with each of the answer choices and determine which one is the most appropriate. Remember to look further into the passage to clarify that they work, because they could still make sense out of context.
   a. Once or twice she <u>made a high pitched cry</u> into the book her sister was reading
   b. Once or twice she <u>smacked</u> into the book her sister was reading
   c. Once or twice she <u>looked curiously</u> into the book her sister was reading
   d. Once or twice she <u>pouted</u> into the book her sister was reading

For Choice A, it does not make much sense in any context for a person to yell into a book, unless maybe something terrible has happened in the story. Given that afterward Alice thinks to herself how useless a book without pictures is, this option does not make sense within context.

For Choice B, smacking a book someone is reading may make sense if the rest of the passage indicates a reason for doing so. If Alice was angry or her sister had shoved it in her face, then maybe smacking the book would make sense within context. However, since whatever she does with the book causes her to think, "what is the use of a book without pictures or conversations?" then answer Choice B is not an appropriate answer. Answer Choice C fits well within context, given her subsequent thoughts on the matter. Answer Choice D does not make sense in context or grammatically, as people do not "pout into" things.

This is a simple example to illustrate the techniques outlined above. There may, however, be a question in which all of the definitions are correct and also make sense out of context, in which the appropriate context clues will really need to be honed in in order to determine the correct answer. For example, here is another passage from *Alice in Wonderland*:

> . . . but when the Rabbit actually took a watch out of its waistcoat pocket, and looked at it, and then hurried on, Alice <u>started</u> to her feet, for it flashed across her mind that she had never before seen a rabbit with either a waistcoat-pocket or a watch to take out of it, and burning with curiosity, she ran across the field after it, and was just in time to see it pop down a large rabbit-hole under the hedge.

Q: As it is used in the passage, the word started means
   a. To turn on
   b. To begin
   c. To move quickly
   d. To be surprised

All of these words qualify as a definition of "start," but using context clues, the correct answer can be identified using one of the two techniques above. It's easy to see that one does not turn on, begin, or be surprised to one's feet. The selection also states that she "ran across the field after it," indicating that she was in a hurry. Therefore, to move quickly would make the most sense in this context.

The same strategies can be applied to vocabulary that may be completely unfamiliar. In this case, focus on the words before or after the unknown word in order to determine its definition. Take this sentence, for example:

> Sam was such a <u>miser</u> that he forced Andrew to pay him twelve cents for the candy, even though he had a large inheritance and he knew his friend was poor.

Unlike with assertion questions, for vocabulary questions, it may be necessary to apply some critical thinking skills that may not be explicitly stated within the passage. Think about the implications of the passage, or what the text is trying to say. With this example, it is important to realize that it is considered unusually stingy for a person to demand so little money from someone instead of just letting their friend have the candy, especially if this person is already wealthy. Hence, a <u>miser</u> is a greedy or stingy individual.

Questions about complex vocabulary may not be explicitly asked, but this is a useful skill to know. If there is an unfamiliar word while reading a passage and its definition goes unknown, it is possible to miss out on a critical message that could inhibit the ability to appropriately answer the questions. Practicing this technique in daily life will sharpen this ability to derive meanings from context clues with ease.

Idiomatic Usage and Misused Words

A figure of speech, sometimes called an **idiom**, is a rhetorical device. It's a phrase that is not intended to be taken literally.

When the writer uses a figure of speech, their intention must be clear if it's to be used effectively. Some phrases can be interpreted in a number of ways, causing confusion for the reader. Look for clues to the writer's true intention to determine the best replacement. Likewise, some figures of speech may seem out of place in a more formal piece of writing. To show this, here is another example involving seat belts:

> Seat belts save more lives than any other automobile safety feature. Many studies show that airbags save lives as well, however not all cars have airbags. For example, some older cars don't. In addition, air bags aren't entirely reliable. For example, studies show that in 15 percent of accidents, airbags don't deploy as designed, but, on the other hand, seat belt malfunctions happen once in a blue moon.

Most people know that "once in a blue moon" refers to something that rarely happens. However, because the rest of the paragraph is straightforward and direct, using this figurative phrase distracts the reader. In this example, the earlier version is much more effective.

Now it's important to take a moment and review the meaning of the word *literally*. This is because it's one of the most misunderstood and misused words in the English language. *Literally* means that something is exactly what it says it is, and there can be no interpretation or exaggeration. Unfortunately, *literally* is often used for emphasis as in the following example:

> This morning, I literally couldn't get out of bed.

This sentence meant to say that the person was extremely tired and wasn't able to get up. However, the sentence can't *literally* be true unless that person was tied down to the bed, paralyzed, or affected by a strange situation that the writer (most likely) didn't intend. Here's another example:

> I literally died laughing.

The writer tried to say that something was very funny. However, unless they're writing this from beyond the grave, it can't *literally* be true.

Note that this doesn't mean that writers can't use figures of speech. The colorful use of language and idioms make writing more interesting and draw in the reader. However, for these kinds of expressions to be used correctly, they cannot include the word *literally*.

Diction

An author's choice of words—also referred to as **diction**—helps to convey their meaning in a particular way. Through diction, an author can convey a particular tone—e.g., a humorous tone, a serious tone—in order to support the thesis in a meaningful way to the reader.

Identifying Variation in Dialect and Diction

Language arts educators often seem to be in the position of teaching the "right" way to use English, particularly in lessons about grammar and vocabulary. However, all it takes is back-to-back viewings of speeches by the queen of England and the president of the United States or side-by-side readings of a contemporary poem and one written in the 1600s to come to the conclusion that there is no single, fixed, correct form of spoken or written English. Instead, language varies and evolves across different regions and time periods. It also varies between cultural groups depending on factors such as race, ethnicity, age, and socioeconomic status. Students should come away from a language arts class with more than a strictly prescriptive view of language; they should have an appreciation for its rich diversity.

It is important to understand some key terms in discussing linguistic variety.

Language is a tool for communication. It may be spoken, unspoken—as with body language—written, or codified in other ways. Language is symbolic in the sense that it can describe objects, ideas, and events that are not actually present, have not actually occurred, or only exist in the mind of the speaker. All languages are governed by systematic rules of grammar and semantics. These rules allow speakers to manipulate a finite number of elements, such as sounds or written symbols, to create an infinite number of meanings.

A **dialect** is a distinct variety of a language in terms of patterns of grammar, vocabulary, and/or **phonology**—the sounds used by its speakers—that distinguish it from other forms of that language. Two dialects are not considered separate languages if they are **mutually intelligible**—if speakers of each dialect are able to understand one another. A dialect is not a subordinate version of a language. Examples of English dialects include Scottish English and American Southern English.

By definition, **Standard English** is a dialect. It is one variety of English with its own usage of grammar, vocabulary, and pronunciation. Given that Standard English is taught in schools and used in places like government, journalism, and other professional workplaces, it is often elevated above other English dialects. Linguistically, though, there is nothing that makes Standard English more correct or advanced than other dialects.

A **pidgin** is formed when speakers of different languages begin utilizing a simplified mixture of elements from both languages to communicate with each other. In North America, pidgins occurred when Africans were brought to European colonies as slaves, leading to a mixture of African and European languages. Historically, pidgins also sprung up in areas of international trade. A pidgin is communication born of necessity and lacks the full complexity or standardized rules that govern a language.

When a pidgin becomes widely used and is taught to children as their native language, it becomes a **Creole**. An example is Haitian Creole, a language based on French and including elements of West African languages.

An **accent** is a unique speech pattern, particularly in terms of tone or intonation. Speakers from different regions tend to have different accents, as do learners of English from different native languages. In some cases, accents are mutually intelligible, but in other cases, speakers with different accents might have some difficulty in understanding one another.

Colloquial language is language that is used conversationally or familiarly—e.g., "What's up?"—in contrast to formal, professional, or academic language—"How are you this evening?"

Vernacular refers to the native, everyday language of a place. Historically, for instance, Bibles and religious services across Europe were primarily offered in Latin, even centuries after the fall of the Roman Empire. After the revolution of the printing press and the widespread availability of vernacular translations of the Bible in the fifteenth and sixteenth centuries, everyday citizens were able to study from Bibles in their own language without needing specialized training in Latin.

A **regionalism** is a word or expression used in a particular region. In the United States, for instance, examples of regionalisms might be *soda*, *pop*, or *Coke*—terms that vary in popularity according to region.

Jargon is vocabulary used within a specialized field, such as computer programming or mechanics. Jargon may consist of specialized words or of everyday words that have a different meaning in this specialized context.

Slang refers to non-standard expressions that are not used in elevated speech and writing. Slang creates linguistic in-groups and out-groups of people, those who can understand the slang terms and those who can't. Slang is often tied to a specific time period. For example, "groovy" and "far out" are connected to the 1970s, and "as if!" and "4-1-1-" are connected to the 1990s.

Understanding Dialect and its Appropriateness

Certain forms of language are viewed differently depending on the context. Lessons learned in the classroom have a real-life application to a student's future, so he or she should know where, when, and how to utilize different forms of language.

Awareness of dialect can help students as readers. Many writers of literary fiction and nonfiction utilize dialect and colloquialisms to add verisimilitude to their writing. This is especially true for authors who focus on a particular region or cultural group in their works, also known as **regionalism** or **local color literature**. Examples include Zora Neale Hurston's *Their Eyes Were Watching God* and the short stories of Kate Chopin. Students can be asked to consider how the speech patterns in a text affect a reader's understanding of the characters—how the pattern reflects a character's background and place in society. They might consider a reader's impression of the region—how similar or different it is from the reader's region or what can be inferred about the region based on how people speak. In some cases,

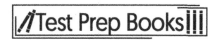

unfamiliar dialect may be very difficult for readers to understand on the page but becomes much more intelligible when read aloud—as in the reading of Shakespeare.

Standard English Conventions

Identifying Parts of Speech

Verbs

A verb is the part of speech that describes an action, state of being, or occurrence. A verb forms the main part of a predicate of a sentence. This means that the verb explains what the noun (which will be discussed shortly) is doing. A simple example is *time flies*. The verb *flies* explains what the action of the noun, *time*, is doing. This example is a **main** verb.

Helping, or **auxiliary**, **verbs** are words like *have, do, be, can, may, should, must,* and *will.* "I *should* go to the store." Helping verbs assist main verbs in expressing tense, ability, possibility, permission, or obligation.

Particles are minor function words like *not, in, out, up,* or *down* that become part of the verb itself. "I might *not.*"

Participles are words formed from verbs that are often used to modify a noun, noun phrase, verb, or verb phrase.

The *running* teenager collided with the cyclist.

Participles can also create compound verb forms.

He is *speaking*.

Verbs have five basic forms:

- Base form
- -s form
- -ing form
- Past form
- Past participle form

The *past* forms are either *regular* (*love/loved; hate/hated*) or *irregular* because they don't end by adding the common past tense suffix "-ed" (*go/went; fall/fell; set/set*).

Verb Forms

Shifting verb forms entails **conjugation**, which is used to indicate tense, voice, or mood.

Verb tense is used to show when the action in the sentence took place. There are several different verb tenses, and it is important to know how and when to use them. Some verb tenses can be achieved by changing the form of the verb, while others require the use of helping verbs (e.g., *is, was,* or *has*).

Present tense shows the action is happening currently or is ongoing:

I walk to work every morning.

25

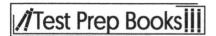

She is stressed about the deadline.

Past tense shows that the action happened in the past or that the state of being is in the past:

I walked to work yesterday morning.

She was stressed about the deadline.

Future tense shows that the action will happen in the future or is a future state of being:

I will walk to work tomorrow morning.

She will be stressed about the deadline.

Present perfect tense shows action that began in the past, but continues into the present:

I have walked to work all week.

She has been stressed about the deadline.

Past perfect tense shows an action was finished before another took place:

I had walked all week until I sprained my ankle.

She had been stressed about the deadline until we talked about it.

Future perfect tense shows an action that will be completed at some point in the future:

By the time the bus arrives, I will have walked to work already.

Agreement

In English writing, certain words connect to other words. People often learn these connections (or **agreements**) as young children and use the correct combinations without a second thought. However, the questions on the test dealing with agreement probably aren't simple ones.

Subject-Verb Agreement

Which of the following sentences is correct?

A large crowd of protesters was on hand.

A large crowd of protesters were on hand.

Many people would say the second sentence is correct, but they'd be wrong. However, they probably wouldn't be alone. Most people just look at two words: *protesters were*. Together they make sense. They sound right. The problem is that the verb *were* doesn't refer to the word *protesters*. Here, the word *protesters* is part of a prepositional phrase that clarifies the actual subject of the sentence (*crowd*). Take the phrase "of protesters" away and re-examine the sentences:

A large crowd was on hand.

A large crowd were on hand.

Without the prepositional phrase to separate the subject and verb, the answer is obvious. The first sentence is correct. On the test, look for confusing prepositional phrases when answering questions about subject-verb agreement. Take the phrase away, and then recheck the sentence.

Noun Agreement

Nouns that refer to other nouns must also match in number. Take the following example:

John and Emily both served as an intern for Senator Wilson.

Two people are involved in this sentence: John and Emily. Therefore, the word *intern* should be plural to match. Here is how the sentence should read:

John and Emily both served as interns for Senator Wilson.

Shift in Noun-Pronoun Agreement

Pronouns are used to replace nouns so that sentences don't have a lot of unnecessary repetition. This repetition can make a sentence seem awkward as in the following example:

Seat belts are important because seat belts save lives, but seat belts can't do so unless seat belts are used.

Replacing some of the nouns (*seat belts*) with a pronoun (*they*) improves the flow of the sentence:

Seat belts are important because they save lives, but they can't do so unless they are used.

A pronoun should agree in number (singular or plural) with the noun that precedes it. Another common writing error is the shift in **noun-pronoun agreement**. Here's an example:

When people are getting in a car, he should always remember to buckle his seatbelt.

The first half of the sentence talks about a plural (*people*), while the second half refers to a singular person (*he* and *his*). These don't agree, so the sentence should be rewritten as:

When people are getting in a car, they should always remember to buckle their seatbelt.

Nouns

A **noun** is a person, place, thing, or idea. All nouns fit into one of two types: common or proper.

A **common noun** is a word that identifies any of a class of people, places, or things. Examples include numbers, objects, animals, feelings, concepts, qualities, and actions. *A, an,* or *the* usually precede the common noun. These parts of speech are called **articles**. Here are some examples of sentences using nouns preceded by articles.

A building is under construction.

The girl would like to move to the city.

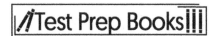

A **proper noun** is used for the specific name of an individual person, place, or organization. The first letter in a proper noun is capitalized.

My name is *Mary*.

I work for *Walmart*.

Pronouns

A word used in place of a noun is known as a **pronoun**. Pronouns are words like *I, mine, hers,* and *us*.

Pronouns can be split into different classifications (see below) which make them easier to learn; however, it's not important to memorize the classifications.

- **Personal pronouns**: refer to people
- **First person**: *we, I, our, mine*
- **Second person**: *you, yours*
- **Third person**: *she, he, them*
- **Possessive pronouns**: demonstrate ownership (mine, his, hers, its, ours, theirs, yours)
- **Interrogative pronouns**: ask questions (*what, which, who, whom, whose*)
- **Relative pronouns**: include the five interrogative pronouns and others that are relative (*whoever, whomever, that, when, where*)
- **Demonstrative pronouns**: replace something specific (*this, that, those, these*)
- *Reciprocal pronouns*: indicate something was done or given in return (*each other, one another*)
- *Indefinite pronouns*: have a nonspecific status (*anybody, whoever, someone, everybody, somebody*)

Indefinite pronouns such as *anybody, whoever, someone, everybody*, and *somebody* command a singular verb form, but others such as *all, none,* and *some* could require a singular or plural verb form.

Antecedents

An **antecedent** is the noun to which a pronoun refers; it needs to be written or spoken before the pronoun is used. For many pronouns, antecedents are imperative for clarity. In particular, many of the personal, possessive, and demonstrative pronouns need antecedents. Otherwise, it would be unclear who or what someone is referring to when they use a pronoun like *he* or *this*.

Pronoun reference means that the pronoun should refer clearly to one, clear, unmistakable noun (the antecedent).

Pronoun-antecedent agreement refers to the need for the antecedent and the corresponding pronoun to agree in gender, person, and number. Here are some examples:

The *kidneys* (plural antecedent) are part of the urinary system. *They* (plural pronoun) serve several roles.

The kidneys are part of the *urinary system* (singular antecedent). *It* (singular pronoun) is also known as the renal system.

28

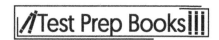

Pronoun Cases

The **subjective pronouns**—*I, you, he/she/it, we, they,* and *who*—are the subjects of the sentence.

Example: *They* have a new house.

The **objective pronouns**—*me, you* (*singular*), *him/her, us, them,* and *whom*—are used when something is being done for or given to someone; they are objects of the action.

Example: The teacher has an apple for *us.*

The **possessive pronouns**—*mine, my, your, yours, his, hers, its, their, theirs, our,* and *ours*—are used to denote that something (or someone) belongs to someone (or something).

Example: It's *their* chocolate cake.
Even Better Example: It's *my* chocolate cake!

One of the greatest challenges and worst abuses of pronouns concerns *who* and *whom.* Just knowing the following rule can eliminate confusion. *Who* is a subjective-case pronoun used only as a subject or subject complement. *Whom* is only objective-case and, therefore, the object of the verb or preposition.

Hint: When using *who* or *whom,* think of whether someone would say *he* or *him.* If the answer is *he,* use *who.* If the answer is *him,* use *whom.* This trick is easy to remember because *he* and *who* both end in vowels, and *him* and *whom* both end in the letter *M.*

Adjectives

Adjectives are words used to modify nouns and pronouns. They can be used alone or in a series and are used to further describe the nouns they modify.

Mark made us a delicious, four-course meal.

The words *delicious* and *four-course* are adjectives that describe the kind of meal Mark made.

Articles are also considered adjectives because they help to describe nouns. Articles can be general or specific. The three articles in English are: *a, an,* and *the.*

Indefinite articles *(a, an)* are used to refer to nonspecific nouns. The article *a* proceeds words beginning with consonant sounds, and the article *an* proceeds words beginning with vowel sounds.

A car drove by our house.

An alligator was loose at the zoo.

He has always wanted a guitar.

Note that *a* and *an* should only proceed nonspecific nouns that are also singular. If a nonspecific noun is plural, it does not need a preceding article.

Alligators were loose at the zoo.

The **definite article** (*the*) is used to refer to specific nouns:

The car pulled into our driveway.

29

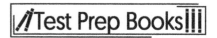

Note that *the* should proceed all specific nouns regardless of whether they are singular or plural.

The cars pulled into our driveway.

Comparative adjectives are used to compare nouns. When they are used in this way, they take on positive, comparative, or superlative form.

The **positive form** is the normal form of the adjective:

Alicia is tall.

The **comparative form** shows a comparison between two things:

Alicia is taller than Maria.

The **superlative form** shows comparison between more than two things:

Alicia is the tallest girl in her class.

Usually, the comparative and superlative can be made by adding *–er* and *–est* to the positive form, but some verbs call for the helping verbs *more* or *most*. Other exceptions to the rule include adjectives like *bad*, which uses the comparative *worse* and the superlative *worst*.

Finally, an **adjective phrase** is a group of words that describes a noun or pronoun and, thus, functions as an adjective. Very happy is an adjective phrase; so are way too hungry and passionate about traveling.

Adverbs

Adverbs have more functions than adjectives because they modify or qualify verbs, adjectives, or other adverbs as well as word groups that express a relation of place, time, circumstance, or cause. Therefore, adverbs answer any of the following questions: *How, when, where, why, in what way, how often, how much, in what condition,* and/or *to what degree.*

Here are some examples of adverbs for different situations:

- how: quickly
- when: daily
- where: there
- in what way: easily
- how often: often
- how much: much
- in what condition: badly
- what degree: hardly

As one can see, for some reason, many adverbs end in *-ly.*

Adverbs do things like emphasize (*really, simply,* and *so*), amplify (*heartily, completely,* and *positively*), and tone down (*almost, somewhat,* and *mildly*).

Adverbs also come in phrases.

The dog ran as <u>though his life depended on it.</u>

30

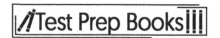

Spelling

Both spoken and written words have rhythm that might be defined as **inflection**. This serves to help writers in their choice of words, expression, and correct spelling. When creating original works, do at least one reading aloud. Some inflection is intrinsic to the words, some are added by writers, and some will be inferred when later read. If the written words are not spelled correctly, then what the author intended is not conveyed. Use rhythm as a spelling tool.

Saying and listening to a word serves as the beginning of knowing how to spell it. Keep these subsequent guidelines in mind, remembering there are often exceptions, because the English language is replete with them.

Guideline #1: syllables must have a vowel
Every syllable in every English word has a vowel. Examples: d*o*g, h*ay*st*a*ck, *a*nsw*e*r*i*ng, *a*bst*e*nt*iou*s (the longest word that uses the five vowels in order), and s*i*mpl*e*.

In addition to this vowel guideline is a built-in bonus: Guideline #1 helps one see whether the word looks right.

Guideline #2: the silent final *-e*
The final word example in Guideline #1, s*i*mpl*e*, provides the opportunity to see another guideline with multiple types:

- Because every syllable has a vowel, words like *simple* require the final silent -e.

- In a word that has a vowel-consonant-e combination like the short, simple word ate, the silent –e at the end shapes the sound of the earlier vowel. The technical term for this is it "makes the vowel say its name." There are thousands of examples of this guideline; just for starters, look at *cute, mate,* and *tote.*

- Let's *dance*...after we leave the *range*! Look what the final silent –e does for the –c and –g: each provides the word's soft sound.

- Other than to *rev* a car's engine, are there other words that ends in a –v? How about a word that ends in a –u? Well some like their cheese *bleu*, there's one, but, while there are more (well, okay, *you*), they are few and far between, and consider words having the ending of the letter –i. Yes, English words generally do not end in –v's, –u's, and –i's, so silent –e to the rescue! Note that it does not change the pronunciation. Examples: *believe, love,* and *active; blue* and *true;* and two very important –i examples, *brownie* and *cookie*. (Exceptions to this rule are generally words from other languages.)

Guideline #3: the long and short of it
When the vowel has a short vowel sound as in *mad* or *bed,* only the single vowel is needed. If the word has a long vowel sound, add another vowel, either alongside it or separated by a consonant: bed/*bead*; mad/*made.* When the second vowel is separated by two spaces—*madder*—it does not affect the first vowel's sound.

Guideline #4: what about the –fixes (pre- and suf-)?
Review the prefix and suffix examples.

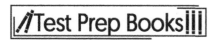

Guideline #5: which came first, the –*i* or the –*e*?

"When the letter 'c' you spy, put the 'e' before the 'i.' (Do not be) dec*e*ived; when the letter 's' you see, put the 'i' before the 'e' (or you might be under) s*i*ege." This old adage still holds up today regarding words where the "c" and "s" *precede* the "i." Another variation is, "'*i*' before '*e*' except after '*c*' or when sounded as '*a*' as in *neighbor* or *weigh*." Keep in mind that these are only guidelines and that there are always exceptions to every rule.

Guideline #6: vowels in the right order

A different helpful ditty is, "When two vowels go walking, the first one does the talking." Usually, when two vowels are in a row, the first one often has a long vowel sound and the other is silent. An example is *team*.

Punctuation

End Punctuation

Periods (.) are used to end a sentence that is a statement (**declarative**) or a command (**imperative**). They should not be used in a sentence that asks a question or is an exclamation. Periods are also used in abbreviations, which are shortened versions of words.

- Declarative: The boys refused to go to sleep.
- Imperative: Walk down to the bus stop.
- Abbreviations: Joan Roberts, M.D., Apple Inc., Mrs. Adamson
- If a sentence ends with an abbreviation, it is inappropriate to use two periods. It should end with a single period after the abbreviation.

    The chef gathered the ingredients for the pie, which included apples, flour, sugar, etc.

Question marks (?) are used with direct questions (**interrogative**). An **indirect question** can use a period:

    Interrogative: When does the next bus arrive?

    Indirect Question: I wonder when the next bus arrives.

An **exclamation point** (!) is used to show strong emotion or can be used as an interjection. This punctuation should be used sparingly in formal writing situations.

    What an amazing shot!

    Whoa!

Capitalization Rules

- Capitalize the first word in a sentence and the first word in a quotation:

    The realtor showed them the house.

    Robert asked, "When can we get together for dinner again?"

- Capitalize proper nouns and words derived from them:

32

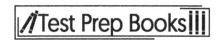

We are visiting Germany in a few weeks.

We will stay with our German relatives on our trip.

- Capitalize days of the week, months of the year, and holidays:

    The book club meets the last Thursday of every month.

    The baby is due in June.

    I decided to throw a Halloween party this year.

- Capitalize the main words in titles (referred to as **title case**), but not the articles, conjunctions, or prepositions:

    A Raisin in the Sun

    To Kill a Mockingbird

- Capitalize directional words that are used as names, but not when referencing a direction:

    The North won the Civil War.

    After making a left, go north on Rt. 476.

    She grew up on the West Coast.

    The winds came in from the west.

- Capitalize titles that go with names:

    Mrs. McFadden   Sir Alec Guinness   Lt. Madeline Suarez

- Capitalize familial relationships when referring to a *specific* person:

    I worked for my Uncle Steven last summer.

    Did you work for your uncle last summer?

Practice Quiz

1. DIRECTIONS: Choose the sentence that shows correct word usage.
   a. Your going to have to put you're jacket over their.
   b. You're going to have to put your jacket over there.
   c. Your going to have to put you're jacket over they're.
   d. You're going to have to put your jacket over their.

2. DIRECTIONS: Choose the option that corrects an error in the underlined portion. If no error exists, choose "No change is necessary."

   Christopher Columbus is often credited for discovering America. This is incorrect.

   a. Christopher Columbus is often credited for discovering America: this is incorrect.
   b. Christopher Columbus is often credited for discovering America this is incorrect.
   c. Christopher Columbus is often credited for discovering America, this is incorrect.
   d. No change is necessary.

3. DIRECTIONS: Choose the option that corrects an error in the underlined portion. If no error exists, choose "No change is necessary."

   Leif Erikson, the son of Erik the Red (a famous Viking outlaw and explorer in his own right), was born in either 970 or 980. Depending on which historian you seek.

   a. 970 or 980; depending on which historian you seek.
   b. 970 or 980! depending on which historian you seek.
   c. 970 or 980, depending on which historian you seek.
   d. No change is necessary.

4. DIRECTIONS: Choose the option that corrects an error in the underlined portion. If no error exists, choose "No change is necessary."

   Later trying to return home, Leif with the intention of taking supplies and spreading Christianity to Greenland, however his ship was blown off course and he arrived in a strange new land: present day Newfoundland, Canada.

   a. Leif to return home tried later
   b. To return home later, Leif
   c. Leif later tried to return home
   d. No change is necessary.

34

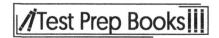

5. DIRECTIONS: Choose the option that corrects an error in the underlined portion. If no error exists, choose "No change is necessary."

During their time in present-day Newfoundland, Leif's expedition made contact with the natives whom they referred to as Skraelings <u>(which translates to 'wretched ones' in Norse).</u>

a. (which translates to "wretched ones" in Norse).
b. (which translates to "wretched ones" in Norse.)
c. (which translates to 'wretched ones' in Norse.)
d. No change is necessary.

Answer Explanations

1. B: Choice *B* correctly uses the contraction for *you are* as the subject of the sentence, and it correctly uses the possessive pronoun *your* to indicate ownership of the jacket. It also correctly uses the adverb *there*, indicating place. Choice *A* is incorrect because it reverses the possessive pronoun *your* and the contraction for *you are*. It also uses the possessive pronoun *their* instead of the adverb *there*. Choice *C* is incorrect because it reverses *your* and *you're* and uses the contraction for *they are* in place of the adverb *there*. Choice *D* incorrectly uses the possessive pronoun *their* instead of the adverb *there*.

2. D: There should be no change here. Both underlined sentences are complete and do not need changing. Choice *A* is incorrect. The underlined portion could *possibly* act with a colon. However, it's not the best choice, so omit Choice *A*. Choice *B* is incorrect because there is no punctuation between the two independent clauses, it is considered a run-on. Choice *C* is incorrect because placing a comma between two independent clauses creates a comma splice.

3. C: Choice *C* is correct; the underlined phrase consists of part of an independent clause and a dependent clause ("Depending on which historian you seek.") The dependent clause cannot stand by itself. Thus, the best choice is to connect the two clauses with a comma. Choices *A* and *D* do not work because you must have two independent clauses on either side of a period as well as a semicolon. Choice *B* is incorrect because an exclamation point is used to show excitement and does not fit the tone here.

4. C: To find out the best answer, try out each answer choice. Choice *A* is not a good answer choice because it inverts words that are otherwise clear with Choice *C*, "Leif later tried to return home with the intention of taking supplies." Choice *B* is also incorrect because we would have the same problem with "Leif with the intention of taking supplies." Choice *D* is incorrect; it might make sense that Leif is "later trying to return home." However, the next sentence says "Leif with the intention of taking supplies," and is not grammatically correct.

5. A: Choice *A* uses the correct punctuation. American English uses double quotes unless placing quotes within a quote (which would then require single quotes). Thus, Choices *C* and *D* are incorrect. Choice *B* is incorrect because the period should go outside of the parenthesis, not inside.

Math

Number Sense, Concepts, and Operations

Real Numbers

A **number line** is a visual representation of all **real numbers**. It is a straight line on which any number can be plotted. The origin is zero, and the values to the right of the origin represent positive numbers. Values to the left of the origin represent negative numbers. Both sides extend forever. Here is an example of a number line:

Number lines can be utilized for addition and subtraction. For example, it could be used to add $1 + 3$. Starting at one on the line, adding 3 to one means moving three units to the right to end up at 4. Therefore, $3 + 1$ is equal to 4. $5 - 2$ can also be determined. Start at 5 on the number line. Subtract 2 from 5. This means moving to the left two units from 5 to end up at 3. Therefore, $5 - 2$ is equal to 3.

The number line can also be used to show the identity property of addition and subtraction. What happens on the number line when you add or subtract zero? There is no movement along the line. For example, $5 + 0$ is equal to 5 and $4 - 0$ is equal to 4. Zero is known as both the **additive** and **subtractive identity.** This is because when you add or subtract zero from a number, that number does not change.

Addition adheres to the commutative property. This is because the order of the numbers being added does not matter. For example, both $4 + 5$ and $5 + 4$ equal 9. The **commutative property of addition** states that for any whole numbers a and b, it is true that $a + b = b + a$. Also, addition follows the associative property because the sum of three or more numbers results in the same answer, no matter what order the numbers are in. Let's look at the following example. Remember that numbers inside parentheses are always calculated first: $1 + (2 + 3)$ and $(1 + 2) + 3$ both equal 6. The **associative property of addition** states that for any whole numbers a, b, and c, $(a + b) + c = a + (b + c)$.

Order of Rational Numbers

A common question type asks to order rational numbers from least to greatest or greatest to least. The numbers will come in a variety of formats, including decimals, percentages, roots, fractions, and whole numbers. These questions test for knowledge of different types of numbers and the ability to determine their respective values.

Whether the question asks to order the numbers from greatest to least or least to greatest, the crux of the question is the same—convert the numbers into a common format. Generally, it's easiest to write the numbers as whole numbers and decimals so they can be placed on a number line. Follow these examples to understand this strategy.

1) Order the following rational numbers from greatest to least:

$$\sqrt{36}, 0.65, 78\%, \frac{3}{4}, 7, 90\%, \frac{5}{2}$$

Of the seven numbers, the whole number (7) and decimal (0.65) are already in an accessible form, so concentrate on the other five.

First, the square root of 36 equals 6. (If the test asks for the root of a non-perfect root, determine which two whole numbers the root lies between.) Next, convert the percentages to decimals. A percentage means "per hundred," so this conversion requires moving the decimal point two places to the left, leaving 0.78 and 0.9. Lastly, evaluate the fractions:

$$\frac{3}{4} = \frac{75}{100} = 0.75; \frac{5}{2} = 2\frac{1}{2} = 2.5$$

Now, the only step left is to list the numbers in the request order:

$$7, \sqrt{36}, \frac{5}{2}, 90\%, 78\%, \frac{3}{4}, 0.65$$

2) Order the following rational numbers from least to greatest:

$$2.5, \sqrt{9}, -10.5, 0.853, 175\%, \sqrt{4}, \frac{4}{5}$$

$$\sqrt{9} = 3$$

$$175\% = 1.75$$

$$\sqrt{4} = 2$$

$$\frac{4}{5} = 0.8$$

From least to greatest, the answer is: -10.5, $\frac{4}{5}$, 0.853, 175%, $\sqrt{4}$, 2.5, $\sqrt{9}$.

Basic Addition, Subtraction, Multiplication, and Division

Addition

Gaining more of something relates to addition. Vocabulary words such as *total*, *sum*, and *more* are common when working with these problems. Addition can also be defined in equation form. For example, $4 + 5 = 9$ shows that $4 + 5$ is the same as 9. Therefore, $9 = 9$, and "four plus five equals nine." When two quantities are being added together, the result is called the *sum*. Therefore, the sum of 4 and 5 is 9. The numbers being added, such as 4 and 5, are known as the *addends*.

Subtraction

Taking something away relates to subtraction. Vocabulary words such as *less, left*, and *remain* are common when working with these problems. Subtraction can also be in equation form. For example, $9 - 5 = 4$ shows that $9 - 5$ is the same as 4 and that "9 minus 5 is 4." The result of subtraction is known as a *difference*. The difference of $9 - 5$ is 4. 4 represents the amount that is left once the subtraction is done. The order in which subtraction is completed does matter. For example, $9 - 5$ and $5 - 9$ do not result in the same answer. $5 - 9$ results in a negative number. So, subtraction does not adhere to the commutative or associative property. The order in which subtraction is completed is important.

Multiplication

Multiplication involves adding together multiple copies of a number. It is indicated by an $\times$ symbol or a number immediately outside of a parenthesis. For example:

$$5(8 - 2)$$

The two numbers being multiplied together are called factors, and their result is called a product. For example, $9 \times 6 = 54$. This can be shown alternatively by expansion of either the 9 or the 6:

$$9 \times 6 = 9 + 9 + 9 + 9 + 9 + 9 = 54$$

$$9 \times 6 = 6 + 6 + 6 + 6 + 6 + 6 + 6 + 6 + 6 = 54$$

Like addition, multiplication holds the commutative and associative properties:

$$115 = 23 \times 5 = 5 \times 23 = 115$$

$$84 = 3 \times (7 \times 4) = (3 \times 7) \times 4 = 84$$

Multiplication also follows the distributive property, which allows the multiplication to be distributed through parentheses. The formula for distribution is $a \times (b + c) = ab + ac$. This is clear after the examples:

$$45 = 5 \times 9 = 5(3 + 6) = (5 \times 3) + (5 \times 6) = 15 + 30 = 45$$

$$20 = 4 \times 5 = 4(10 - 5) = (4 \times 10) - (4 \times 5) = 40 - 20 = 20$$

For larger-number multiplication, how the numbers are lined up can ease the process. It is simplest to put the number with the most digits on top and the number with fewer digits on the bottom. If they have the same number of digits, select one for the top and one for the bottom. Line up the problem and begin by multiplying the far-right column on the top and the far-right column on the bottom. If the answer to a column is more than 9, the ones place digit will be written below that column and the tens place digit will carry to the top of the next column to be added after those digits are multiplied. Write the answer below that column. Move to the next column to the left on the top and multiply it by the same far right column on the bottom. Keep moving to the left one column at a time on the top number until the end.

Example
Multiply 37×8

Line up the numbers, placing the one with the most digits on top.

$$
\begin{array}{r}
3\ 7 \\
\times \quad 8 \\
\hline
\end{array}
$$

Multiply the far-right column on the top with the far right column on the bottom (7 x 8). Write the answer, 56, as below: The ones value, 6, gets recorded, the tens value, 5, is carried.

$$
\begin{array}{r}
{\scriptstyle +5} \\
3\ 7 \\
\times \quad 8 \\
\hline
6
\end{array}
$$

Move to the next column left on the top number and multiply with the far-right bottom (3 x 8). Remember to add any carry over after multiplying: 3 x 8 = 24, 24 + 5 = 29. Since there are no more digits on top, write the entire number below.

$$
\begin{array}{r}
{\scriptstyle +5} \\
3\ 7 \\
\times \quad 8 \\
\hline
2\ 9\ 6
\end{array}
$$

The solution is 296

If there is more than one column to the bottom number, move to the row below the first strand of answers, mark a zero in the far-right column, and then begin the multiplication process again with the far right column on top and the second column from the right on the bottom. For each digit in the bottom number, there will be a row of answers, each padded with the respective number of zeros on the right. Finally, add up all of the answer rows for one total number.

Example: Multiply 512×36.

Line up the numbers (the one with the most digits on top) to multiply.

Begin with the right column on top and the right column on bottom (2×6).

$$
\begin{array}{r}
5\ 1\ 2 \\
\times \quad 3\ 6 \\
\hline
\end{array}
$$

Move one column left on top and multiply by the far-right column on the bottom (1×6). Add the carry over after multiplying: $1 \times 6 = 6, 6 + 1 = 7$.

$$
\begin{array}{r}
{\scriptstyle +1} \\
5\ 1\ 2 \\
\times \quad 3\ 6 \\
\hline
7\ 2
\end{array}
$$

Move one column left on top and multiply by the far-right column on the bottom (5×6). Since this is the last digit on top, write the whole answer below.

$$
\begin{array}{r}
5\ 1\ 2 \\
\times \quad 3\ 6 \\
\hline
3\ 0\ 7\ 2
\end{array}
$$

40

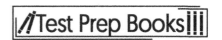

Now move on to the second column on the bottom number. Starting on the far right column on the top, repeat this pattern for the next number left on the bottom (2×3). Write the answers below the first line of answers; remember to begin with a zero placeholder on the far right.

```
      5 1 2
 X      3 6
 3 0 7 2
      6 0
```

Continue the pattern (1×3).

```
      5 1 2
 X      3 6
 3 0 7 2
    3 6 0
```

Since this is the last digit on top, write the whole answer below.

```
      5 1 2
 x      3 6
 3 0 7 2
 1 5 3 6 0
```

Now add the answer rows together. Pay attention to ensure they are aligned correctly.

```
        5 1 2
 x        3 6
   3 0 7 2
 1 5 3 6 0
 1 8 4 3 2
```

The solution is 18,432.

Multiplication becomes slightly more complicated when multiplying numbers with decimals. The easiest way to answer these problems is to ignore the decimals and multiply as if they were whole numbers. After multiplying the factors, place a decimal in the product. The placement of the decimal is determined by taking the cumulative number of decimal places in the factors.

For example:

```
   0 . 7          2 . 6          1 . 5
 x 3            x 4 . 2        x 6 . 4
 ---------      -----------    -----------
   2 . 1        1 0 . 9 2        9 . 6 0
```

Let's tackle the first example. First, ignore the decimal and multiply the numbers as though they were whole numbers to arrive at a product: 21. Second, count the number of digits that follow a decimal (one). Finally, move the decimal place that many positions to the left, as the factors have only one decimal place. The second example works the same way, except that there are two total decimal places in the factors, so the product's decimal is moved two places over. In the third example, the decimal should be moved over two digits, but the digit zero is no longer needed, so it is erased, and the final answer is 9.6.

Division
Division and multiplication are inverses of each other in the same way that addition and subtraction are opposites. The signs designating a division operation are the ÷ and / symbols. In division, the second number divides into the first.

The number before the division sign is called the dividend or, if expressed as a fraction, the numerator. For example, in $a \div b$, a is the dividend, while in $\frac{a}{b}$, a is the numerator.

The number after the division sign is called the divisor or, if expressed as a fraction, the denominator. For example, in $a \div b$, b is the divisor, while in $\frac{a}{b}$, b is the denominator.

Like subtraction, division doesn't follow the commutative property, as it matters which number comes before the division sign, and division doesn't follow the associative or distributive properties for the same reason. For example:

$$\frac{3}{2} = 9 \div 6 \neq 6 \div 9 = \frac{2}{3}$$

$$2 = 10 \div 5 = (30 \div 3) \div 5 \neq 30 \div (3 \div 5) = 30 \div \frac{3}{5} = 50$$

$$25 = 20 + 5 = (40 \div 2) + (40 \div 8) \neq 40 \div (2 + 8) = 40 \div 10 = 4$$

If a divisor doesn't divide into a dividend an integer number of times, whatever is left over is termed the remainder. The remainder can be further divided out into decimal form by using long division; however, this doesn't always give a quotient with a finite number of decimal places, so the remainder can also be expressed as a fraction over the original divisor.

Example
Divide 1050/42 or 1050 ÷ 42.

Set up the problem with the denominator being divided into the numerator.

$$4\,2\,\overline{)1\,0\,5\,0}$$

Check for divisibility into the first unit of the numerator, 1.

42 cannot go into 1, so add on the next unit in the denominator, 0.

42 cannot go into 10, so add on the next unit in the denominator, 5.

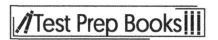

42 can be divided into 105 two times. Write the 2 over the 5 in 105 and multiply 42 x 2. Write the 84 under 105 for subtraction and note the remainder, 21 is less than 42.

$$
\begin{array}{r}
2 \\
4\,2\,\overline{)\,1\,0\,5\,0} \\
-\,8\,4 \\
\hline
2\,1
\end{array}
$$

Drop the next digit in the numerator down to the remainder (making 21 into 210) to create a number 42 can divide into. 42 divides into 210 five times. Write the 5 over the 0 and multiply 42×5.

$$
\begin{array}{r}
2\,5 \\
4\,2\,\overline{)\,1\,0\,5\,0} \\
-\,8\,4 \\
\hline
2\,1\,0
\end{array}
$$

Write the 210 under 210 for subtraction. The remainder is 0.

$$
\begin{array}{r}
2\,5 \\
4\,2\,\overline{)\,1\,0\,5\,0} \\
-\,8\,4 \\
\hline
2\,1\,0 \\
-\,2\,1\,0 \\
\hline
0
\end{array}
$$

The solution is 25.

Example
Divide 375/4 or $375 \div 4$.

Set up the problem.

$$
4\,\overline{)\,3\,7\,5}
$$

4 cannot divide into 3, so add the next unit from the numerator, 7. 4 divides into 37 nine times, so write the 9 above the 7. Multiply $4 \times 9 = 36$. Write the 36 under the 37 for subtraction. The remainder is 1 (1 is less than 4).

$$
\begin{array}{r}
9 \\
4\,\overline{)\,3\,7\,5} \\
-\,3\,6 \\
\hline
1
\end{array}
$$

43

Drop the next digit in the numerator, 5, making the remainder 15. 4 divides into 15, three times, so write the 3 above the 5. Multiply 4×3. Write the 12 under the 15 for subtraction, remainder is 3 (3 is less than 4).

$$
\begin{array}{r}
9\ 3 \\
4\overline{\smash{)}3\ 7\ 5} \\
-\ 3\ 6 \\
\hline
1\ 5 \\
-\ 1\ 2 \\
\hline
3
\end{array}
$$

The solution is 93 remainder 3 or 93 ¾ (the remainder can be written over the original denominator).

Division with decimals is similar to multiplication with decimals in that when dividing a decimal by a whole number, ignore the decimal and divide as if it were a whole number.

Upon finding the answer, or quotient, place the decimal at the decimal place equal to that in the dividend.

$$15.75 \div 3 = 5.25$$

When the divisor is a decimal number, multiply both the divisor and dividend by 10. Repeat this until the divisor is a whole number, then complete the division operation as described above.

$$17.5 \div 2.5 = 175 \div 25 = 7$$

Word Problems and Applications

In **word problems**, multiple quantities are often provided with a request to find some kind of relation between them. This often will mean that one variable (the dependent variable whose value needs to be found) can be written as a function of another variable (the independent variable whose value can be figured from the given information). The usual procedure for solving these problems is to start by giving each quantity in the problem a variable, and then figuring the relationship between these variables.

For example, suppose a car gets 25 miles per gallon. How far will the car travel if it uses 2.4 gallons of fuel? In this case, y would be the distance the car has traveled in miles, and x would be the amount of fuel burned in gallons (2.4). Then the relationship between these variables can be written as an algebraic equation, $y = 25x$. In this case, the equation is $y = 25 \times 2.4 = 60$, so the car has traveled 60 miles.

Some word problems require more than just one simple equation to be written and solved. Consider the following situations and the linear equations used to model them.

Suppose Margaret is 2 miles to the east of John at noon. Margaret walks to the east at 3 miles per hour. How far apart will they be at 3 p.m.? To solve this, x would represent the time in hours past noon, and y would represent the distance between Margaret and John. Now, noon corresponds to the equation where x is 0, so the y-intercept is going to be 2. It's also known that the slope will be the rate at which the distance is changing, which is 3 miles per hour. This means that the slope will be 3 (be careful at this point: if units were used, other than miles and hours, for x- and y-variables, a conversion of the given information to the appropriate units would be required first).

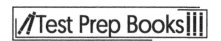

The simplest way to write an equation given the y-intercept and the slope is the **Slope-Intercept form**, $y = mx + b$. Recall that m here is the slope and b is the y intercept. So, $m = 3$ and $b = 2$. Therefore, the equation will be $y = 3x + 2$. The word problem asks how far to the east Margaret will be from John at 3 p.m., which means when x is 3. So, substitute $x = 3$ into this equation to obtain:

$$y = 3 \times 3 + 2 = 9 + 2 = 11$$

Therefore, she will be 11 miles to the east of him at 3 p.m.

For another example, suppose that a box with 4 cans in it weighs 6 lbs., while a box with 8 cans in it weighs 12 lbs. Find out how much a single can weighs. To do this, let x denote the number of cans in the box, and y denote the weight of the box with the cans in lbs. This line touches two pairs: $(4, 6)$ and $(8, 12)$. A formula for this relation could be written using the two-point form, with:

$$x_1 = 4, y_1 = 6, x_2 = 8, y_2 = 12$$

This would yield $\frac{y-6}{x-4} = \frac{12-6}{8-4}$, or $\frac{y-6}{x-4} = \frac{6}{4} = \frac{3}{2}$. However, only the slope is needed to solve this problem, since the slope will be the weight of a single can. From the computation, the slope is $\frac{3}{2}$. Therefore, each can weighs $\frac{3}{2}$ lb.

Translating Words into Math

To translate a word problem into an expression, look for a series of key words indicating addition, subtraction, multiplication, or division:

Addition: *add, altogether, together, plus, increased by, more than, in all, sum*, and *total*

Subtraction: *minus, less than, difference, decreased by, fewer than, remain*, and *take away*

Multiplication: *times, twice, of, double*, and *triple*

Division: *divided by, cut up, half, quotient of, split*, and *shared equally*

If a question asks to give words to a mathematical expression and says "equals," then an = sign must be included in the answer. Similarly, "less than or equal to" is expressed by the inequality symbol ≤, and "greater than or equal" to is expressed as ≥. Furthermore, "less than" is represented by <, and "greater than" is expressed by >.

Working with Money

Walter's Coffee Shop sells a variety of drinks and breakfast treats.

Price List	
Hot Coffee	$2.00
Slow-Drip Iced Coffee	$3.00
Latte	$4.00
Muffin	$2.00
Crepe	$4.00
Egg Sandwich	$5.00

Costs	
Hot Coffee	$0.25
Slow-Drip Iced Coffee	$0.75
Latte	$1.00
Muffin	$1.00
Crepe	$2.00
Egg Sandwich	$3.00

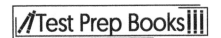

Walter's utilities, rent, and labor costs him $500 per day. Today, Walter sold 200 hot coffees, 100 slow-drip iced coffees, 50 lattes, 75 muffins, 45 crepes, and 60 egg sandwiches. What was Walter's total profit today?

To accurately answer this type of question, determine the total cost of making his drinks and treats, then determine how much revenue he earned from selling those products. After arriving at these two totals, the profit is measured by deducting the total cost from the total revenue.

Walter's costs for today:

Item	Quantity	Cost Per Unit	Total Cost
Hot Coffee	200	$0.25	$50
Slow-Drip Iced Coffee	100	$0.75	$75
Latte	50	$1.00	$50
Muffin	75	$1.00	$75
Crepe	45	$2.00	$90
Egg Sandwich	60	$3.00	$180
Utilities, rent, and labor			$500
Total Costs			$1,020

Walter's revenue for today:

Item	Quantity	Revenue Per Unit	Total Revenue
Hot Coffee	200	$2.00	$400
Slow-Drip Iced Coffee	100	$3.00	$300
Latte	50	$4.00	$200
Muffin	75	$2.00	$150
Crepe	45	$4.00	$180
Egg Sandwich	60	$5.00	$300
Total Revenue			$1,530

Walter's Profit = *Revenue − Costs* = $1,530 − $1,020 = $510

This strategy is applicable to other question types. For example, calculating salary after deductions, balancing a checkbook, and calculating a dinner bill are common word problems similar to business planning. Just remember to use the correct operations. When a balance is increased, use addition. When a balance is decreased, use subtraction. Common sense and organization are your greatest assets when answering word problems.

Order of Operations

When working with longer expressions, parentheses are used to show the order in which the operations should be performed. Operations inside the parentheses should be completed first. Thus, $(3 − 1) \div 2$ means one should first subtract 1 from 3, and then divide that result by 2.

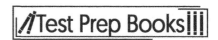

The **order of operations** gives an order for how a mathematical expression is to be simplified:

- Parentheses
- Exponents
- Multiplication
- Division
- Addition
- Subtraction

To help remember this, many students like to use the mnemonic PEMDAS. Some students associate this word with a phrase to help them, such as "Pirates Eat Many Donuts at Sea." Here is a quick example:

Evaluate $2^2 \times (3 - 1) \div 2 + 3$.

Parenthesis: $2^2 \times 2 \div 2 + 3$.

Exponents: $4 \times 2 \div 2 + 3$

Multiply: $8 \div 2 + 3$.

Divide: $4 + 3$.

Addition: 7

Geometry and Measurement

Plane Geometry

Locations on the plane that have no width or breadth are called **points**. These points usually will be denoted with capital letters such as P.

Any pair of points A, B on the plane will determine a unique straight line between them. This line is denoted AB. Sometimes to emphasize a line is being considered, this will be written as $\overleftrightarrow{AB}$.

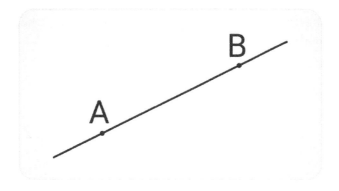

If the Cartesian coordinates for A and B are known, then the distance $d(A, B)$ along the line between them can be measured using the *Pythagorean formula*, which states that if $A = (x_1, y_1)$ and $B = (x_2, y_2)$, then the distance between them is:

$$d(A, B) = \sqrt{(x_2 - x_1)^2 + (y_2 - y_1)^2}$$

The part of a line that lies between A and B is called a **line segment**. It has two endpoints, one at A and one at B. *Rays* also can be formed. Given points A and B, a *ray* is the portion of a line that starts at one of these points, passes through the other, and keeps on going. Therefore, a ray has a single endpoint, but the other end goes off to infinity.

Given a pair of points A and B, a circle centered at A and passing through B can be formed. This is the set of points whose distance from A is exactly $d(A, B)$. The radius of this circle will be $d(A, B)$.

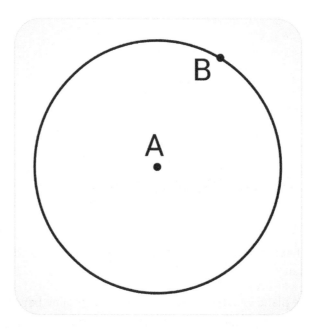

The **circumference** of a circle is the distance traveled by following the edge of the circle for one complete revolution, and the length of the circumference is given by $2\pi r$, where r is the radius of the circle. The formula for circumference is $C = 2\pi r$.

This material is provided for exam preparation purposes only and does not indicate an endorsement of any specific scientific, political, or religious point of view. © TPB Publishing. You have been licensed one copy of this document for personal use only. Any other reproduction or redistribution is strictly prohibited. All rights reserved.

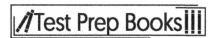

When two lines cross, they form an **angle**. The point where the lines cross is called the *vertex* of the angle. The angle can be named by either just using the vertex, ∠A, or else by listing three points ∠BAC, as shown in the diagram below.

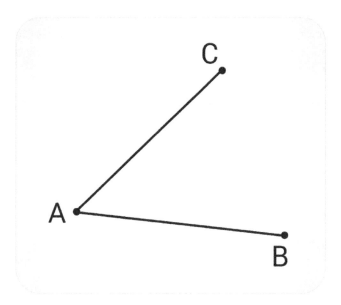

The measurement of an angle can be given in degrees or in radians. In degrees, a full circle is 360 degrees, written 360°. In radians, a full circle is 2π radians.

Given two points on the circumference of a circle, the path along the circle between those points is called an **arc** of the circle. For example, the arc between B and C is denoted by a thinner line:

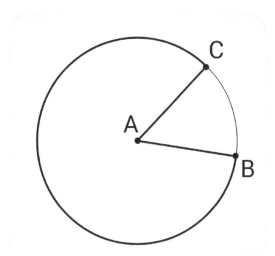

The length of the path along an arc is called the **arc length**. If the circle has radius r, then the arc length is given by multiplying the measure of the angle in radians by the radius of the circle.

Two lines are said to be **parallel** if they never intersect. If the lines are AB and CD, then this is written as $AB \parallel CD$.

If two lines cross to form four quarter-circles, that is, 90° angles, the two lines are **perpendicular**. If the point at which they cross is *B*, and the two lines are *AB* and *BC*, then this is written as $AB \perp BC$.

A **polygon** is a closed figure (meaning it divides the plane into an inside and an outside) consisting of a collection of line segments between points. These points are called the **vertices** of the polygon. These line segments must not overlap one another. Note that the number of sides is equal to the number of angles, or vertices of the polygon. The angles between line segments meeting one another in the polygon are called **interior angles**.

A **regular polygon** is a polygon whose edges are all the same length and whose interior angles are all of equal measure.

A **triangle** is a polygon with three sides. A **quadrilateral** is a polygon with four sides.

A **right triangle** is a triangle that has one 90° angle.

The sum of the interior angles of any triangle must add up to 180°.

An **isosceles triangle** is a triangle in which two of the sides are the same length. In this case, it will always have two congruent interior angles. If a triangle has two congruent interior angles, it will always be isosceles.

An **equilateral triangle** is a triangle whose sides are all the same length and whose angles are all equivalent to one another, equal to 60°. Equilateral triangles are examples of regular polygons. Note that equilateral triangles are also isosceles.

A **rectangle** is a quadrilateral whose interior angles are all 90°. A rectangle has two sets of sides that are equal to one another.

A **square** is a rectangle whose width and height are equal. Therefore, squares are regular polygons.

A **parallelogram** is a quadrilateral in which the opposite sides are parallel and equivalent to each other.

Transformations of a Plane

Given a figure drawn on a plane, many changes can be made to that figure, including **rotation**, **translation**, and **reflection**. Rotations turn the figure about a point, translations slide the figure, and reflections flip the figure over a specified line. When performing these transformations, the original figure is called the **pre-image**, and the figure after transformation is called the **image**.

More specifically, **translation** means that all points in the figure are moved in the same direction by the same distance. In other words, the figure is slid in some fixed direction. Of course, while the entire figure is slid by the same distance, this does not change any of the measurements of the figures involved. The result will have the same distances and angles as the original figure.

In terms of Cartesian coordinates, a translation means a shift of each of the original points (x, y) by a fixed amount in the *x* and *y* directions, to become $(x + a, y + b)$.

Another procedure that can be performed is called **reflection**. To do this, a line in the plane is specified, called the **line of reflection**. Then, take each point and flip it over the line so that it is the same distance from the line but on the opposite side of it. This does not change any of the distances or angles involved, but it does reverse the order in which everything appears.

To reflect something over the x-axis, the points (x, y) are sent to $(x, -y)$. To reflect something over the y-axis, the points (x, y) are sent to the points $(-x, y)$. Flipping over other lines is not something easy to express in Cartesian coordinates. However, by drawing the figure and the line of reflection, the distance to the line and the original points can be used to find the reflected figure.

Example: Reflect this triangle with vertices (-1, 0), (2, 1), and (2, 0) over the y-axis. The pre-image is shown below.

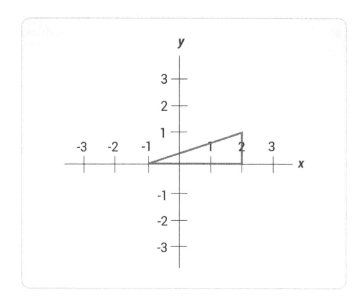

To do this, flip the x values of the points involved to the negatives of themselves, while keeping the y-values the same. The image is shown here.

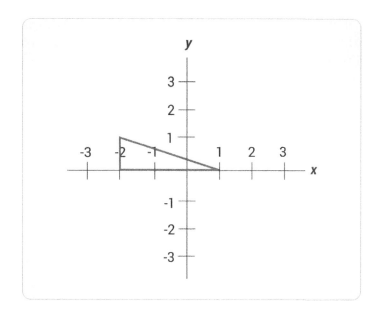

51

The new vertices will be $(1, 0)$, $(-2, 1)$, and $(-2, 0)$.

Another procedure that does not change the distances and angles in a figure is **rotation**. In this procedure, pick a center point, then rotate every vertex along a circle around that point by the same angle. This procedure is also not easy to express in Cartesian coordinates, and this is not a requirement on this test. However, as with reflections, it's helpful to draw the figures and see what the result of the rotation would look like. This transformation can be performed using a compass and protractor.

Each one of these transformations can be performed on the coordinate plane without changes to the original dimensions or angles.

If two figures in the plane involve the same distances and angles, they are called **congruent figures**. In other words, two figures are congruent when they go from one form to another through reflection, rotation, and translation, or a combination of these.

Remember that rotation and translation will give back a new figure that is identical to the original figure, but reflection will give back a mirror image of it.

To recognize that a figure has undergone a rotation, check to see that the figure has not been changed into a mirror image, but that its orientation has changed (that is, whether the parts of the figure now form different angles with the x- and y-axes).

To recognize that a figure has undergone a translation, check to see that the figure has not been changed into a mirror image, and that the orientation remains the same.

To recognize that a figure has undergone a reflection, check to see that the new figure is a mirror image of the old figure.

Keep in mind that sometimes a combination of translations, reflections, and rotations may be performed on a figure.

Dilation

A **dilation** is a transformation that preserves angles, but not distances. This can be thought of as stretching or shrinking a figure. If a dilation makes figures larger, it is called an **enlargement**. If a dilation makes figures smaller, it is called a **reduction**. The easiest example is to dilate around the origin. In this case, multiply the x- and y-coordinates by a **scale factor**, k, sending points (x, y) to (kx, ky).

As an example, draw a dilation of the following triangle, whose vertices will be the points $(-1, 0)$, $(1, 0)$, and $(1, 1)$.

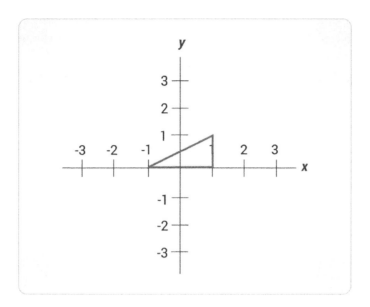

For this problem, dilate by a scale factor of 2, so the new vertices will be $(-2, 0)$, $(2, 0)$, and $(2, 2)$.

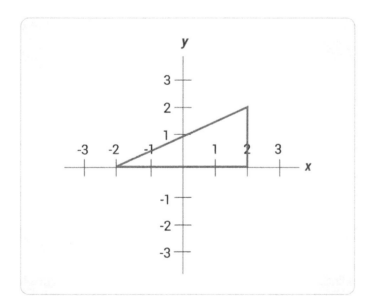

Note that after a dilation, the distances between the vertices of the figure will have changed, but the angles will remain the same. The two figures that are obtained by dilation, along with possibly translation, rotation, and reflection, are all similar to one another. Another way to think of this is that similar figures have the same number of vertices and edges, and their angles are all the same. Similar figures have the same basic shape but are different in size.

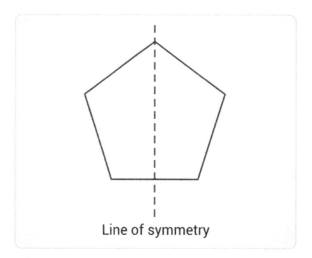

Symmetry

Using the types of transformations above, if an object can undergo these changes and not appear to have changed, then the figure is symmetrical. If an object can be split in half by a line and flipped over that line to lie directly on top of itself, it is said to have **line symmetry**. An example of both types of figures is seen below.

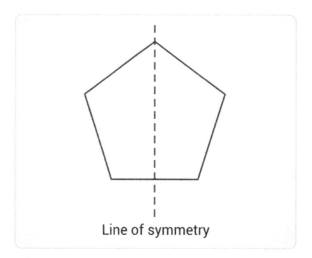

Line of symmetry

If an object can be rotated about its center to any degree smaller than 360, and it lies directly on top of itself, the object is said to have **rotational symmetry**. An example of this type of symmetry is shown below. The pentagon has an order of 5.

The rotational symmetry lines in the figure above can be used to find the angles formed at the center of the pentagon. Knowing that all of the angles together form a full circle, at 360 degrees, the figure can be split into 5 angles equally. By dividing the 360° by 5, each angle is 72°.

Given the length of one side of the figure, the perimeter of the pentagon can also be found using rotational symmetry. If one side length was 3 cm, that side length can be rotated onto each other side length four times. This would give a total of 5 side lengths equal to 3 cm. To find the perimeter, or distance around the figure, multiply 3 by 5. The perimeter of the figure would be 15 cm.

54

If a line cannot be drawn anywhere on the object to flip the figure onto itself or rotated less than or equal to 180 degrees to lay on top of itself, the object is asymmetrical. Examples of these types of figures are shown below.

No line of symmetry

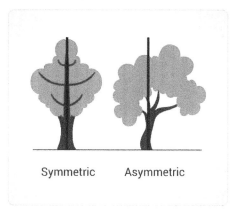

Symmetric   Asymmetric

Perimeters and Areas

The **perimeter** of a polygon is the total length of a trip around the whole polygon, starting and ending at the same point. It is found by adding up the lengths of each line segment in the polygon. For a rectangle with sides of length x and y, the perimeter will be $2x + 2y$.

The area of a polygon is the area of the region that it encloses. Regarding the area of a rectangle with sides of length x and y, the area is given by xy. For a triangle with a base of length b and a height of length h, the area is $\frac{1}{2}bh$.

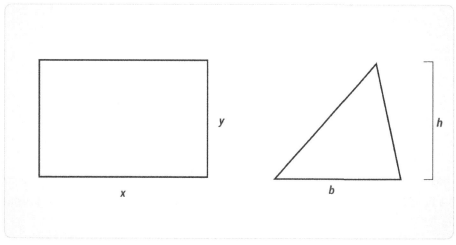

To find the areas of more general polygons, it is usually easiest to break up the polygon into rectangles and triangles. For example, find the area of the following figure whose vertices are $(-1, 0)$, $(-1, 2)$, $(1, 3)$, and $(1, 0)$.

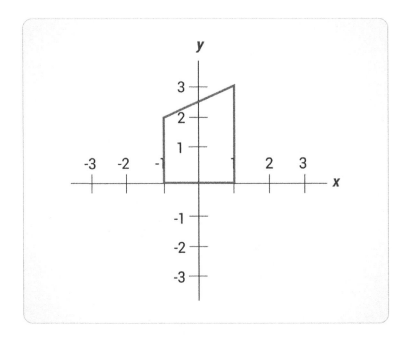

Separate this into a rectangle and a triangle as shown:

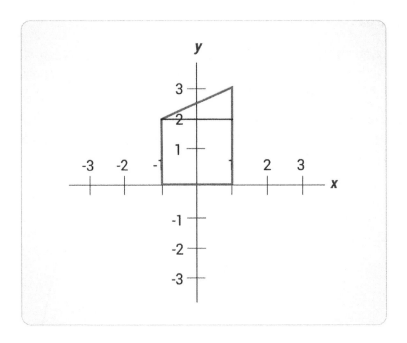

The rectangle has a height of 2 and a width of 2, so it has a total area of $2 \times 2 = 4$. The triangle has a width of 2 and a height of 1, so it has an area of $\frac{1}{2} 2 \times 1 = 1$. Therefore, the entire quadrilateral has an area of $4 + 1 = 5$.

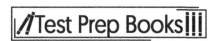

As another example, suppose someone wants to tile a rectangular room that is 10 feet by 6 feet using triangular tiles that are 12 inches by 6 inches. How many tiles would be needed? To figure this, first find the area of the room, which will be $10 \times 6 = 60$ square feet. The dimensions of the triangle are 1 foot by ½ foot, so the area of each triangle is $\frac{1}{2} \times 1 \times \frac{1}{2} = \frac{1}{4}$ square feet. Notice that the dimensions of the triangle had to be converted to the same units as the rectangle. Now, take the total area divided by the area of one tile to find the answer:

$$\frac{60}{\frac{1}{4}} = 60 \times 4 = 240 \text{ tiles required}$$

Volumes and Surface Areas

Geometry in three dimensions is similar to geometry in two dimensions. The main new feature is that three points now define a unique **plane** that passes through each of them. Three dimensional objects can be made by putting together two-dimensional figures in different surfaces. Below, some of the possible three-dimensional figures will be provided, along with formulas for their volumes and surface areas.

A rectangular prism is a box whose sides are all rectangles meeting at 90° angles. Such a box has three dimensions: length, width, and height. If the length is x, the width is y, and the height is z, then the volume is given by $V = xyz$.

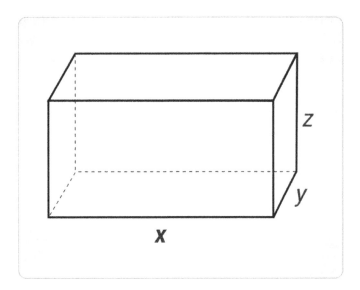

The surface area will be given by computing the surface area of each rectangle and adding them together. There are a total of six rectangles. Two of them have sides of length x and y, two have sides of length y and z, and two have sides of length x and z. Therefore, the total surface area will be given by:

$$SA = 2xy + 2yz + 2xz$$

A **rectangular pyramid** is a figure with a rectangular base and four triangular sides that meet at a single vertex. If the rectangle has sides of length x and y, then the volume will be given by:

$$V = \frac{1}{3}xyh$$

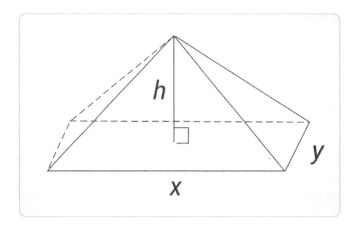

To find the surface area, the dimensions of each triangle need to be known. However, these dimensions can differ depending on the problem in question. Therefore, there is no general formula for calculating total surface area.

A **sphere** is a set of points all of which are equidistant from some central point. It is like a circle, but in three dimensions. The volume of a sphere of radius r is given by $V = \frac{4}{3}\pi r^3$. The surface area is given by $A = 4\pi r^2$.

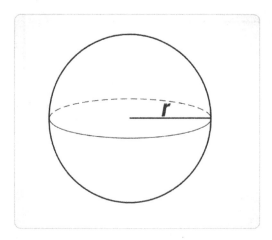

The Pythagorean Theorem

The **Pythagorean** theorem is an important concept in geometry. It states that for right triangles, the sum of the squares of the two shorter sides will be equal to the square of the longest side (also called the **hypotenuse**). The longest side will always be the side opposite to the 90° angle. If this side is called c, and the other two sides are a and b, then the Pythagorean theorem states that $c^2 = a^2 + b^2$. Since

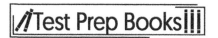

lengths are always positive, this also can be written as $c = \sqrt{a^2 + b^2}$. A diagram to show the parts of a triangle using the Pythagorean theorem is below.

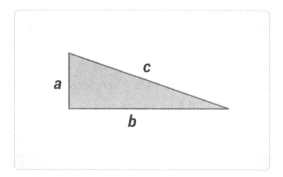

As an example of the theorem, suppose that Shirley has a rectangular field that is 5 feet wide and 12 feet long, and she wants to split it in half using a fence that goes from one corner to the opposite corner. How long will this fence need to be? To figure this out, note that this makes the field into two right triangles, whose hypotenuse will be the fence dividing it in half. Therefore, the fence length will be given by:

$$\sqrt{5^2 + 12^2} = \sqrt{169} = 13 \text{ feet long}$$

Similar Figures and Proportions

Sometimes, two figures are similar, meaning they have the same basic shape and the same interior angles, but they have different dimensions. If the ratio of two corresponding sides is known, then that ratio, or scale factor, holds true for all of the dimensions of the new figure.

Here is an example of applying this principle. Suppose that Lara is 5 feet tall and is standing 30 feet from the base of a light pole, and her shadow is 6 feet long. How high is the light on the pole? To figure this, it helps to make a sketch of the situation:

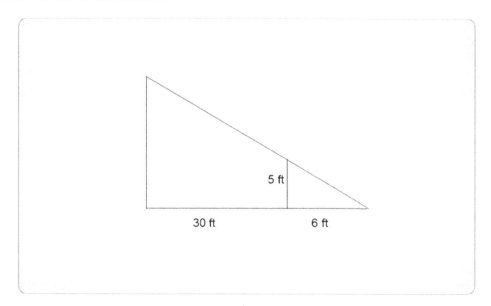

The light pole is the left side of the triangle. Lara is the 5-foot vertical line. Notice that there are two right triangles here, and that they have all the same angles as one another. Therefore, they form similar triangles. So, the ratio of proportionality between them must be determined.

The bases of these triangles are known. The small triangle, formed by Lara and her shadow, has a base of 6 feet. The large triangle formed by the light pole along with the line from the base of the pole out to the end of Lara's shadow is $30 + 6 = 36$ feet long. So, the ratio of the big triangle to the little triangle will be $\frac{36}{6} = 6$. The height of the little triangle is 5 feet. Therefore, the height of the big triangle will be $6 \times 5 = 30$ feet, meaning that the light is 30 feet up the pole.

Notice that the perimeter of a figure changes by the ratio of proportionality between two similar figures, but the area changes by the **square** of the ratio. This is because if the length of one side is doubled, the area is quadrupled.

As an example, suppose two rectangles are similar, but the edges of the second rectangle are three times longer than the edges of the first rectangle. The area of the first rectangle is 10 square inches. How much more area does the second rectangle have than the first?

To answer this, note that the area of the second rectangle is $3^2 = 9$ times the area of the first rectangle, which is 10 square inches. Therefore, the area of the second rectangle is going to be $9 \times 10 = 90$ square inches. This means it has $90 - 10 = 80$ square inches more area than the first rectangle.

As a second example, suppose X and Y are similar right triangles. The hypotenuse of X is 4 inches. The area of Y is $\frac{1}{4}$ the area of X. What is the hypotenuse of Y?

First, realize the area has changed by a factor of $\frac{1}{4}$. The area changes by a factor that is the **square** of the ratio of changes in lengths, so the ratio of the lengths is the square root of the ratio of areas. That means that the ratio of lengths must be $\sqrt{\frac{1}{4}} = \frac{1}{2}$, and the hypotenuse of Y must be $\frac{1}{2} \times 4 = 2$ inches.

Volumes between similar solids change like the cube of the change in the lengths of their edges. Likewise, if the ratio of the volumes between similar solids is known, the ratio between their lengths is known by finding the cube root of the ratio of their volumes.

For example, suppose there are two similar rectangular pyramids X and Y. The base of X is 1 inch by 2 inches, and the volume of X is 8 inches. The volume of Y is 64 inches. What are the dimensions of the base of Y?

To answer this, first find the ratio of the volume of Y to the volume of X. This will be given by $\frac{64}{8} = 8$. Now the ratio of lengths is the cube root of the ratio of volumes, or $\sqrt[3]{8} = 2$. So, the dimensions of the base of Y must be 2 inches by 4 inches.

Ratios and Proportions

A **ratio** is a comparison of two quantities in a particular order. Example: If there are 14 computers in a lab, and the class has 20 students, there is a student to computer ratio of 20 to 14, commonly written as 20:14. Ratios are normally reduced to their smallest whole number representation, so 20:14 would be reduced to 10:7 by dividing both sides by 2.

A proportion is a relationship between two quantities that dictates how one changes when the other changes. A direct proportion describes a relationship in which a quantity increases by a set amount for every increase in the other quantity, or decreases by that same amount for every decrease in the other quantity. Example: Assuming a constant driving speed, the time required for a car trip increases as the distance of the trip increases. The distance to be traveled and the time required to travel are directly proportional.

Inverse proportion is a relationship in which an increase in one quantity is accompanied by a decrease in the other, or vice versa. Example: the time required for a car trip decreases as the speed increases, and increases as the speed decreases, so the time required is inversely proportional to the speed of the car.

Solving for x in a Proportion

Solve for x in this proportion: $\frac{10}{15} = \frac{x}{30}$.

There are two ways to solve for x.

Method 1: Cross multiply; then, solve for x.

$$\frac{10}{15} = \frac{x}{30}$$

$$10(30) = 15(x)$$

$$300 = 15x$$

$$300 \div 15 = 15x \div 15$$

$$x = 20$$

Method 2: Notice that 30 is twice as much as 15, so x should be twice as much as 10. Therefore, $x = 10 \times 2 = 20$.

American Measuring System

The measuring system used today in the United States developed from the British units of measurement during colonial times. The most typically used units in this customary system are those used to measure weight, liquid volume, and length, whose common units are found below. In the customary system, the basic unit for measuring weight is the ounce (oz.); there are 16 ounces (oz.) in 1 pound (lb.) and 2000 pounds in 1 ton. The basic unit for measuring liquid volume is the ounce (oz.); 1 ounce is equal to 2 tablespoons (tbsp.) or 6 teaspoons (tsp), and there are 8 ounces in 1 cup, 2 cups in 1 pint (pt.), 2 pints in 1 quart (qt.), and 4 quarts in 1 gallon (gal). For measurements of length, the inch (in) is the base unit; 12 inches make up 1 foot (ft.), 3 feet make up 1 yard (yd.), and 5280 feet make up 1 mile (mi). However, as

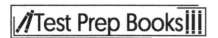

there are only a set number of units in the customary system, with extremely large or extremely small amounts of material, the numbers can become awkward and difficult to compare.

Common Customary Measurements		
Length	Weight	Capacity
1 foot = 12 inches	1 pound = 16 ounces	1 cup = 8 fluid ounces
1 yard = 3 feet	1 ton = 2,000 pounds	1 pint = 2 cups
1 yard = 36 inches		1 quart = 2 pints
1 mile = 1,760 yards		1 quart = 4 cups
1 mile = 5,280 feet		1 gallon = 4 quarts
		1 gallon = 16 cups

Metric System

Aside from the United States, most countries in the world have adopted the metric system embodied in the International System of Units (SI). The three main SI base units used in the metric system are the meter (m), the kilogram (kg), and the liter (L); meters measure length, kilograms measure mass, and liters measure volume.

These three units can use different prefixes, which indicate larger or smaller versions of the unit by powers of ten. This can be thought of as making a new unit, which is sized by multiplying the original unit in size by a factor.

These prefixes and associated factors are:

Metric Prefixes			
Prefix	Symbol	Multiplier	Exponential
giga	G	1,000,000,000	10^9
mega	M	1,000,000	10^6
kilo	k	1,000	10^3
hecto	h	100	10^2
deca	da	10	10^1
no prefix		1	10^0
deci	d	0.1	10^{-1}
centi	c	0.01	10^{-2}
milli	m	0.001	10^{-3}
micro	μ	0.000001	10^{-6}
nano	n	0.000000001	10^{-9}

The correct prefix is then attached to the base. Some examples:

1 milliliter equals .001 liters.
1,000,000,000 nanometers equals 1 meter.
1 kilogram equals 1,000 grams.

Choosing the Appropriate Measuring Unit

Some units of measure are represented as square or cubic units depending on the solution. For example, perimeter is measured in linear units, area is measured in square units, and volume is measured in cubic units.

It is important to use the most appropriate unit for the thing being measured. A building's height might be measured in feet or meters while the length of a nail might be measured in inches or centimeters. Additionally, for SI units, the prefix should be chosen to provide the most succinct available value. For example, the mass of a bag of fruit would likely be measured in kilograms rather than grams or milligrams, and the length of a bacteria cell would likely be measured in micrometers rather than centimeters or kilometers.

Algebraic Thinking and the Coordinate Plane

Algebraic Expressions and Equations

Algebraic expressions look similar to equations, but they do not include the equal sign. Algebraic expressions are comprised of numbers, variables, and mathematical operations. Some examples of algebraic expressions are $8x + 7y - 12z$, $3a^2$, and $5x^3 - 4y^4$.

Algebraic expressions and equations can be used to represent real-life situations and model the behavior of different variables. For example, $2x + 5$ could represent the cost to play games at an arcade. In this case, 5 represents the price of admission to the arcade, and 2 represents the cost of each game played. To calculate the total cost, use the number of games played for x, multiply it by 2, and add 5.

Properties Involving Algebraic Expressions

Properties such as associativity and commutativity that hold among operations between real numbers also hold between algebraic expressions. Addition and multiplication are associative and commutative; therefore, addition and multiplication can be completed in any order inside an algebraic expression. This is helpful when it comes to solving equations. The addition and multiplication principles state that anything can be added to or multiplied by both sides of an equation to maintain equality. This process is helpful when it comes to isolating the variable. The only time there might be an issue is multiplying times a rational expression with a variable in the denominator. One must make sure that the denominator cannot equal zero. Therefore, it would not be appropriate to multiply both sides of the equation $x^2 = 1$ by $\frac{1}{x}$ to solve for x. The solution $x = 0$ would be lost.

Rewriting Expressions

Algebraic expressions are made up of numbers, variables, and combinations of the two, using mathematical operations. Expressions can be rewritten based on their factors. For example, the expression $6x + 4$ can be rewritten as $2(3x + 2)$ because 2 is a factor of both $6x$ and 4. More complex expressions can also be rewritten based on their factors. The expression $x^4 - 16$ can be rewritten as $(x^2 - 4)(x^2 + 4)$. This is a different type of factoring, where a difference of squares is factored into a sum and difference of the same two terms. With some expressions, the factoring process is simple and

63

only leads to a different way to represent the expression. With others, factoring and rewriting the expression leads to more information about the given problem.

In the following quadratic equation, factoring the binomial leads to finding the zeros of the function:

$$x^2 - 5x + 6 = y$$

This equations factors into $(x - 3)(x - 2) = y$, where 2 and 3 are found to be the zeros of the function when y is set equal to zero. The zeros of any function are the x-values where the graph of the function on the coordinate plane crosses the x-axis.

Factoring an equation is a simple way to rewrite the equation and find the zeros, but factoring is not possible for every quadratic. Completing the square is one way to find zeros when factoring is not an option. The following equation cannot be factored:

$$x + 10x - 9 = 0$$

The first step in this method is to move the constant to the right side of the equation, making it $x^2 + 10x = 9$. Then, the coefficient of x is divided by 2 and squared. This number is then added to both sides of the equation, to make the equation still true. For this example, $\left(\frac{10}{2}\right)^2 = 25$ is added to both sides of the equation to obtain:

$$x^2 + 10x + 25 = 9 + 25$$

This expression simplifies to $x^2 + 10x + 25 = 34$, which can then be factored into:

$$(x + 5)^2 = 34$$

Solving for x then involves taking the square root of both sides and subtracting 5. This leads to two zeros of the function:

$$x = \pm\sqrt{34} - 5$$

Depending on the type of answer the question seeks, a calculator may be used to find exact numbers.

Given a quadratic equation in standard form— $ax^2 + bx + c = 0$—the sign of a tells whether the function has a minimum value or a maximum value. If $a > 0$, the graph opens up and has a minimum value. If $a < 0$, the graph opens down and has a maximum value. Depending on the way the quadratic equation is written, multiplication may need to occur before a max/min value is determined.

Exponential expressions can also be rewritten, just as quadratic equations. Properties of exponents must be understood. Multiplying two exponential expressions with the same base involves adding the exponents:

$$a^m a^n = a^{m+n}$$

Dividing two exponential expressions with the same base involves subtracting the exponents:

$$\frac{a^m}{a^n} = a^{m-n}$$

64

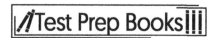

Raising an exponential expression to another exponent includes multiplying the exponents:

$$(a^m)^n = a^{mn}$$

The zero power always gives a value of 1: $a^0 = 1$. Raising either a product or a fraction to a power involves distributing that power:

$$(ab)^m = a^m b^m \text{ and } \left(\frac{a}{b}\right)^m = \frac{a^m}{b^m}$$

Finally, raising a number to a negative exponent is equivalent to the reciprocal including the positive exponent:

$$a^{-m} = \frac{1}{a^m}$$

Defining Linear Equations

A function is called **linear** if it can take the form of the equation $f(x) = ax + b$, or $y = ax + b$, for any two numbers a and b. A linear equation forms a straight line when graphed on the coordinate plane. An example of a linear function is shown below on the graph.

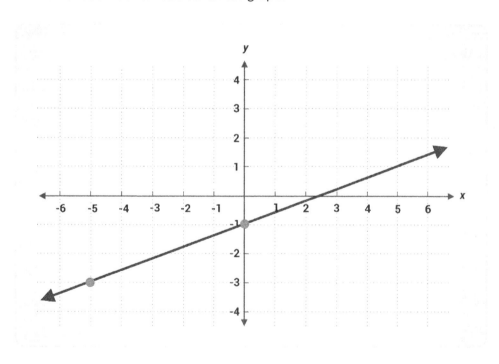

This is a graph of the following function: $y = \frac{2}{5}x - 1$. A table of values that satisfies this function is shown below.

x	y
-5	-3
0	-1
5	1
10	3

These points can be found on the graph using the form (x, y). For more on graphing in the coordinate plane, refer to the Graphing section below.

Graphing Functions and Relations

To graph relations and functions, the Cartesian plane is used. This means to think of the plane as being given a grid of squares, with one direction being the x-axis and the other direction the y-axis. Generally, the independent variable is placed along the horizontal axis, and the dependent variable is placed along the vertical axis. Any point on the plane can be specified by saying how far to go along the x-axis and how far along the y-axis with a pair of numbers (x, y). Specific values for these pairs can be given names such as $C = (-1, 3)$. Negative values mean to move left or down; positive values mean to move right or up. The point where the axes cross one another is called the **origin**. The origin has coordinates $(0, 0)$ and is usually called O when given a specific label. An illustration of the Cartesian plane, along with the plotted points $(2, 1)$ and $(-1, -1)$, is below.

Relations also can be graphed by marking each point whose coordinates satisfy the relation. If the relation is a function, then there is only one value of y for any given value of x. This leads to the **vertical line test**: if a relation is graphed, then the relation is a function if any possible vertical line drawn anywhere along the graph would only touch the graph of the relation in no more than one place. Conversely, when graphing a function, then any possible vertical line drawn will not touch the graph of the function at any point or will touch the function at just one point. This test is made from the definition of a function, where each x-value must be mapped to one and only one y-value.

Forms of Linear Equations

When graphing a linear function, note that the ratio of the change of the y coordinate to the change in the x coordinate is constant between any two points on the resulting line, no matter which two points are chosen. In other words, in a pair of points on a line, (x_1, y_1) and (x_2, y_2), with $x_1 \neq x_2$ so that the two points are distinct, then the ratio $\frac{y_2 - y_1}{x_2 - x_1}$ will be the same, regardless of which particular pair of points are chosen. This ratio, $\frac{y_2 - y_1}{x_2 - x_1}$, is called the **slope** of the line and is frequently denoted with the letter m. If slope m is positive, then the line goes upward when moving to the right, while if slope m is negative, then the line goes downward when moving to the right. If the slope is 0, then the line is called **horizontal**, and the y coordinate is constant along the entire line. In lines where the x-coordinate is constant along the entire line, y is not actually a function of x. For such lines, the slope is not defined. These lines are called **vertical** lines.

Linear functions may take forms other than $y = ax + b$. The most common forms of linear equations are explained below:

1. Standard Form: $Ax + By = C$, in which the slope is given by $m = \frac{-A}{B}$, and the y-intercept is given by $\frac{C}{B}$.

2. Slope-Intercept Form: $y = mx + b$, where the slope is m and the y intercept is b.

3. Point-Slope Form: $y - y_1 = m(x - x_1)$, where the slope is m and (x_1, y_1) is any point on the chosen line.

4. Two-Point Form: $\frac{y - y_1}{x - x_1} = \frac{y_2 - y_1}{x_2 - x_1}$, where (x_1, y_1) and (x_2, y_2) are any two distinct points on the chosen line. Note that the slope is given by $m = \frac{y_2 - y_1}{x_2 - x_1}$.

5. Intercept Form: $\frac{x}{x_1} + \frac{y}{y_1} = 1$, in which x_1 is the x-intercept and y_1 is the y-intercept.

These five ways to write linear equations are all useful in different circumstances. Depending on the given information, it may be easier to write one of the forms over another.

If $y = mx$, y is directly proportional to x. In this case, changing x by a factor changes y by that same factor. If $y = \frac{m}{x}$, y is inversely proportional to x. For example, if x is increased by a factor of 3, then y will be decreased by the same factor, 3.

Solving Linear Equations

Sometimes, rather than a situation where there's an equation such as $y = ax + b$ and finding y for some value of x is requested, the result is given and finding x is requested.

The key to solving any equation is to remember that from one true equation, another true equation can be found by adding, subtracting, multiplying, or dividing both sides by the same quantity. In this case, it's necessary to manipulate the equation so that one side only contains x. Then the other side will show what x is equal to.

For example, in solving $3x - 5 = 2$, adding 5 to each side results in $3x = 7$. Next, dividing both sides by 3 results in $x = \frac{7}{3}$. To ensure the calculated results of x is correct, this calculated value can be substituted into the original equation and solved to see if it makes a true statement. For example, $3(\frac{7}{3}) - 5 = 2$ can be simplified by cancelling out the two 3s. This yields $7 - 5 = 2$, which is a true statement.

Sometimes an equation may have more than one x term. For example, consider the following equation:

$$3x + 2 = x - 4$$

Moving all of the x terms to one side by subtracting x from both sides results in $2x + 2 = -4$. Next, subtract 2 from both sides so that there is no constant term on the left side. This yields $2x = -6$. Finally, divide both sides by 2, which leaves $x = -3$.

Solving Linear Inequalities

Solving linear inequalities is very similar to solving equations, except for one rule: when multiplying or dividing an inequality by a negative number, the inequality symbol changes direction. Given the following inequality, solve for x: $-2x + 5 < 13$. The first step in solving this equation is to subtract 5 from both sides. This leaves the inequality: $-2x < 8$. The last step is to divide both sides by -2. By using the rule, the answer to the inequality is $x > -4$.

Since solutions to inequalities include more than one value, number lines are often used to model the answer. For the previous example, the answer is modelled on the number line below. It shows that any number greater than -4, not including -4, satisfies the inequality.

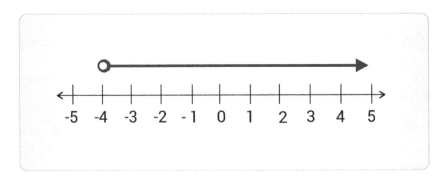

Linear Systems of Equations

A problem sometimes involves multiple variables and multiple equations. These are called **systems of equations**. In this case, try to manipulate them until an expression is found that provides the value of one of the variables. There are a couple of different approaches to this, and some of them can be used together in some cases. The three basic rules to keep in mind are the following.

> 1. Manipulate a set of equations by doing the same operation to both equations, just as is done when working with just one equation.

> 2. If one of the equations can be changed so that it expresses one variable in terms of the others, then that expression can be substituted into the other equations and the variable can be eliminated. This means the other equations will have one less variable in them. This is called the method of substitution.

> 3. If two equations of the form $a = b, c = d$ are included, then a new equation can be formed by adding the left sides and adding the right sides, $a + c = b + d$, or $a - c = b - d$. This enables the elimination of one of the variables from an equation. This is called the method of elimination.

The simplest case is the case of a **linear** system of equations. Although the equations may be written in more complicated forms, linear systems of equations with two variables can always be written in the form $ax + by = c, dx + ey = f$. The two basic approaches to solving these systems are substitution and elimination.

Consider the system $3x - y = 2$ and $2x + 2y = 3$. This can be solved in two ways.

> 1. By substitution: start by solving the first equation for y. First, subtract $3x$ from both sides to obtain $-y = 2 - 3x$. Next, divide both sides by -1, to obtain $y = 3x - 2$. Then substitute this value for y into the second equation. This yields:

$$2x + 2(3x - 2) = 3$$

This can be simplified to $2x + 6x - 4 = 3$, or $8x = 7$, which means $x = \frac{7}{8}$. By plugging in this value for x into $y = 3x - 2$, the result is

$$y = 3\left(\frac{7}{8}\right) - 2 = \frac{21}{8} - \frac{16}{8} = \frac{5}{8}$$

So, this results in $x = \frac{7}{8}, y = \frac{5}{8}$.

> 2. By elimination: first, multiply the first equation by 2. This results in $-2y$, which could cancel out the $+2y$ in the second equation. Multiplying both sides of the first equation by 2 gives results in $2(3x - y) = 2(2)$, or $6x - 2y = 4$. Adding the left sides and the right sides of the two equations and setting the results equal to one another results in:

$$(6x + 2x) + (-2y + 2y) = 4 + 3$$

This simplifies to $8x = 7$, so again $x = \frac{7}{8}$. Plug this back into either of the original equations and the result is $3\left(\frac{7}{8}\right) - y = 2$ or:

$$y = 3\left(\frac{7}{8}\right) - 2 = \frac{21}{8} - \frac{16}{8} = \frac{5}{8}$$

This again yields $x = \frac{7}{8}, y = \frac{5}{8}$.

As this shows, both methods will give the same answer. However, one method is sometimes preferred over another simply because of the amount of work required. To check the answer, the values can be substituted into the given system to make sure they form two true statements.

Rate of Change

Rate of change for any line calculates the steepness of the line over a given interval. Rate of change is also known as the slope or rise/run. The rates of change for nonlinear functions vary depending on the interval being used for the function. The rate of change over one interval may be zero, while the next interval may have a positive rate of change.

The equation plotted on the graph below, $y = x^2$, is a quadratic function and non-linear. The average rate of change from points $(0, 0)$ to $(1, 1)$ is 1 because the vertical change is 1 over the horizontal change of 1. For the next interval, $(1, 1)$ to $(2, 4)$, the average rate of change is 3 because the slope is $\frac{3}{1}$.

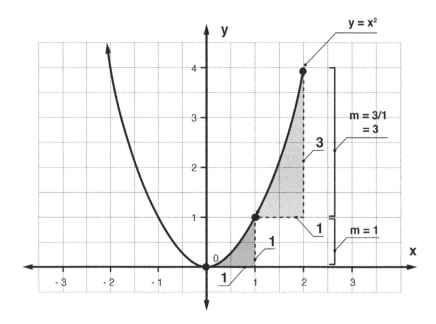

The rate of change for a linear function is constant and can be determined based on a few representations. One method is to place the equation in slope-intercept form: $y = mx + b$. Thus, m is the slope, and b is the y-intercept. In the graph below, the equation is $y = x + 1$, where the slope is 1 and the y-intercept is 1. For every vertical change of 1 unit, there is a horizontal change of 1 unit. The x-intercept is -1, which is the point where the line crosses the x-axis.

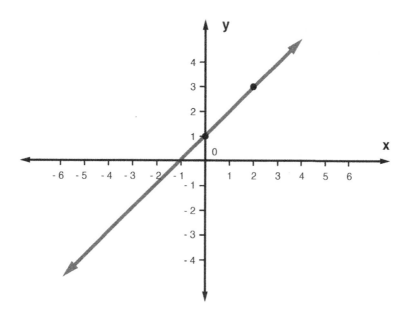

Relations and Functions

First, it's important to understand the definition of a relation. Given two variables, x and y, which stand for unknown numbers, a **relation** between x and y is an object that splits all of the pairs (x, y) into those for which the relation is true and those for which it is false. For example, consider the relation of $x^2 = y^2$. This relationship is true for the pair $(1, 1)$ and for the pair $(-2, 2)$, but false for $(2, 3)$. Another example of a relation is $x \leq y$. This is true whenever x is less than or equal to y.

A **function** is a special kind of relation where, for each value of x, there is only a single value of y that satisfies the relation. So, $x^2 = y^2$ is *not* a function because in this case, if x is 1, y can be either 1 or -1: the pair $(1, 1)$ and $(1, -1)$ both satisfy the relation. More generally, for this relation, any pair of the form $(a, \pm a)$ will satisfy it. On the other hand, consider the following relation: $y = x^2 + 1$. This is a function because for each value of x, there is a unique value of y that satisfies the relation. Notice, however, there are multiple values of x that give us the same value of y. This is perfectly acceptable for a function. Therefore, y is a function of x.

To determine if a relation is a function, check to see if every x value has a unique corresponding y-value.

A function can be viewed as an object that has x as its input and outputs a unique y-value. It is sometimes convenient to express this using **function notation**, where the function itself is given a name, often f. To emphasize that f takes x as its input, the function is written as $f(x)$. In the above example, the equation could be rewritten as $f(x) = x^2 + 1$. To write the value that a function yields for some specific value of x, that value is put in place of x in the function notation. For example, $f(3)$ means the value that the function outputs when the input value is 3. If $f(x) = x^2 + 1$, then $f(3) = 3^2 + 1 = 10$.

71

A function can also be viewed as a table of pairs (x, y), which lists the value for y for each possible value of x.

The set of all possible values for x in $f(x)$ is called the **domain** of the function, and the set of all possible outputs is called the **range** of the function. Note that usually the domain is assumed to be all real numbers, except those for which the expression for $f(x)$ is not defined, unless the problem specifies otherwise. An example of how a function might not be defined is in the case of $f(x) = \frac{1}{x+1}$, which is not defined when $x = -1$ (which would require dividing by zero). Therefore, in this case the domain would be all real numbers except $x = -1$.

If y is a function of x, then x is the **independent variable** and y is the **dependent variable**. This is because in many cases, the problem will start with some value of x and then see how y changes depending on this starting value.

Evaluating Functions

To **evaluate functions**, plug in the given value everywhere the variable appears in the expression for the function. For example, find $g(-2)$ where $g(x) = 2x^2 - \frac{4}{x}$. To complete the problem, plug in -2 in the following way:

$$g(-2) = 2(-2)^2 - \frac{4}{-2}$$

$$2 \times 4 + 2 = 8 + 2 = 10$$

Finding the Zeros of a Function

The **zeros of a function** are the points where its graph crosses the x-axis. At these points, $y = 0$. One way to find the zeros is to analyze the graph. If given the graph, the x-coordinates can be found where the line crosses the x-axis. Another way to find the zeros is to set $y = 0$ in the equation and solve for x. Depending on the type of equation, this could be done by using opposite operations, by factoring the equation, by completing the square, or by using the quadratic formula. If a graph does not cross the x-axis, then the function may have complex roots.

Probability, Statistics, and Data Interpretation

Interpretation of Graphs

Data can be represented in many ways including picture graphs, bar graphs, line plots, and tally charts. It is important to be able to organize the data into categories that could be represented using one of these methods. Equally important is the ability to read these types of diagrams and interpret their meaning.

A **picture graph** is a diagram that shows pictorial representation of data being discussed. The symbols used can represent a certain number of objects. Notice how each fruit symbol in the following graph represents a count of two fruits. One drawback of picture graphs is that they can be less accurate if each symbol represents a large number. For example, if each banana symbol represented ten bananas, and

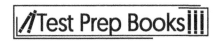

students consumed 22 bananas, it may be challenging to draw and interpret two and one-fifth bananas as a frequency count of 22.

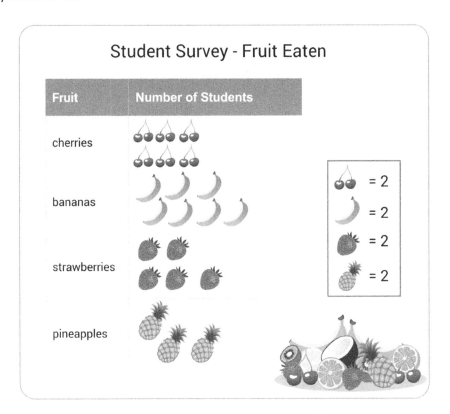

A **bar graph** is a diagram in which the quantity of items within a specific classification is represented by the height of a rectangle. Each type of classification is represented by a rectangle of equal width. Here is an example of a bar graph:

A **line plot** is a diagram that shows quantity of data along a number line. It is a quick way to record data in a structure similar to a bar graph without needing to do the required shading of a bar graph. Here is an example of a line plot:

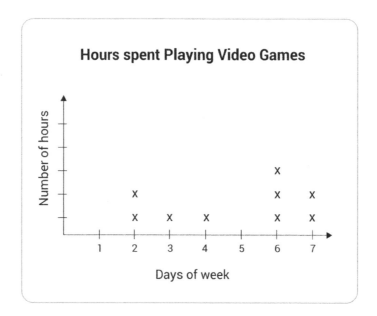

A **tally chart** is a diagram in which tally marks are utilized to represent data. Tally marks are a means of showing a quantity of objects within a specific classification. Here is an example of a tally chart:

Number of days with rain	Number of weeks
0	II
1	IIII
2	IIII
3	IIII
4	IIII IIII IIII IIII
5	IIII I
6	IIII I
7	IIII

Data is often recorded using fractions, such as half a mile, and understanding fractions is critical because of their popular use in real-world applications. Also, it is extremely important to label values with their units when using data. For example, regarding length, the number 2 is meaningless unless it is attached to a unit. Writing 2 cm shows that the number refers to the length of an object.

A **circle graph**, also called a pie chart, shows categorical data with each category representing a percentage of the whole data set. To make a circle graph, the percent of the data set for each category must be determined. To do so, the frequency of the category is divided by the total number of data points and converted to a percent. For example, if 80 people were asked what their favorite sport is and

74

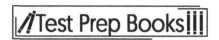

20 responded basketball, basketball makes up 25% of the data ($\frac{20}{80} = 0.25 = 25\%$). Each category in a data set is represented by a *slice* of the circle proportionate to its percentage of the whole.

FAVORITE SPORT

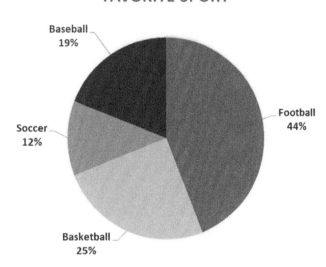

A **scatter plot** displays the relationship between two variables. Values for the independent variable, typically denoted by *x*, are paired with values for the dependent variable, typically denoted by *y*. Each set of corresponding values are written as an ordered pair (*x*, *y*). To construct the graph, a coordinate grid is labeled with the *x*-axis representing the independent variable and the *y*-axis representing the dependent variable. Each ordered pair is graphed.

Like a scatter plot, a **line graph** compares two variables that change continuously, typically over time. Paired data values (ordered pair) are plotted on a coordinate grid with the x- and y-axis representing the two variables. A line is drawn from each point to the next, going from left to right. A double line graph simply displays two sets of data that contain values for the same two variables. The double line graph below displays the profit for given years (two variables) for Company A and Company B (two data sets).

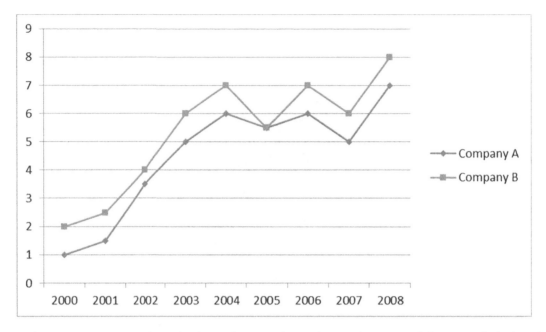

Choosing the appropriate graph to display a data set depends on what type of data is included in the set and what information must be shown. Histograms and box plots can be used for data sets consisting of individual values across a wide range. Examples include test scores and incomes. Histograms and box plots will indicate the center, spread, range, and outliers of a data set. A histogram will show the shape of the data set, while a box plot will divide the set into quartiles (25% increments), allowing for comparison between a given value and the entire set.

Scatter plots and line graphs can be used to display data consisting of two variables. Examples include height and weight, or distance and time. A correlation between the variables is determined by examining the points on the graph. Line graphs are used if each value for one variable pairs with a distinct value for the other variable. Line graphs show relationships between variables.

Comparing Data

Comparing data sets within statistics can mean many things. The first way to compare data sets is by looking at the center and spread of each set. The **center** of a data set can mean two things: median or mean. The **median** is the value that's halfway into each data set, and it splits the data into two intervals. The **mean** is the average value of the data within a set. It's calculated by adding up all of the data in the set and dividing the total by the number of data points. **Outliers** can significantly impact the mean. Additionally, two completely different data sets can have the same mean. For example, a data set with values ranging from 0 to 100 and a data set with values ranging from 44 to 56 can both have means of 50. The first data set has a much wider range, which is known as the **spread** of the data. This measures how varied the data is within each set. Spread can be defined further as either interquartile range or standard deviation.

The **interquartile range (IQR)** is the range of the middle 50 percent of the data set. This range can be seen in the large rectangle on a box plot. The **standard deviation (s or σ)** quantifies the amount of variation with respect to the mean. A lower standard deviation shows that the data set doesn't differ greatly from the mean. A larger standard deviation shows that the data set is spread out farther from

76

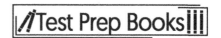

the mean. The formula used for standard deviation depends on whether it's being used for a population or a sample (a subset of a population). The formula for sample standard deviation is:

$$s = \sqrt{\frac{\sum(x - \bar{x})^2}{n - 1}}$$

In this formula, s represents the standard deviation value, x is each value in the data set, $\bar{x}$ is the sample mean, and n is the total number of data points in the set. Note that sample standard deviations use *one less than the total* in the denominator. The population standard deviation formula is similar:

$$\sigma = \sqrt{\frac{\sum(x - \mu)^2}{N}}$$

For population standard deviations, sigma (σ) represents the standard deviation, x represents each value in the data set, mu (μ) is the population mean, and N is the total number of data points for the population.

Interpreting Data
The shape of a data set is another way to compare two or more sets of data. If a data set isn't symmetric around its mean, it's said to be **skewed**. If the tail to the left of the mean is longer, it's said to be **skewed to the left**. In this case, the mean is less than the median. Conversely, if the tail to the right of the mean is longer, it's said to be **skewed to the right** and the mean is greater than the median. When classifying a data set according to its shape, its overall *skewness* is being discussed. If the mean and median are equal, the data set isn't *skewed*; it is *symmetric*, and is considered normally distributed.

An outlier is a data point that lies a great distance away from the majority of the data set. It also can be labeled as an extreme value. Technically, an outlier is any value that falls 1.5 times the IQR above the upper quartile or 1.5 times the IQR below the lower quartile. The effect of outliers in the data set is seen visually because they affect the mean. If there's a large difference between the mean and mode, outliers are the cause. The mean shows bias towards the outlying values. However, the median won't be affected as greatly by outliers.

Normal Distribution
A **normal distribution** of data follows the shape of a bell curve and the data set's median, mean, and mode are equal. Therefore, 50 percent of its values are less than the mean and 50 percent are greater than the mean. Data sets that follow this shape can be generalized using normal distributions. Normal distributions are described as **frequency distributions** in which the data set is plotted as percentages rather than true data points. A **relative frequency distribution** is one where the y-axis is between zero and 1, which is the same as 0% to 100%.

Within a standard deviation, 68 percent of the values are within 1 standard deviation of the mean, 95 percent of the values are within 2 standard deviations of the mean, and 99.7 percent of the values are within 3 standard deviations of the mean. The number of standard deviations that a data point falls from the mean is called the **z-score**. The formula for the z-score is $Z = \frac{x - \mu}{\sigma}$, where μ is the mean, σ is the standard deviation, and x is the data point. This formula is used to fit any data set that resembles a normal distribution to a standard normal distribution in a process known as **standardizing**.

Here is a normal distribution with labeled z-scores:

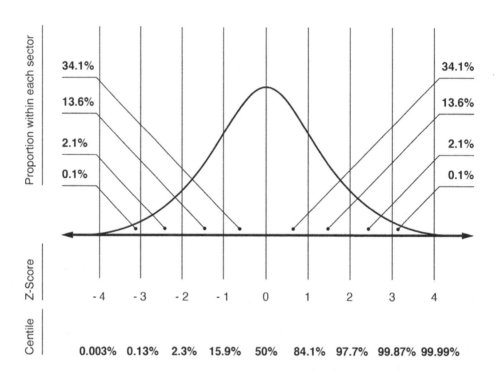

Normal Distribution with Labelled Z-Scores

Population percentages can be estimated using normal distributions. For example, the probability that a data point will be less than the mean, or that the z-score will be less than 0, is 50%. Similarly, the probability that a data point will be within 1 standard deviation of the mean, or that the z-score will be between -1 and 1, is about 68.2%. When using a z-table, the left column states how many standard deviations (to one decimal place) away from the mean the point is, and the row heading states the second decimal place. The entries in the table corresponding to each column and row give the probability, which is equal to the area.

Areas Under the Curve

The area under the curve of a standard normal distribution is equal to 1. Areas under the curve can be estimated using the z-score and a table. The area is equal to the probability that a data point lies in that region in decimal form. For example, the area under the curve from $z = -1$ to $z = 1$ is 0.682.

Mean, Median, Mode, and Range

Mean

Suppose that you have a set of data points and some description of the general properties of this data need to be found.

78

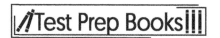

The first property that can be defined for this set of data is the **mean**. This is the same as the average. To find the mean, add up all the data points, then divide by the total number of data points. For example, suppose that in a class of 10 students, the scores on a test were 50, 60, 65, 65, 75, 80, 85, 85, 90, 100. Therefore, the average test score will be:

$$\frac{50 + 60 + 65 + 65 + 75 + 80 + 85 + 85 + 90 + 100}{10} = 75.5$$

The mean is a useful number if the distribution of data is normal (more on this later), which roughly means that the frequency of different outcomes has a single peak and is roughly equally distributed on both sides of that peak. However, it is less useful in some cases where the data might be split or where there are some **outliers**. Outliers are data points that are far from the rest of the data. For example, suppose there are 10 executives and 90 employees at a company. The executives make $1000 per hour, and the employees make $10 per hour.

Therefore, the average pay rate will be:

$$\frac{\$1000 \times 10 + \$10 \times 90}{100} = \$109 \text{ per hour}$$

In this case, this average is not very descriptive since it's not close to the actual pay of the executives or the employees.

Median

Another useful measurement is the **median**. In a data set, the median is the point in the middle. The middle refers to the point where half the data comes before it and half comes after, when the data is recorded in numerical order. For instance, these are the speeds of the fastball of a pitcher during the last inning that he pitched (in order from least to greatest):

90, 92, 93, 93, 95, 96, 97, 97, 97

There are nine total numbers, so the middle or median number is the 5th one, which is 95.

In cases where the number of data points is an even number, then the average of the two middle points is taken. In the previous example of test scores, the two middle points are 75 and 80. Since there is no single point, the average of these two scores needs to be found. The average is:

$$\frac{75 + 80}{2} = 77.5$$

The median is generally a good value to use if there are a few outliers in the data. It prevents those outliers from affecting the "middle" value as much as when using the mean.

Since an outlier is a data point that is far from most of the other data points in a data set, this means an outlier also is any point that is far from the median of the data set. The outliers can have a substantial effect on the mean of a data set, but they usually do not change the median or mode, or do not change them by a large quantity. For example, consider the data set (3, 5, 6, 6, 6, 8). This has a median of 6 and a mode of 6, with a mean of $\frac{34}{6} \approx 5.67$. Now, suppose a new data point of 1000 is added so that the data set is now (3, 5, 6, 6, 6, 8, 1000). The median and mode, which are both still 6, remain unchanged.

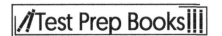

However, the average is now $\frac{1034}{7}$, which is approximately 147.7. In this case, the median and mode will be better descriptions for most of the data points.

Outliers in a given data set are sometimes the result of an error by the experimenter, but oftentimes, they are perfectly valid data points that must be taken into consideration.

Mode

One additional measure to define for X is the **mode**. This is the data point that appears most frequently. If two or more data points all tie for the most frequent appearance, then each of them is considered a mode. In the case of the test scores, where the numbers were 50, 60, 65, 65, 75, 80, 85, 85, 90, 100, there are two modes: 65 and 85.

Range

Range refers to the difference between the highest and lowest digits in a set of numbers. To find the range of a set of numbers, simply subtract the lowest number in the set from the highest number in the set.

$$34, 56, 23, 78, 94, 15$$

To find the range of these numbers, subtract 15 from 94.

$$94-15= 79$$

The range of this set of numbers is 79.

Quartiles and Percentiles

The **first quartile** of a set of data X refers to the largest value from the first ¼ of the data points. In practice, there are sometimes slightly different definitions that can be used, such as the median of the first half of the data points (excluding the median itself if there are an odd number of data points). The term also has a slightly different use: when it is said that a data point lies *in the first quartile*, it means it is less than or equal to the median of the first half of the data points. Conversely, if it lies *at* the first quartile, then it is equal to the first quartile.

When it is said that a data point lies in the **second quartile**, it means it is between the first quartile and the median.

The **third quartile** refers to data that lies between ½ and ¾ of the way through the data set. Again, there are various methods for defining this precisely, but the simplest way is to include all of the data that lie between the median and the median of the top half of the data.

Data that lies in the **fourth quartile** refers to all of the data above the third quartile.

Percentiles may be defined in a similar manner to quartiles. Generally, this is defined in the following manner:

If a data point lies *in the n-th percentile*, this means it lies in the range of the first n% of the data.

If a data point lies *at* the n-th percentile, then it means that n% of the data lies below this data point.

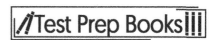

Standard Deviation

Given a data set X consisting of data points $(x_1, x_2, x_3, \dots x_n)$, the **variance** of X is defined to be:

$$\frac{\sum_{i=1}^{n}(x_i - \bar{X})^2}{n}$$

This means that the variance of X is the average of the squares of the differences between each data point and the mean of X. In the formula, $\bar{X}$ is the mean of the values in the data set, and x_i represents each individual value in the data set. The sigma notation indicates that the sum should be found with n being the number of values to add together. $i = 1$ means that the values should begin with the first value.

Given a data set X consisting of data points $(x_1, x_2, x_3, \dots x_n)$, the **standard deviation** of X is defined to be:

$$s_x = \sqrt{\frac{\sum_{i=1}^{n}(x_i - \bar{X})^2}{n}}$$

In other words, the standard deviation is the square root of the variance.

Both the variance and the standard deviation are measures of how much the data tend to be spread out. When the standard deviation is low, the data points are mostly clustered around the mean. When the standard deviation is high, this generally indicates that the data are quite spread out, or else that there are a few substantial outliers.

As a simple example, compute the standard deviation for the data set (1, 3, 3, 5). First, compute the mean, which will be:

$$\frac{1+3+3+5}{4} = \frac{12}{4} = 3$$

Now, find the variance of X with the formula:

$$\sum_{i=1}^{4}(x_i - \bar{X})^2 = (1-3)^2 + (3-3)^2 + (3-3)^2 + (5-3)^2$$

$$-2^2 + 0^2 + 0^2 + 2^2 = 8$$

Therefore, the variance is $\frac{8}{4} = 2$. Taking the square root, the standard deviation will be $\sqrt{2}$.

Note that the standard deviation only depends upon the mean, not upon the median or mode(s). Generally, if there are multiple modes that are far apart from one another, the standard deviation will be high. A high standard deviation does not always mean there are multiple modes, however.

Fitting Functions to Data

Sometimes, when data are measured, it is not simply measuring the frequency of a given outcome, but rather measuring a relationship between two different quantities. In these cases, there is usually one

81

variable that is controlled, the **independent variable**, and one that depends on this variable, the **dependent variable**. If there is a relationship between the two variables, then they are said to be **correlated**.

There are two caveats to these terms. First, the independent variable is not necessarily controlled by the experimenters. It is simply the one chosen to organize the data. In other words, the data are divided up based on the value of an independent variable. Second, finding a significant relationship between the dependent variable and the independent variable does not necessarily imply that there is a causal relationship between the two variables. It only means that once the independent variable is known, a fairly accurate prediction of the dependent variable can be made. This is often expressed with the phrase *correlation does not imply causation*. In other words, just because there is a relationship between two variables does not mean that one is the cause of the other. There could be other factors involved that are the real cause.

Consider some examples. An experimenter could do an experiment in which the independent variable is the number of hours that a student studies for a given test, and the dependent variable is the score the student receives when he or she actually takes the test. Such an experiment would attempt to measure whether there is a relationship between the time spent studying and the score a student receives when taking the test. The expectation would be that the larger value of the independent variable would yield a larger value for the dependent variable. Another experimenter might do an experiment with runners, where the independent variable is the length of the runner's leg, and the dependent variable is the time it takes for the runner to run a fixed distance. In this experiment, as the independent variable increases, the dependent variable would be expected to decrease.

As an example of the phenomenon that correlation does not imply causation, consider an experiment where the independent variable is the value of a person's house, and the dependent variable is their income. Although people in more expensive houses are expected to make more money, it is clear that their expensive houses are not the cause of them making more money. This illustrates one example of why it is important for experimenters to be careful when drawing conclusions about causation from their data.

Linear Data Fitting

The simplest type of correlation between two variables is a **linear correlation**. If the independent variable is x and the dependent variable is y, then a linear correlation means $y = mx + b$. If m is positive, then y will increase as x increases. While if m is negative, then y decreases while x increases. The variable b represents the value of y when x is 0.

As one example of such a correlation, consider a manufacturing plant. Suppose x is the number of units produced by the plant, and y is the cost to the company. In this example, b will be the cost of the plant itself. The plant will cost money even if it is never used, just by buying the machinery. For each unit produced, there will be a cost for the labor and the material. Let m represent this cost to produce one unit of the product.

For a more concrete example, suppose a computer factory costs $100,000. It requires $100 of parts and $50 of labor to make one computer. How much will it cost for a company to make 1000 computers? To figure this, let y be the amount of money the company spends, and let x be the number of computers. The cost of the factory is $100,000, so $b = 100,000$. On the other hand, the cost of producing a

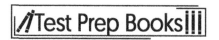

computer is the parts plus labor, or $150, so $m = 150$. Therefore, $y = 150x + 100{,}000$. Substitute 1000 for x and get:

$$y = 150 \times 1000 + 100{,}000 = 150{,}000 + 1000 = 250{,}000$$

It will cost the company $250,000 to make 1000 computers.

Probabilities

Given a set of possible outcomes X, a **probability distribution** on X is a function that assigns a probability to each possible outcome. If the outcomes are $(x_1, x_2, x_3, \ldots x_n)$, and the probability distribution is p, then the following rules are applied.

- $0 \leq p(x_i) \leq 1$, for any i.

- $\sum_{i=1}^{n} p(x_i) = 1$.

In other words, the probability of a given outcome must be between zero and 1, while the total probability must be 1.

If $p(x_i)$ is constant, then this is called a **uniform probability distribution**, and $p(x_i) = \frac{1}{n}$. For example, on a six-sided die, the probability of each of the six outcomes will be $\frac{1}{6}$.

If seeking the probability of an outcome occurring in some specific range A of possible outcomes, written $P(A)$, add up the probabilities for each outcome in that range. For example, consider a six-sided die, and figure the probability of getting a 3 or lower when it is rolled. The possible rolls are 1, 2, 3, 4, 5, and 6. So, to get a 3 or lower, a roll of 1, 2, or 3 must be completed. The probabilities of each of these is $\frac{1}{6}$, so add these to get:

$$p(1) + p(2) + p(3) = \frac{1}{6} + \frac{1}{6} + \frac{1}{6} = \frac{1}{2}$$

Conditional Probabilities

An outcome occasionally lies within some range of possibilities B, and the probability that the outcomes also lie within some set of possibilities A needs to be figured. This is called a **conditional probability**. It is written as $P(A|B)$, which is read "the probability of A given B." The general formula for computing conditional probabilities is:

$$P(A|B) = \frac{P(A \cap B)}{P(B)}$$

However, when dealing with uniform probability distributions, simplify this a bit. Write $|A|$ to indicate the number of outcomes in A. Then, for uniform probability distributions, write $P(A|B) = \frac{|A \cap B|}{|B|}$ (recall that $A \cap B$ means "A intersect B," and consists of all of the outcomes that lie in both A and B). This means that all possible outcomes do not need to be known. To see why this formula works, suppose

83

that the set of outcomes X is $(x_1, x_2, x_3, \ldots x_n)$, so that $|X| = n$. Then, for a uniform probability distribution, $P(A) = \frac{|A|}{n}$. However, this means:

$$(A|B) = \frac{P(A \cap B)}{P(B)} = \frac{\frac{|A \cap B|}{n}}{\frac{|B|}{n}} = \frac{|A \cap B|}{|B|}$$

Since the n's cancel out.

For example, suppose a die is rolled, and it is known that it will land between 1 and 4. However, how many sides the die has is unknown. Figure the probability that the die is rolled higher than 2. To figure this, $P(3)$ or $P(4)$ does not need to be determined, or any of the other probabilities, since it is known that a fair die has a uniform probability distribution. Therefore, apply the formula $\frac{|A \cap B|}{|B|}$. So, in this case B is (1, 2, 3, 4) and $A \cap B$ is (3, 4). Therefore:

$$\frac{|A \cap B|}{|B|} = \frac{2}{4} = \frac{1}{2}$$

Conditional probability is an important concept because, in many situations, the likelihood of one outcome can differ radically depending on how something else comes out. The probability of passing a test given that one has studied all of the material is generally much higher than the probability of passing a test given that one has not studied at all. The probability of a person having heart trouble is much lower if that person exercises regularly. The probability that a college student will graduate is higher when their SAT scores are higher, and so on. For this reason, there are many people who are interested in conditional probabilities.

Note that in some practical situations, changing the order of the conditional probabilities can make the outcome very different. For example, the probability that a person with heart trouble has exercised regularly is quite different than the probability that a person who exercises regularly will have heart trouble. The probability of a person receiving a military-only award, given that he or she is or was a soldier, is generally not very high, but the probability that a person being or having been a soldier, given that he or she received a military-only award, is 1.

However, in some cases, the outcomes do not influence one another this way. If the probability of A is the same regardless of whether B is given; that is, if $P(A|B) = P(A)$, then A and B are considered **independent**. In this case, $P(A|B) = \frac{P(A \cap B)}{P(B)} = P(A)$, so $P(A \cap B) = P(A)P(B)$. In fact, if $P(A \cap B) = P(A)P(B)$, it can be determined that $P(A|B) = P(A)$ and $P(A|B) = P(B)$ by working backward. Therefore, B is also independent of A.

An example of something being independent can be seen in rolling dice. In this case, consider a red die and a green die. It is expected that when the dice are rolled, the outcome of the green die should not depend in any way on the outcome of the red die. Or, to take another example, if the same die is rolled repeatedly, then the next number rolled should not depend on which numbers have been rolled previously. Similarly, if a coin is flipped, then the next flip's outcome does not depend on the outcomes of previous flips.

This can sometimes be counter-intuitive, since when rolling a die or flipping a coin, there can be a streak of surprising results. If, however, it is known that the die or coin is fair, then these results are just the

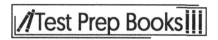

result of the fact that over long periods of time, it is very likely that some unlikely streaks of outcomes will occur. Therefore, avoid making the mistake of thinking that when considering a series of independent outcomes, a particular outcome is "due to happen" simply because a surprising series of outcomes has already been seen.

There is a second type of common mistake that people tend to make when reasoning about statistical outcomes: the idea that when something of low probability happens, this is surprising. It would be surprising that something with low probability happened after just one attempt. However, with so much happening all at once, it is easy to see at least something happen in a way that seems to have a very low probability. In fact, a lottery is a good example. The odds of winning a lottery are very small, but the odds that somebody wins the lottery each week are actually fairly high. Therefore, no one should be surprised when low probability things happen.

Representations of Probability

Probability can be represented in a few different ways. One of these ways is through the use of a **tree diagram**. A probability tree is useful for determining when one should add or multiply information. They can also help the student to see the problem more clearly. They help to map out multiple probabilities in a graph form without using overly complex formulas. See the probability tree below to understand the outcomes of a toss between blue and red. Each column represents a toss.

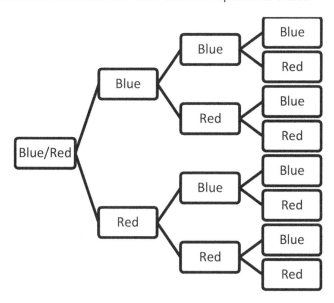

The outcomes from the three tosses would be: (B,B,B), (B,B,R), (B,R,B), (B,R,R) (R,B,B) (R,B,R), (R,R,B) and (R,R,R). Using the probability table helps the student to the likeliness of certain combinations of blue and red being rolled together.

In addition to a probability tree, a student could use a **probability table**. A probability table is another way to determine the likeliness of an event to occur. Here's how to make one:

1. Identify how many possible outcomes are in the first event. Create that many columns plus two.

2. Identify how many possible outcomes are in the second event. Create that many rows plus two.

3. Create your table according the number of needed rows and columns.

4. Label the columns with your known information.

5. Label the rows with your known information.

6. The total of all of the probabilities must be one. Put 1 in the "total/total" box.

7. Identify the probability of one event, and write it in the corresponding "total" box.

8. Identify the probability of the combined event, and write it in the corresponding box.

9. Fill out the rest of the table.

A probability table for the probability of red or blue might look like:

	Red	Blue	Total
Red	.25	.25	.50
Blue	.25	.25	.50
Total	.50	.50	1

Addition Rule

The **addition rule** for probabilities states that the probability of A or B happening is:

$$P(A \cup B) = P(A) + P(B) - P(A \cap B)$$

Note that the subtraction of $P(A \cap B)$ must be performed, or else it would result in double counting any outcomes that lie in both A and in B. For example, suppose that a 20-sided die is being rolled. Fred bets that the outcome will be greater than 10, while Helen bets that it will be greater than 4 but less than 15. What is the probability that at least one of them is correct?

We apply the rule $P(A \cup B) = P(A) + P(B) - P(A \cap B)$, where A is that outcome x is in the range $x > 10$, and B is that outcome x is in the range $4 < x < 15$.

$$P(A) = 10 \times \frac{1}{20} = \frac{1}{2}$$

$$P(B) = 10 \times \frac{1}{20} = \frac{1}{2}$$

$P(A \cap B)$ can be computed by noting that $A \cap B$ means the outcome x is in the range $10 < x < 15$, so:

$$P(A \cap B) = 4 \times \frac{1}{20} = \frac{1}{5}$$

Therefore:

$$P(A \cup B) = P(A) + P(B) - P(A \cap B)$$

$$\frac{1}{2} + \frac{1}{2} - \frac{1}{5} = \frac{4}{5}$$

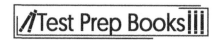

Note that in this particular example, we could also have directly reasoned about the set of possible outcomes $A \cup B$, by noting that this would mean that x must be in the range $5 \leq x$. However, this is not always the case, depending on the given information.

Multiplication Rule

The **multiplication rule** for probabilities states the probability of A and B both happening is:

$$P(A \cap B) = P(A)P(B|A)$$

As an example, suppose that when Jamie wears black pants, there is a ½ probability that she wears a black shirt as well, and that she wears black pants ¾ of the time. What is the probability that she is wearing both a black shirt and black pants?

To figure this, use the above formula, where A will be "Jamie is wearing black pants," while B will be "Jamie is wearing a black shirt." It is known that $P(A)$ is ¾. It is also known that $P(B|A) = \frac{1}{2}$. Multiplying the two, the probability that she is wearing both black pants and a black shirt is:

$$P(A)P(B|A) = \frac{3}{4} \times \frac{1}{2} = \frac{3}{8}$$

What are Statistics?

The field of statistics describes relationships between quantities that are related, but not necessarily in a deterministic manner. For example, a graduating student's salary will often be higher when the student graduates with a higher GPA, but this is not always the case. Likewise, people who smoke tobacco are more likely to develop lung cancer, but, in fact, it is possible for non-smokers to develop the disease as well. **Statistics** describes these kinds of situations, where the likelihood of some outcome depends on the starting data.

Descriptive statistics involves analyzing a collection of data to describe its broad properties such as average (or mean), what percent of the data falls within a given range, and other such properties. An example of this would be taking all of the test scores from a given class and calculating the average test score. **Inferential statistics** attempts to use data about a subset of some population to make inferences about the rest of the population. An example of this would be taking a collection of students who received tutoring and comparing their results to a collection of students who did not receive tutoring, then using that comparison to try to predict whether the tutoring program in question is beneficial.

To be sure that inferences have a high probability of being true for the whole population, the subset that is analyzed needs to resemble a miniature version of the population as closely as possible. For this reason, statisticians like to choose random samples from the population to study, rather than picking a specific group of people based on some similarity. For example, studying the incomes of people who live in Portland does not reveal anything useful about the incomes of people who live in Tallahassee.

Statistical Processes

Statistics involves making decisions and predictions about larger data sets based on smaller data sets. Basically, the information from one part or subset can help predict what happens in the entire data set or population at large. The entire process involves guessing, and the predictions and decisions may not be 100 percent correct all of the time; however, there is some truth to these predictions, and the decisions do have mathematical support. The smaller data set is called a **sample** and the larger data set (in which the decision is being made) is called a **population.** A **random sample** is used as the sample, which is an unbiased collection of data points that represents the population as well as it can. There are many methods of forming a random sample, and all adhere to the fact that every potential data point has a predetermined probability of being chosen.

Making Inferences and Justifying Conclusions from Samples, Experiments, and Observational Studies

Data Gathering Techniques

The three most common types of data gathering techniques are sample surveys, experiments, and observational studies. **Sample surveys** involve collecting data from a random sample of people from a desired population. The measurement of the variable is only performed on this set of people. To have accurate data, the sampling must be unbiased and random. For example, surveying students in an advanced calculus class on how much they enjoy math classes is not a useful sample if the population should be all college students based on the research question. An **experiment** is the method by which a hypothesis is tested using a controlled process called the scientific method. A cause and the effect of that cause are measured, and the hypothesis is accepted or rejected.

Experiments are usually completed in a controlled environment where the results of a control population are compared to the results of a test population. The groups are selected using a randomization process in which each group has a representative mix of the population being tested. Finally, an **observational study** is similar to an experiment. However, this design is used when circumstances prevent or do not allow for a designated control group and experimental group (e.g., lack of funding or unrealistic expectations). Instead, existing control and test populations must be used, so this method has a lack of randomization.

Population Mean and Proportion

Both the population mean and proportion can be calculated using data from a sample. The **population mean** (μ) is the average value of the parameter for the entire population. Due to size constraints, finding the exact value of μ is impossible, so the mean of the sample population is used as an estimate instead. The larger the sample size, the closer the sample mean gets to the population mean. An alternative to finding μ is to find the **proportion** of the population, which is the part of the population with the given characteristic. The proportion can be expressed as a decimal, a fraction, or a percentage, and can be given as a single value or a range of values. Because the population mean and proportion are both estimates, there's a **margin of error**, which is the difference between the actual value and the expected value.

Evaluating Completed Tests

In addition to applying statistical techniques to actual testing, evaluating completed tests is another important aspect of statistics. Reports can be read that already have conclusions, and the process can be evaluated using learned concepts (for example, deciding if a sample being used is appropriate). Other things that can be evaluated include determining if the samples are randomized or the results are significant. Once statistical concepts are understood, the knowledge can be applied to many applications.

Practice Quiz

1. A piggy bank contains 12 dollars' worth of nickels. A nickel weighs 5 grams, and the empty piggy bank weighs 1,050 grams. What is the total weight of the full piggy bank?
   a. 1,110 grams
   b. 1,200 grams
   c. 2,250 grams
   d. 2,200 grams

2. Last year, the New York City area received approximately $27\frac{3}{4}$ inches of snow. The Denver area received approximately 3 times as much snow as New York City. How much snow fell in Denver?
   a. $71\frac{3}{4}$ inches

   b. $27\frac{1}{4}$ inches

   c. $89\frac{1}{4}$ inches

   d. $83\frac{1}{4}$ inches

3. Which of the following would be an instance in which ordinal numbers are used?
   a. Katie scored a 9 out of 10 on her quiz.
   b. Matthew finished second in the spelling bee.
   c. Jacob missed one day of school last month.
   d. Kim was 5 minutes late to school this morning.

4. The graph shows the position of a car over a 10-second time interval. Which of the following is the correct interpretation of the graph for the interval 1 to 3 seconds?

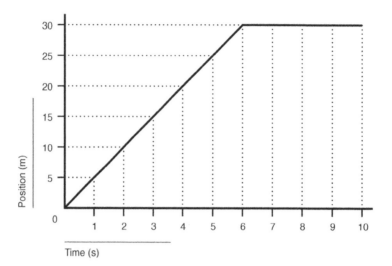

Time (s)

   a. The car remains in the same position.
   b. The car is traveling at a speed of 5m/s.
   c. The car is traveling up a hill.
   d. The car is traveling at 5 mph.

5. A data set contains the following values: 2, 3, 5, 6. What is the standard deviation of the set?
   a. 2.5
   b. 1.58
   c. 1.82
   d. 2.25

Answer Explanations

1. C: A dollar contains 20 nickels. Therefore, if there are 12 dollars' worth of nickels, there are $12 \times 20 = 240$ nickels. Each nickel weighs 5 grams. Therefore, the weight of the nickels is:

$$240 \times 5 = 1{,}200 \text{ grams}$$

Adding in the weight of the empty piggy bank, the filled bank weighs 2,250 grams.

2. D: To find Denver's total snowfall, 3 must be multiplied by $27\frac{3}{4}$. In order to easily do this, the mixed number should be converted into an improper fraction.

$$27\frac{3}{4} = \frac{27 \times 4 + 3}{4} = \frac{111}{4}$$

Therefore, Denver had approximately $\frac{3 \times 111}{4} = \frac{333}{4}$ inches of snow. The improper fraction can be converted back into a mixed number through division.

$$\frac{333}{4} = 83\frac{1}{4} \text{ inches}$$

3. B: Ordinal numbers represent a ranking. Placing second in a competition is a ranking among the other participants of the spelling bee.

4. B: The car is traveling at a speed of five meters per second. On the interval from one to three seconds, the position changes by ten meters. By making this change in position over time into a rate, the speed becomes ten meters in two seconds or five meters in one second.

5. A: First, the population mean must be calculated.

$$\overline{X} = \frac{1}{4}(2 + 3 + 5 + 6) = 4$$

The standard deviation of the data set is:

$$\sigma = \sqrt{\frac{\sum (x - \overline{X})^2}{n}}$$

$n = 4$ represents the number of data points. Therefore:

$$\sigma = \sqrt{\frac{1}{4}[(2-4)^2 + (3-4)^2 + (5-4)^2 + (6-4)^2]}$$

$$\sqrt{\frac{1}{4}(4 + 1 + 1 + 4)} = 1.58$$

Reading

Key Ideas Based on Text Selections

Drawing Conclusions

When drawing conclusions about texts or passages, readers should do two main things: 1) Use the information that they already know and 2) Use the information they have learned from the text or passage. Authors write with an intended purpose, and it is the readers' responsibility to understand and form logical conclusions of authors' ideas. It is important to remember that the readers' conclusions should be supported by information directly from the text. Readers cannot simply form conclusions based off information they already know.

There are several ways readers can draw conclusions from authors' ideas and points to consider when doing so, such as text evidence, text credibility, and directly stated information versus implications.

Text Evidence

Text evidence is the information readers find in a text or passage that supports the main idea or point(s) in a story. In turn, text evidence can help readers draw conclusions about the text or passage. The information should be taken directly from the text or passage and placed in quotation marks. Text evidence provides readers with information to support ideas about the text or passage so that they simply do not just rely on their own thoughts. Details should be precise, descriptive, and factual. Statistics are a great piece of text evidence because they provide readers with exact numbers and not just a generalization. For example, instead of saying "Asia has a larger population than Europe," authors could provide detailed information such as "In Asia there are over 7 billion people, whereas in Europe there are a little over 750 million." More definitive information provides better evidence to readers to help support their conclusions about texts or passages.

Text Credibility

Credible sources are important when drawing conclusions because readers need to be able to trust what they are reading. Authors should always use credible sources to help gain the trust of their readers. A text is **credible** when it is believable and the author is objective and unbiased. If readers do not trust authors' words, they may simply dismiss the text completely. For example, if an author writes a persuasive essay, he or she is outwardly trying to sway readers' opinions to align with their own, providing readers with the liberty to do what they please with the text. Readers may agree or disagree with the author, which may, in turn, lead them to believe that the author is credible or not credible. Also, readers should keep in mind the source of the text. If readers review a journal about astronomy, would a more reliable source be a NASA employee or a plumber? Overall, text credibility is important when drawing conclusions because readers want reliable sources that support the decisions they have made about the author's ideas.

Inferences in a Text

Readers should be able to make **inferences**. Making an inference requires the reader to read between the lines and look for what is implied rather than what is explicitly stated. That is, using information that is known from the text, the reader is able to make a logical assumption about information that is not explicitly stated but is probably true. Read the following passage:

"Hey, do you wanna meet my new puppy?" Jonathan asked.

"Oh, I'm sorry but please don't—" Jacinta began to protest, but before she could finish, Jonathan had already opened the passenger side door of his car and a perfect white ball of fur came bouncing towards Jacinta.

"Isn't he the cutest?" beamed Jonathan.

"Yes—achoo!—he's pretty—aaaachooo!!—adora—aaa—aaaachoo!" Jacinta managed to say in between sneezes. "But if you don't mind, I—I—achoo!—need to go inside."

Which of the following can be inferred from Jacinta's reaction to the puppy?
    a. she hates animals
    b. she is allergic to dogs
    c. she prefers cats to dogs
    d. she is angry at Jonathan

An inference requires the reader to consider the information presented and then form their own idea about what is probably true. Based on the details in the passage, what is the best answer to the question? Important details to pay attention to include the tone of Jacinta's dialogue, which is overall polite and apologetic, as well as her reaction itself, which is a long string of sneezes. Choices *A* and *D* both express strong emotions ("hates" and "angry") that are not evident in Jacinta's speech or actions. Choice *C* mentions cats, but there is nothing in the passage to indicate Jacinta's feelings about cats. Choice *B*, "she is allergic to dogs," is the most logical choice—based on the fact that she began sneezing as soon as a fluffy dog approached her, it makes sense to guess that Jacinta might be allergic to dogs. So even though Jacinta never directly states, "Sorry, I'm allergic to dogs!" using the clues in the passage, it is still reasonable to guess that this is true.

Making inferences is crucial for readers of literature because literary texts often avoid presenting complete and direct information to readers about characters' thoughts or feelings, or they present this information in an unclear way, leaving it up to the reader to interpret clues given in the text. In order to make inferences while reading, readers should ask themselves:

- What details are being presented in the text?
- Is there any important information that seems to be missing?
- Based on the information that the author does include, what else is probably true?
- Is this inference reasonable based on what is already known?

Bias and Stereotypes

Not only can authors state facts or opinions in their writing, they sometimes intentionally or unintentionally show bias or portray a stereotype. A **bias** is when someone demonstrates a prejudice in favor of or against something or someone in an unfair manner. When an author is biased in their writing, readers should be skeptical despite the fact that the author's bias may be correct. For example, two athletes competed for the same position. One athlete is related to the coach and is a mediocre athlete, while the other player excels and deserves the position. The coach chose the less talented player who is related to him for the position. This is a biased decision because it favors someone in an unfair way.

Similar to a bias, a **stereotype** shows favoritism or opposition but toward a specific group or place. Stereotypes create an oversimplified or overgeneralized idea about a certain group, person, or place. For example:

> Women are horrible drivers.

This statement basically labels *all* women as horrible drivers. While there may be some terrible female drivers, the stereotype implies that *all* women are bad drivers when, in fact, not *all* women are. While many readers are aware of several vile ethnic, religious, and cultural stereotypes, audiences should be cautious of authors' flawed assumptions because they can be less obvious than the despicable examples that are pervasive in society.

Topic Versus the Main Idea

It is very important to know the difference between the topic and the main idea of the text. Even though these two are similar because they both present the central point of a text, they have distinctive differences. A **topic** is the subject of the text; it can usually be described in a one- to two-word phrase and appears in the simplest form. On the other hand, the **main idea** is more detailed and provides the author's central point of the text. It can be expressed through a complete sentence and is often found in the beginning, middle, or end of a paragraph. In most nonfiction books, the first sentence of the passage usually (but not always) states the main idea. Review the passage below to explore the topic versus the main idea.

> Cheetahs are one of the fastest mammals on the land, reaching up to 70 miles an hour over short distances. Even though cheetahs can run as fast as 70 miles an hour, they usually only have to run half that speed to catch up with their choice of prey. Cheetahs cannot maintain a fast pace over long periods of time because their bodies will overheat. After a chase, cheetahs need to rest for approximately 30 minutes prior to eating or returning to any other activity.

In the example above, the topic of the passage is "Cheetahs" simply because that is the subject of the text. The main idea of the text is "Cheetahs are one of the fastest mammals on the land but can only maintain a fast pace for shorter distances." While it covers the topic, it is more detailed and refers to the text in its entirety. The text continues to provide additional details called supporting details, which will be discussed in the next section.

Supporting Details

Supporting details help readers better develop and understand the main idea. Supporting details answer questions like *who, what, where, when, why,* and *how*. Different types of supporting details include examples, facts and statistics, anecdotes, and sensory details.

Persuasive and informative texts often use supporting details. In persuasive texts, authors attempt to make readers agree with their points of view, and supporting details are often used as "selling points." If authors make a statement, they need to support the statement with evidence in order to adequately persuade readers. Informative texts use supporting details such as examples and facts to inform readers. Review the previous "Cheetahs" passage to find examples of supporting details.

Cheetahs are one of the fastest mammals on the land, reaching up to 70 miles an hour over short distances. Even though cheetahs can run as fast as 70 miles an hour, they usually only have to run half that speed to catch up with their choice of prey. Cheetahs cannot maintain a fast pace over long periods of time because their bodies will overheat. After a chase, cheetahs need to rest for approximately 30 minutes prior to eating or returning to any other activity.

In the example, supporting details include:

- Cheetahs reach up to 70 miles per hour over short distances.
- They usually only have to run half that speed to catch up with their prey.
- Cheetahs will overheat if they exert a high speed over longer distances.
- Cheetahs need to rest for 30 minutes after a chase.

Look at the diagram below (applying the cheetah example) to help determine the hierarchy of topic, main idea, and supporting details.

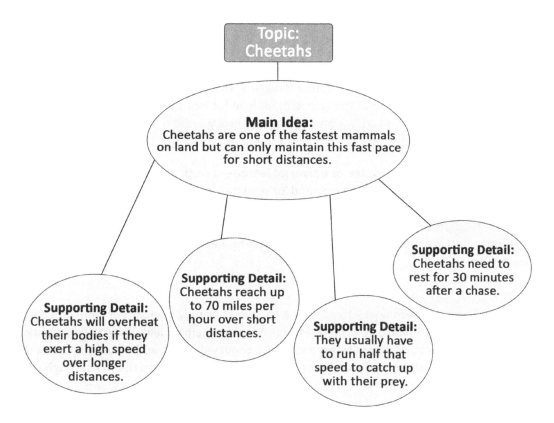

Understanding the Development of Themes

Identifying Theme or Central Message
The **theme** is the central message of a fictional work, whether that work is structured as prose, drama, or poetry. It is the heart of what an author is trying to say to readers through the writing, and theme is largely conveyed through literary elements and techniques.

95

In literature, a theme can often be determined by considering the over-arching narrative conflict within the work. Though there are several types of conflicts and several potential themes within them, the following are the most common:

- Individual against the self—relevant to themes of self-awareness, internal struggles, pride, coming of age, facing reality, fate, free will, vanity, loss of innocence, loneliness, isolation, fulfillment, failure, and disillusionment

- Individual against nature—relevant to themes of knowledge vs. ignorance, nature as beauty, quest for discovery, self-preservation, chaos and order, circle of life, death, and destruction of beauty

- Individual against society—relevant to themes of power, beauty, good, evil, war, class struggle, totalitarianism, role of men/women, wealth, corruption, change vs. tradition, capitalism, destruction, heroism, injustice, and racism

- Individual against another individual—relevant to themes of hope, loss of love or hope, sacrifice, power, revenge, betrayal, and honor

For example, in Hawthorne's *The Scarlet Letter*, one possible narrative conflict could be the individual against the self, with a relevant theme of internal struggles. This theme is alluded to through characterization—Dimmesdale's moral struggle with his love for Hester and Hester's internal struggles with the truth and her daughter, Pearl. It's also alluded to through plot—Dimmesdale's suicide and Hester helping the very townspeople who initially condemned her.

Sometimes, a text can convey a **message** or **universal lesson**—a truth or insight that the reader infers from the text, based on analysis of the literary and/or poetic elements. This message is often presented as a statement. For example, a potential message in Shakespeare's *Hamlet* could be "Revenge is what ultimately drives the human soul." This message can be immediately determined through plot and characterization in numerous ways, but it can also be determined through the setting of Norway, which is bordering on war.

How Authors Develop Theme

Authors employ a variety of techniques to present a theme. They may compare or contrast characters, events, places, ideas, or historical or invented settings to speak thematically. They may use analogies, metaphors, similes, allusions, or other literary devices to convey the theme. An author's use of diction, syntax, and tone can also help convey the theme. Authors will often develop themes through the development of characters, use of the setting, repetition of ideas, use of symbols, and through contrasting value systems. Authors of both fiction and nonfiction genres will use a variety of these techniques to develop one or more themes.

Regardless of the literary genre, there are commonalities in how authors, playwrights, and poets develop themes or central ideas.

Authors often do research, the results of which contributes to theme. In prose fiction and drama, this research may include real historical information about the setting the author has chosen or include elements that make fictional characters, settings, and plots seem realistic to the reader. In nonfiction, research is critical since the information contained within this literature must be accurate and, moreover, accurately represented.

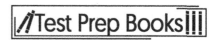

In fiction, authors present a narrative conflict that will contribute to the overall theme. In fiction, this conflict may involve the storyline itself and some trouble within characters that needs resolution. In nonfiction, this conflict may be an explanation or commentary on factual people and events.

Authors will sometimes use character motivation to convey theme, such as in the example from *Hamlet* regarding revenge. In fiction, the characters an author creates will think, speak, and act in ways that effectively convey the theme to readers. In nonfiction, the characters are factual, as in a biography, but authors pay particular attention to presenting those motivations to make them clear to readers.

Authors also use literary devices as a means of conveying theme. For example, the use of moon symbolism in Mary Shelley's *Frankenstein* is significant as its phases can be compared to the phases that the Creature undergoes as he struggles with his identity.

The selected point of view can also contribute to a work's theme. The use of first-person point of view in a fiction or non-fiction work engages the reader's response differently than third person point of view. The central idea or theme from a first-person narrative may differ from a third-person limited text.

In literary nonfiction, authors usually identify the purpose of their writing, which differs from fiction, where the general purpose is to entertain. The purpose of nonfiction is usually to inform, persuade, or entertain the audience. The stated purpose of a non-fiction text will drive how the central message or theme, if applicable, is presented.

Authors identify an audience for their writing, which is critical in shaping the theme of the work. For example, the audience for J.K. Rowling's *Harry Potter* series would be different than the audience for a biography of George Washington. The audience an author chooses to address is closely tied to the purpose of the work. The choice of an audience also drives the choice of language and level of diction an author uses. Ultimately, the intended audience determines the level to which that subject matter is presented and the complexity of the theme.

Summarizing and Paraphrasing a Passage

Creating an outline that identifies the main ideas of a passage as well as the supporting details is a helpful tool in effectively summarizing a text. Most outlines will include a title that reveals the topic of the text, and is usually a single phrase or word, such as "whales." If the passage is divided up into paragraphs, or the paragraphs into sections, each paragraph or section will have its own main idea. These "main ideas" are usually depicted in outlines as roman numerals. Next, writers use supporting details in order to support or prove the main ideas. The supporting details should be listed underneath each main idea in the outline. For example:

Title: Whales
I. Killer whales
       a. Highly social
       b. Apex predator
II. Humpback whales
       a. Males produce "song"
       b. Targeted for whaling industry
III. Beluga whales
       a. Complex sense of hearing
       b. Slow swimmers

Making an outline is a useful method of summarization because it forces the reader to deconstruct the text as a whole and to identify only the most important parts of the text.

Ideas from a text can also be organized using graphic organizers. A **graphic organizer** is a way to simplify information and take key points from the text. A graphic organizer such as a timeline may have an event listed for a corresponding date on the timeline while an outline may have an event listed under a key point that occurs in the text. Each reader needs to create the type of graphic organizer that works the best in terms of being able to recall information from a story. Examples include a **spider-map**, which takes a main idea from the story and places it in a bubble with supporting points branching off the main idea. An **outline** is useful for diagramming the main and supporting points of the entire story, and a **Venn diagram** classifies information as separate or overlapping.

Writing a summary is similar to creating an outline. In both instances, the reader wants to relay the most important parts of the text without being too verbose. A summary of a text should begin with stating the main idea of that text. Then, the reader must decide which supporting details are absolutely essential to the main idea of the text and leave any irrelevant information out of the summary. A summary shouldn't be too brief—readers should include important details depicted in the text—but it also shouldn't be too long either. The appeal of a summary to an audience is that they are able to receive the message of the text without being distracted by the style or detours of the author.

Another effective reading comprehension strategy is paraphrasing. **Paraphrasing** is usually longer than a summary. Paraphrasing is taking the author's text and rewriting, or "translating," it into their own words. A tip for paraphrasing is to read a passage over three times. Once you've read the passage and understand what the author is saying, cover the original passage and begin to write everything you remember from that passage into your own words. Usually, if you understand the content well enough, you will have translated the main idea of the author into your own words with your own writing style. An effective paraphrase will be as long as the original passage but will have a different writing structure.

Craft and Structure Based on Text Selections

Figurative Language

Literary texts also employ rhetorical devices. **Figurative language** like simile and metaphor is a type of rhetorical device commonly found in literature. In addition to rhetorical devices that play on the meanings of words, there are also rhetorical devices that use the sounds of words. These devices are most often found in poetry but may also be found in other types of literature and in non-fiction writing like speech texts.

Alliteration and **assonance** are both varieties of sound repetition. Other types of sound repetition include: **anaphora**, repetition that occurs at the beginning of the sentences; **epiphora**, repetition occurring at the end of phrases; **antimetabole**, repetition of words in reverse order; and **antiphrasis**, a form of denial of an assertion in a text.

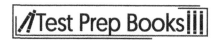

Alliteration refers to the repetition of the first sound of each word. Recall Robert Burns' opening line:

>My love is like a red, red rose

This line includes two instances of alliteration: "love" and "like" (repeated *L* sound), as well as "red" and "rose" (repeated *R* sound). Next, assonance refers to the repetition of vowel sounds, and can occur anywhere within a word (not just the opening sound). Here is the opening of a poem by John Keats:

>When I have fears that I may cease to be
>Before my pen has glean'd my teeming brain

Assonance can be found in the words "fears," "cease," "be," "glean'd," and "teeming," all of which stress the long *E* sound. Both alliteration and assonance create a harmony that unifies the writer's language.

Another sound device is **onomatopoeia**, or words whose spelling mimics the sound they describe. Words such as "crash," "bang," and "sizzle" are all examples of onomatopoeia. Use of onomatopoetic language adds auditory imagery to the text.

Readers are probably most familiar with the technique of pun. A *pun* is a play on words, taking advantage of two words that have the same or similar pronunciation. Puns can be found throughout Shakespeare's plays, for instance:

>Now is the winter of our discontent
>Made glorious summer by this son of York

These lines from *Richard III* contain a play on words. Richard III refers to his brother, the newly crowned King Edward IV, as the "son of York," referencing their family heritage from the house of York. However, while drawing a comparison between the political climate and the weather (times of political trouble were the "winter," but now the new king brings "glorious summer"), Richard's use of the word "son" also implies another word with the same pronunciation, "sun"—so Edward IV is also like the sun, bringing light, warmth, and hope to England. Puns are a clever way for writers to suggest two meanings at once.

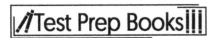

Some examples of figurative language are included in the following table.

Term	Definition	Example
Simile	Compares two things using "like" or "as"	Her hair was like gold.
Metaphor	Compares two things as if they are the same	He was a giant teddy bear.
Idiom	Using words with predictable meanings to create a phrase with a different meaning	The world is your oyster.
Alliteration	Repeating the same beginning sound or letter in a phrase for emphasis	The busy baby babbled.
Personification	Attributing human characteristics to an object or an animal	The house glowered menacingly with a dark smile.
Foreshadowing	Giving an indication that something is going to happen later in the story	I wasn't aware at the time, but I would come to regret those words.
Symbolism	Using symbols to represent ideas and provide a different meaning	The ring represented the bond between us.
Onomatopoeia	Using words that imitate sound	The tire went off with a bang and a crunch.
Imagery	Appealing to the senses by using descriptive language	The sky was painted with red and pink and streaked with orange.
Hyperbole	Using exaggeration not meant to be taken literally	The girl weighed less than a feather.

Figurative language can be used to give additional insight into the theme or message of a text by moving beyond the usual and literal meaning of words and phrases. It can also be used to appeal to the senses of readers and create a more in-depth story.

Connotation and Denotation

Connotation is when an author chooses words or phrases that invoke ideas or feelings other than their literal meaning. An example of the use of connotation is the word *cheap*, which suggests something is poor in value or negatively describes a person as reluctant to spend money. When something or someone is described this way, the reader is more inclined to have a particular image or feeling. Thus, connotation can be a very effective language tool in creating emotion and swaying opinion. However,

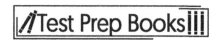

connotations are sometimes hard to pin down because varying emotions can be associated with a word. Generally, though, connotative meanings tend to be fairly consistent within a specific cultural group.

Denotation refers to words or phrases that mean exactly what they say. It is helpful when a writer wants to present hard facts or vocabulary terms with which readers may be unfamiliar. Some examples of denotation are the words *inexpensive* and *frugal*. *Inexpensive* refers to the cost of something, not its value, and *frugal* indicates that a person is conscientiously watching their spending. These terms do not elicit the same emotions that *cheap* does.

Authors sometimes choose to use both, but what they choose and when they use it is what critical readers need to differentiate. One method isn't inherently better than the other; however, one may create a better effect, depending upon an author's intent. If, for example, an author's purpose is to inform, to instruct, and to familiarize readers with a difficult subject, their use of connotation may be helpful. However, it may also undermine credibility and confuse readers. An author who wants to create a credible, scholarly effect in their text would most likely use denotation, which emphasizes literal, factual meaning and examples.

Organization

Good writing is not merely a random collection of sentences. No matter how well written, sentences must relate and coordinate appropriately with one another. If not, the writing seems random, haphazard, and disorganized. Therefore, good writing must be organized, where each sentence fits a larger context and relates to the sentences around it.

Transition Words

The writer should act as a guide, showing the reader how all the sentences fit together. Consider this seat belt example:

> Seat belts save more lives than any other automobile safety feature. Many studies show that airbags save lives as well. Not all cars have airbags. Many older cars don't. Air bags aren't entirely reliable. Studies show that in 15% of accidents, airbags don't deploy as designed. Seat belt malfunctions are extremely rare.

There's nothing wrong with any of these sentences individually, but together they're disjointed and difficult to follow. The best way for the writer to communicate information is through the use of transition words. Here are examples of transition words and phrases that tie sentences together, enabling a more natural flow:

- To show causality: *as a result, therefore,* and *consequently*
- To compare and contrast: *however, but,* and *on the other hand*
- To introduce examples: *for instance, namely,* and *including*
- To show order of importance: *foremost, primarily, secondly,* and *lastly*

Note that this is not a complete list of transitions. There are many more that can be used; however, most fit into these or similar categories. The important point is that the words should clearly show the relationship between sentences, supporting information, and the main idea.

Here is an update to the previous example using transition words. These changes make it easier to read and bring clarity to the writer's points:

> Seat belts save more lives than any other automobile safety feature. Many studies show that airbags save lives as well; however, not all cars have airbags. For instance, some older cars don't. Furthermore, air bags aren't entirely reliable. For example, studies show that in 15% of accidents, airbags don't deploy as designed, but, on the other hand, seat belt malfunctions are extremely rare.

Also, test takers should be prepared to analyze whether the writer is using the best transition word or phrase for the situation. For example, the sentence: "As a result, seat belt malfunctions are extremely rare" doesn't make sense in the context above because the writer is trying to show the contrast between seat belts and airbags, not the causality.

Logical Sequence

Even if the writer includes plenty of information to support their point, the writing is only coherent when the information is in a logical order. First, the writer should introduce the main idea, whether for a paragraph, a section, or the entire piece. Second, they should present evidence to support the main idea by using transitional language. This shows the reader how the information relates to the main idea and to the sentences around it. The writer should then take time to interpret the information, making sure necessary connections are obvious to the reader. Finally, the writer can summarize the information in a closing section.

Though most writing follows this pattern, it isn't a set rule. Sometimes writers change the order for effect. For example, the writer can begin with a surprising piece of supporting information to grab the reader's attention, and then transition to the main idea. Thus, if a passage doesn't follow the logical order, don't immediately assume it's wrong. However, most writing usually settles into a logical sequence after a nontraditional beginning.

Introductions and Conclusions

Examining the writer's strategies for introductions and conclusions puts the reader in the right mindset to interpret the rest of the text. Look for methods the writer might use for introductions such as:

- Stating the main point immediately, followed by outlining how the rest of the piece supports this claim.

- Establishing important, smaller pieces of the main idea first, and then grouping these points into a case for the main idea.

- Opening with a quotation, anecdote, question, seeming paradox, or other piece of interesting information, and then using it to lead to the main point.

Whatever method the writer chooses, the introduction should make their intention clear, establish their voice as a credible one, and encourage a person to continue reading.

Conclusions tend to follow a similar pattern. In them, the writer restates their main idea a final time, often after summarizing the smaller pieces of that idea. If the introduction uses a quote or anecdote to grab the reader's attention, the conclusion often makes reference to it again. Whatever way the writer chooses to arrange the conclusion, the final restatement of the main idea should be clear and simple for the reader to interpret. Finally, conclusions shouldn't introduce any new information.

Text Structure

Depending on what the author is attempting to accomplish, certain formats or text structures work better than others. For example, a sequence structure might work for narration but not for identifying similarities and differences between concepts. Similarly, a comparison-contrast structure is not useful for narration. It's the author's job to put the right information in the correct format.

Readers should be familiar with the five main literary structures:

1. **Sequence** structure (sometimes referred to as the order structure) is when the order of events proceed in a predictable order. In many cases, this means the text goes through the plot elements: exposition, rising action, climax, falling action, and resolution. Readers are introduced to characters, setting, and conflict in the exposition. In the rising action, there's an increase in tension and suspense. The climax is the height of tension and the point of no return. Tension decreases during the falling action. In the resolution, any conflicts presented in the exposition are solved, and the story concludes. An informative text that is structured sequentially will often go in order from one step to the next.

2. In the **problem-solution** structure, authors identify a potential problem and suggest a solution. This form of writing is usually divided into two paragraphs and can be found in informational texts. For example, cell phone, cable, and satellite providers use this structure in manuals to help customers troubleshoot or identify problems with services or products.

3. When authors want to discuss similarities and differences between separate concepts, they arrange thoughts in a **comparison-contrast** paragraph structure. Venn diagrams are an effective graphic organizer for comparison-contrast structures because they feature two overlapping circles that can be used to organize similarities and differences. A comparison-contrast essay organizes one paragraph based on similarities and another based on differences. A comparison-contrast essay can also be arranged with the similarities and differences of individual traits addressed within individual paragraphs. Words such as *however*, *but*, and *nevertheless* help signal a contrast in ideas.

4. **Descriptive** writing structure is designed to appeal to your senses. Much like an artist who constructs a painting, good descriptive writing builds an image in the reader's mind by appealing to the five senses: sight, hearing, taste, touch, and smell. However, overly descriptive writing can become tedious; whereas sparse descriptions can make settings and characters seem flat. Good authors strike a balance by applying descriptions only to passages, characters, and settings that are integral to the plot.

5. Passages that use the **cause and effect** structure are simply asking *why* by demonstrating some type of connection between ideas. Words such as *if, since, because, then, or consequently* indicate a cause-and-effect relationship. By switching the order of a complex sentence, the writer can rearrange the emphasis on different clauses. Saying, *If Sheryl is late, we'll miss the dance*, is different from saying *We'll miss the dance if Sheryl is late*. One emphasizes Sheryl's tardiness while the other emphasizes missing the dance. Paragraphs can also be arranged in a cause and effect format. Since the format—before and after—is sequential, it is useful when authors wish to discuss the impact of choices. Researchers often apply this paragraph structure to the scientific method.

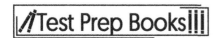

Point of View

In fiction writing, **point of view** refers to who tells the story or from whose perspective readers are observing the story. In non-fiction writing, the point of view refers to whether authors refer to themselves, their readers, or choose not to refer to either. Whether fiction or nonfiction, the author will carefully consider the impact the perspective will have on the purpose and main point of the writing.

- **First-person point of view**: The story is told from the writer's perspective. In fiction, this would mean that the main character is also the narrator. First-person point of view is easily recognized by the use of personal pronouns such as *I, me, we, us, our, my*, and *myself*.

- **Third-person point of view**: In a more formal essay, this would be an appropriate perspective because the focus should be on the subject matter, not the writer or the reader. Third-person point of view is recognized using the pronouns *he, she, they,* and *it*. In fiction writing, third-person point of view has a few variations.

- **Third-person limited point of view**: Refers to a story told by a narrator who has access to the thoughts and feelings of just one character.

- **Third-person omniscient point of view**: The narrator has access to the thoughts and feelings of all the characters.

- **Third-person objective point of view**: the narrator is like a fly on the wall and can see and hear what the characters do and say but does not have access to their thoughts and feelings.

- **Second-person point of view**: This point of view isn't commonly used in fiction or nonfiction writing because it directly addresses the reader using the pronouns *you, your,* and *yourself*. Second-person perspective is more appropriate in direct communication, such as business letters or emails.

Point of View	Pronouns Used
First person	I, me, we, us, our, my, myself
Second person	You, your, yourself
Third person	He, she, it, they

Identifying the Position and Purpose

Readers should always identify the author's position or stance in a text. No matter how objective a piece may seem, assume the author has preconceived beliefs. Reduce the likelihood of accepting an invalid argument by looking for multiple articles on the topic, including those with varying opinions. If several opinions point in the same direction, and are backed by reputable peer-reviewed sources, it's more likely the author has a valid argument. Positions that run contrary to widely held beliefs and existing data should invite scrutiny. There are exceptions to the rule, so be a careful consumer of information.

Though themes, symbols, and motifs are buried deep within the text and can sometimes be difficult to infer, an author's purpose is usually obvious from the beginning. There are four purposes of writing: to inform, to persuade, to describe, and to entertain. Informative writings present facts in an accessible way and are also known as expository writing. Persuasive writing appeals to emotions and logic to inspire the reader to adopt a specific stance. Be wary of this type of writing, as it often lacks objectivity.

104

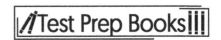

Descriptive writing is designed to paint a picture in the reader's mind, while texts that entertain are often narratives designed to engage and delight the reader.

The various writing styles are usually blended, with one purpose dominating the rest. For example, a persuasive piece might begin with a humorous tale to make readers more receptive to the persuasive message, or a recipe in a cookbook designed to inform might be preceded by an entertaining anecdote that makes the recipe more appealing.

Integration of Information and Ideas

Interpreting Media and Non-Print Text

In the 21st century, rhetoric is evident in a variety of formats. Blogs, vlogs, videos, news footage, advertisements, and live video fill informational feeds, and readers see many shortened images and snapshot texts a day. It's important to note that the majority of these formats use images to appeal to emotion over factual information. Online visuals spread more quickly and are more easily adopted by consumers as fact than printed formats.

Critical readers should be aware that media and non-print text carries some societal weight to the population. In being inundated with pictures and live footage, readers often feel compelled to skip the task of critical reading analysis and accept truth at literal face value. Authors of non-print media are aware of this fact and frequently capitalize on it.

To critically address non-print media requires that the consumer address additional sources and not exclude printed text in order to reach sound conclusions. While it's tempting for consumers to get swept away in the latest viral media, it's important to remember that creators of such have an agenda, and unless the non-print media in question is backed up with sound supporting evidence, any thesis or message cannot be considered valid or factual. Memes, gifs, and looped video cannot tell the whole, truthful story although they may appeal to opinions with which readers already agree. Sharing such non-print media online can precipitate widespread misunderstanding.

When presented with non-print media, critical readers should consider these bits of information as teasers to be investigated for accuracy and veracity. Of course, certain non-print media exists solely for entertainment, but the critical reader should be able to separate out what's generalized for entertainment's sake and what's presented for further verification, before blindly accepting the message. Increasingly, this has become more difficult for readers to do, only because of the onslaught of information to which they are exposed.

If a reader is not to fall prey to strong imagery and non-print media, he or she will need to fact-check. This, of course, requires time and attention on the reader's part, and in current culture, taking the time to fact-check seems counterproductive. However, in order to maintain credibility themselves, readers must be able to evaluate multiple sources of information across media formats and be able to identify the emotional appeal used in the smaller sound bites of non-print media. Readers must view with a discerning eye, listen with a questioning ear, and think with a critical mind.

Synthesis

Synthesis in reading involves the ability to fully comprehend text passages, and then going further by making new connections to see things in a new or different way. It involves a full thought process and

105

requires readers to change the way they think about what they read. The FTCE General Knowledge will require a test taker to integrate new information that they already know and demonstrate an ability to express new thoughts.

Synthesis goes further than summary. When summarizing, a reader collects all of the information an author presents in a text passage and restates it in an effective manner. Synthesis requires that the test taker not only summarize reading material but be able to express new ideas based on the author's message. It is a full culmination of all reading comprehension strategies. It will require the test taker to order, recount, summarize, and recreate information into a whole new idea.

In utilizing synthesis, a reader must be able to form mental images about what they read, recall any background information they have about the topic, ask critical questions about the material, determine the importance of points an author makes, make inferences based on the reading, and finally be able to form new ideas based on all of the above skills. Synthesis requires the reader to make connections, visualize concepts, determine their importance, ask questions, make inferences, then fully synthesize all of this information into new thought.

Making Connections in Reading

There are three helpful thinking strategies to keep in mind when attempting to synthesize text passages:

- Think about how the content of a passage relates to life experience.
- Think about how the content of a passage relates to other text.
- Think about how the content of a passage relates to the world in general.

When reading a given passage, the test taker should actively think about how the content relates to their life experience. While the author's message may express an opinion different from what the reader believes, or express ideas with which the reader is unfamiliar, a good reader will try to relate any of the author's details to their own familiar ground. A reader should use context clues to understand unfamiliar terminology and recognize familiar information they have encountered in prior experience. Bringing prior life experience and knowledge to the test-taking situation is helpful in making connections. The ability to relate an unfamiliar idea to something the reader already knows is critical in understanding unique and new ideas. When trying to make connections while reading, keep the following questions in mind:

- How does this feel familiar in personal experience?
- How is this similar to or different from other reading?
- How is this familiar in the real world?
- How does this relate to the world in general?

Readers should ask themselves these questions in order to actively make connections to past and present experiences. Utilizing the ability to make connections is an important step in achieving synthesis.

Determining Importance in Reading

Being able to determine what is most important while reading is critical to synthesis. It is the difference between being able to tell what is necessary to full comprehension and that which is interesting but not necessary.

When determining the importance of an author's ideas, consider the following:

- Ask how critical an author's particular idea, assertion, or concept is to the overall message.

- Ask "is this an interesting fact or is this information essential to understanding the author's main idea?"

- Make a simple chart. On one side, list all of the important, essential points an author makes and on the other, list all of the interesting yet non-critical ideas.

- Highlight, circle, or underline any dates or data in non-fiction passages. Pay attention to headings, captions, and any graphs or diagrams.

- When reading a fictional passage, delineate important information such as theme, character, setting, conflict (what the problem is), and resolution (how the problem is fixed). Most often, these are the most important aspects contained in fictional text.

- If a non-fiction passage is instructional in nature, take physical note of any steps in the order of their importance as presented by the author. Look for words such as first, next, then, and last.

Determining the importance of an author's ideas is critical to synthesis in that it requires the test taker to parse out any unnecessary information and demonstrate they have the ability to make sound determination on what is important to the author, and what is merely a supporting or less critical detail.

Asking Questions While Reading

A reader must ask questions while reading. This demonstrates their ability to critically approach information and apply higher thinking skills to an author's content. Some of these questions have been addressed earlier in this section. A reader must ask what is or isn't important, what relates to their experience, and what relates to the world in general. However, it's important to ask other questions as well in order to make connections and synthesize reading material. Consider the following partial list of possibilities:

- What type of passage is this? Is it fiction? Non-fiction? Does it include data?
- Based on the type of passage, what information should be noted in order to make connections, visualize details, and determine importance?
- What is the author's message or theme? What is it they want the reader to understand?
- Is this passage trying to convince readers of something? What is it? If so, is the argument logical, convincing, and effective? How so? If not, how not?
- What do readers already know about this topic? Are there other viewpoints that support or contradict it?
- Is the information in this passage current and up to date?
- Is the author trying to teach readers a lesson? If so, what is it? Is there a moral to this story?
- How does this passage relate to experience?
- What is not as understandable in this passage? What context clues can help with understanding?
- What conclusions can be drawn? What predictions can be made?

Again, the above should be considered only a small example of the possibilities. Any question the reader asks while reading will help achieve synthesis and full reading comprehension.

Understanding the Characteristics of Literary Genres

Classifying literature involves an understanding of the concept of genre. A **genre** is a category of literature that possesses similarities in style and in characteristics. Based on form and structure, there are four basic genres.

Fictional Prose
Fictional prose consists of fictional works written in standard form with a natural flow of speech and without poetic structure. Fictional prose primarily utilizes grammatically complete sentences and a paragraph structure to convey its message.

Drama
Drama is fiction that is written to be performed in a variety of media, intended to be performed for an audience, and structured for that purpose. It might be composed using poetry or prose, often straddling the elements of both in what actors are expected to present. Action and dialogue are the tools used in drama to tell the story.

Poetry
Poetry is verse that has a unique focus on the rhythm of language and focuses on intensity of feeling. It is not an entire story, though it may tell one; it is compact in form and in function. Poetry can be considered as a poet's brief word picture for a reader. Poetic structure is primarily composed of lines and stanzas. Together, poetic structure and devices are the methods that poets use to lead readers to feeling an effect and, ultimately, to the interpretive message.

Literary Nonfiction
Literary nonfiction is prose writing that is based on current or past real events or real people and includes straightforward accounts as well as those that offer opinions on facts or factual events. The Praxis exam distinguishes between **literary nonfiction**—a form of writing that incorporates literary styles and techniques to create factually-based narratives—and informational texts, which will be addressed in the next section.

Identifying Characteristics of Major Forms Within Each Genre

Fictional Prose
Fiction written in prose can be further broken down into **fiction genres**—types of fiction. Some of the more common genres of fiction are as follows:

- **Classical fiction**: a work of fiction considered timeless in its message or theme, remaining noteworthy and meaningful over decades or centuries—e.g., Charlotte Brontë's *Jane Eyre*, Mark Twain's *Adventures of Huckleberry Finn*

- **Fables**: short fiction that generally features animals, fantastic creatures, or other forces within nature that assume human-like characters and has a moral lesson for the reader—e.g., *Aesop's Fables*

- **Fairy tales**: children's stories with magical characters in imaginary, enchanted lands, usually depicting a struggle between good and evil, a sub-genre of folklore—e.g., Hans Christian Anderson's *The Little Mermaid*, *Cinderella* by the Brothers Grimm

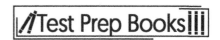

- **Fantasy**: fiction with magic or supernatural elements that cannot occur in the real world, sometimes involving medieval elements in language, usually includes some form of sorcery or witchcraft and sometimes set on a different world—e.g., J.R.R. Tolkien's *The Hobbit*, J.K. Rowling's *Harry Potter and the Sorcerer's Stone*, George R.R. Martin's *A Game of Thrones*

- **Folklore**: types of fiction passed down from oral tradition, stories indigenous to a particular region or culture, with a local flavor in tone, designed to help humans cope with their condition in life and validate cultural traditions, beliefs, and customs—e.g., William Laughead's *Paul Bunyan and The Blue Ox*, the Buddhist story of "The Banyan Deer"

- **Mythology**: closely related to folklore but more widespread, features mystical, otherworldly characters and addresses the basic question of why and how humans exist, relies heavily on allegory and features gods or heroes captured in some sort of struggle—e.g., Greek myths, Genesis I and II in the Bible, Arthurian legends

- **Science fiction**: fiction that uses the principle of extrapolation—loosely defined as a form of prediction—to imagine future realities and problems of the human experience—e.g., Robert Heinlein's *Stranger in a Strange Land*, Ayn Rand's *Anthem*, Isaac Asimov's *I, Robot*, Philip K. Dick's *Do Androids Dream of Electric Sheep?*

- **Short stories**: short works of prose fiction with fully-developed themes and characters, focused on mood, generally developed with a single plot, with a short period of time for settings—e.g., Edgar Allan Poe's "Fall of the House of Usher," Shirley Jackson's "The Lottery," Isaac Bashevis Singer's "Gimpel the Fool"

Drama

Drama refers to a form of literature written for the purpose of performance for an audience. Like prose fiction, drama has several genres. The following are the most common ones:

- **Comedy**: a humorous play designed to amuse and entertain, often with an emphasis on the common person's experience, generally resolved in a positive way—e.g., Richard Sheridan's *School for Scandal*, Shakespeare's *Taming of the Shrew*, Neil Simon's *The Odd Couple*

- **History**: a play based on recorded history where the fate of a nation or kingdom is at the core of the conflict—e.g., Christopher Marlowe's *Edward II*, Shakespeare's *King Richard III*, Arthur Miller's *The Crucible*

- **Tragedy**: a serious play that often involves the downfall of the protagonist. In modern tragedies, the protagonist is not necessarily in a position of power or authority—e.g., Jean Racine's *Phèdre*, Arthur Miller's *Death of a Salesman*, John Steinbeck's *Of Mice and Men*

- **Melodrama**: a play that emphasizes heightened emotion and sensationalism, generally with stereotypical characters in exaggerated or realistic situations and with moral polarization—e.g., Jean-Jacques Rousseau's *Pygmalion*

- **Tragi-comedy**: a play that has elements of both tragedy—a character experiencing a tragic loss—and comedy—the resolution is often positive with no clear distinctive mood for either—e.g., Shakespeare's *The Merchant of Venice*, Anton Chekhov's *The Cherry Orchard*

Poetry

The genre of **poetry** refers to literary works that focus on the expression of feelings and ideas through the use of structure and linguistic rhythm to create a desired effect.

Different poetic structures and devices are used to create the various major forms of poetry. Some of the most common forms are discussed in the following chart.

Type	Poetic Structure	Example
Ballad	A poem or song passed down orally which tells a story and in English tradition usually uses an ABAB or ABCB rhyme scheme	William Butler Yeats' "The Ballad of Father O'Hart"
Epic	A long poem from ancient oral tradition which narrates the story of a legendary or heroic protagonist	Homer's *The Odyssey* Virgil's *The Aeneid*
Haiku	A Japanese poem of three unrhymed lines with five, seven, and five syllables (in English) with nature as a common subject matter	Matsuo Bashō "An old silent pond . . . A frog jumps into the pond, splash! Silence again."
Limerick	A five-line poem written in an AABBA rhyme scheme, with a witty focus	From Edward Lear's *Book of Nonsense*: "There was a Young Person of Smyrna Whose grandmother threatened to burn her . . ."
Ode	A formal lyric poem that addresses and praises a person, place, thing, or idea	Edna St. Vincent Millay's "Ode to Silence"
Sonnet	A fourteen-line poem written in iambic pentameter	Shakespeare's Sonnets 18 and 130

Literary Nonfiction

Nonfiction works are best characterized by their subject matter, which must be factual and real, describing true life experiences. There are several common types of literary non-fiction.

Biography

A **biography** is a work written about a real person (historical or currently living). It involves factual accounts of the person's life, often in a re-telling of those events based on available, researched factual information. The re-telling and dialogue, especially if related within quotes, must be accurate and reflect reliable sources. A biography reflects the time and place in which the person lived, with the goal of creating an understanding of the person and their human experience. Examples of well-known biographies include *The Life of Samuel Johnson* by James Boswell and *Steve Jobs* by Walter Isaacson.

Autobiography

An **autobiography** is a factual account of a person's life written by that person. It may contain some or all of the same elements as a biography, but the author is the subject matter. An autobiography will be told in first person narrative. Examples of well-known autobiographies in literature include *Night* by Elie Wiesel and *Margaret Thatcher: The Autobiography* by Margaret Thatcher.

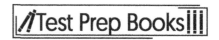

Memoir

A **memoir** is a historical account of a person's life and experiences written by one who has personal, intimate knowledge of the information. The line between memoir, autobiography, and biography is often muddled, but generally speaking, a memoir covers a specific timeline of events as opposed to the other forms of nonfiction. A memoir is less all-encompassing. It is also less formal in tone and tends to focus on the emotional aspect of the presented timeline of events. Some examples of memoirs in literature include *Angela's Ashes* by Frank McCourt and *All Creatures Great and Small* by James Herriot.

Journalism

Some forms of **journalism** can fall into the category of literary non-fiction—e.g., travel writing, nature writing, sports writing, the interview, and sometimes, the essay. Some examples include Elizabeth Kolbert's "The Lost World," in the Annals of Extinction series for *The New Yorker* and Gary Smith's "Ali and His Entourage" for ***Sports Illustrated***.

Identifying Literary Contexts

Understanding that works of literature emerged either because of a particular context—or perhaps despite a context—is key to analyzing them effectively.

Historical Context

The **historical context** of a piece of literature can refer to the time period, setting, or conditions of living at the time it was written as well as the context of the work. For example, Hawthorne's *The Scarlet Letter* was published in 1850, though the setting of the story is 1642–1649. Historically, then, when Hawthorne wrote his novel, the United States found itself at odds as the beginnings of a potential Civil War were in view. Thus, the historical context is potentially significant as it pertains to the ideas of traditions and values, which Hawthorne addresses in his story of Hester Prynne in the era of Puritanism.

Cultural Context

The **cultural context** of a piece of literature refers to cultural factors, such as the beliefs, religions, and customs that surround and are in a work of literature. The Puritan's beliefs, religion, and customs in Hawthorne's novel would be significant as they are at the core of the plot—the reason Hester wears the *A* and why Arthur kills himself. The customs of people in the Antebellum Period, though not quite as restrictive, were still somewhat similar. This would impact how the audience of the time received the novel.

Literary Context

Literary context refers to the consideration of the genre, potentially at the time the work was written. In 1850, Realism and Romanticism were the driving forces in literature in the U.S., with depictions of life as it was at the time in which the work was written or the time it was written *about* as well as some works celebrating the beauty of nature. Thus, an audience in Hawthorne's time would have been well satisfied with the elements of both offered in the text. They would have been looking for details about everyday things and people (Realism), but they also would appreciate his approach to description of nature and the focus on the individual (American Romanticism). The contexts would be significant as they would pertain to evaluating the work against those criteria.

Here are some questions to use when considering context:

- When was the text written?
- What was society like at the time the text was written, or what was it like, given the work's identified time period?
- Who or what influenced the writer?
- What political or social influences might there have been?
- What influences may there have been in the genre that may have affected the writer?

Additionally, test takers should familiarize themselves with literary periods such as Old and Middle English, American Colonial, American Renaissance, American Naturalistic, and British and American Modernist and Post-Modernist movements. Most students of literature will have had extensive exposure to these literary periods in history, and while it is not necessary to recognize every major literary work on sight and associate that work to its corresponding movement or cultural context, the test taker should be familiar enough with the historical and cultural significance of each test passage in order to be able to address test questions correctly.

The following brief description of literary contexts and their associated literary examples follows. It is not an all-inclusive list. The test taker should read each description, then follow up with independent study to clarify each movement, its context, its most familiar authors, and their works.

Metaphysical Poetry
Metaphysical poetry is the descriptor applied to 17th century poets whose poetry emphasized the lyrical quality of their work. These works contain highly creative poetic conceits or metaphoric comparisons between two highly dissimilar things or ideas. Metaphysical poetry is characterized by highly prosaic language and complicated, often layered, metaphor.

Poems such as John Donne's "The Flea," Andrew Marvell's "To His Coy Mistress," George Herbert's "The Collar," Henry Vaughan's "The World," and Richard Crashaw's "A Song" are associated with this type of poetry.

British Romanticism
British Romanticism was a cultural and literary movement within Europe that developed at the end of the 18th century and extended into the 19th century. It occurred partly in response to aristocratic, political, and social norms and partly in response to the Industrial Revolution of the day. Characterized by intense emotion, major literary works of British Romanticism embrace the idea of aestheticism and the beauty of nature. Literary works exalted folk customs and historical art and encouraged spontaneity of artistic endeavor. The movement embraced the heroic ideal and the concept that heroes would raise the quality of society.

Authors who are classified as British Romantics include Samuel Taylor Coleridge, John Keats, George Byron, Mary Shelley, Percy Bysshe Shelley, and William Blake. Well-known works include Samuel Taylor Coleridge's "Kubla Khan," John Keats' "Ode on a Grecian Urn," George Byron's "Childe Harold's Pilgrimage," Mary Shelley's *Frankenstein*, Percy Bysshe Shelley's "Ode to the West Wind," and William Blake's "The Tyger."

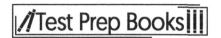

American Romanticism

American Romanticism occurred within the American literary scene beginning early in the 19th century. While many aspects were similar to British Romanticism, it is further characterized as having gothic aspects and the idea that individualism was to be encouraged. It also embraced the concept of the **noble savage**—the idea that indigenous culture uncorrupted by civilization is better than advanced society.

Well-known authors and works include Nathanial Hawthorne's *The House of the Seven Gables*, Edgar Allan Poe's "The Raven" and "The Cask of Amontillado," Emily Dickinson's "I Felt a Funeral in My Brain" and James Fenimore Cooper's *The Last of the Mohicans.*

Transcendentalism

Transcendentalism was a movement that applied to a way of thinking that developed within the United States, specifically New England, around 1836. While this way of thinking originally employed philosophical aspects, transcendentalism spread to all forms of art, literature, and even to the ways people chose to live. It was born out of a reaction to traditional rationalism and purported concepts such as a higher divinity, feminism, humanitarianism, and communal living. Transcendentalism valued intuition, self-reliance, and the idea that human nature was inherently good.

Well-known authors include Ralph Waldo Emerson, Henry David Thoreau, Louisa May Alcott, and Ellen Sturgis Hooper. Works include Ralph Waldo Emerson's "Self-Reliance" and "Uriel," Henry David Thoreau's *Walden* and *Civil Disobedience*, Louisa May Alcott's *Little Women*, and Ellen Sturgis Hooper's "I Slept, and Dreamed that Life was Beauty."

The Harlem Renaissance

The Harlem Renaissance is the descriptor given to the cultural, artistic, and social boom that developed in Harlem, New York, at the beginning of the 20th century, spanning the 1920s and 1930s. Originally termed **The New Negro Movement**, it emphasized African-American urban cultural expression and migration across the United States. It had strong roots in African-American Christianity, discourse, and intellectualism. The Harlem Renaissance heavily influenced the development of music and fashion as well. Its singular characteristic was to embrace Pan-American culturalisms; however, strong themes of the slavery experience and African-American folk traditions also emerged. A hallmark of the Harlem Renaissance was that it laid the foundation for the future Civil Rights Movement in the United States.

Well-known authors and works include Zora Neale Hurston's *Their Eyes Were Watching God*, Richard Wright's *Native Son*, Langston Hughes' "I, Too," and James Weldon Johnson's "God's Trombones: Seven Negro Sermons in Verse" and *The Book of American Negro Poetry.*

Practice Quiz

Questions 1-5 are based upon the following passage:

The Myth of Head Heat Loss

It has recently been brought to my attention that most people believe that 75% of your body heat is lost through your head. I had certainly heard this before, and am not going to attempt to say I didn't believe it when I first heard it. It is natural to be gullible to anything said with enough authority. But the "fact" that the majority of your body heat is lost through your head is a lie.

Let me explain. Heat loss is proportional to surface area exposed. An elephant loses a great deal more heat than an anteater because it has a much greater surface area than an anteater. Each cell has mitochondria that produce energy in the form of heat, and it takes a lot more energy to run an elephant than an anteater.

So, each part of your body loses its proportional amount of heat in accordance with its surface area. The human torso probably loses the most heat, though the legs lose a significant amount as well. Some people have asked, "Why does it feel so much warmer when you cover your head than when you don't?" Well, that's because your head, because it is not clothed, is losing a lot of heat while the clothing on the rest of your body provides insulation. If you went outside with a hat and pants but no shirt, not only would you look stupid but your heat loss would be significantly greater because so much more of you would be exposed. So, if given the choice to cover your chest or your head in the cold, choose the chest. It could save your life.

1. What is the primary purpose of this passage?
    a. To provide evidence that disproves a myth
    b. To compare elephants and anteaters
    c. To explain why it is appropriate to wear clothes in winter
    d. To show how people are gullible

2. Which of the following best describes the main idea of the passage?
    a. It is better to wear a shirt than a hat
    b. Heat loss is proportional to surface area exposed
    c. It is natural to be gullible
    d. The human chest loses the most heat

3. Why does the author compare elephants and anteaters?
    a. To express an opinion
    b. To give an example that helps clarify the main point
    c. To show the differences between them
    d. To persuade why one is better than the other

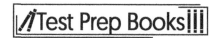

4. The statement, "If you went outside with a hat and pants but no shirt, not only would you look stupid, but your heat loss would be significantly greater because so much more of you would be exposed" is which of the following?

    a. An opinion
    b. A fact
    c. An opinion within a fact
    d. Neither

5. Which of the following best describes the tone of the passage?

    a. Harsh
    b. Angry
    c. Casual
    d. Indifferent

Answer Explanations

1. A: Not only does the article provide examples to disprove a myth, the title also suggests that the article is trying to disprove a myth. Further, the sentence, "But the 'fact' that the majority of your body heat is lost through your head is a lie," and then the subsequent "let me explain," demonstrates the author's intention in disproving a myth. *B* is incorrect because although the selection does compare elephants and anteaters, it does so in order to prove a point, and is not the primary reason that the selection was written. *C* is incorrect because even though the article mentions somebody wearing clothes in the winter, and that doing so could save your life, wearing clothes in the winter is not the primary reason this article was written. *D* is incorrect because the article only mentions that people are gullible once, and makes no further comment on the matter, so this cannot be the primary purpose.

2. B: If the myth is that most of one's body heat is lost through their head, then the fact that heat loss is proportional to surface area exposed is the best evidence that disproves it, since one's head is a great deal less surface area than the rest of the body, making *B* the correct choice. "It is better to wear a shirt than a hat" does not provide evidence that disproves the fact that the head loses more heat than the rest of the body. Thus, *A* is incorrect. *C* is incorrect because gullibility is mentioned only once in this passage and the rest of the article ignores this statement, so clearly it is not the main idea. Finally, *D* is incorrect because though the article mentions that the human chest probably loses the most heat, it is to provide an example of the evidence that heat loss is proportional to surface area exposed, so this is not the main idea of the passage.

3. B: Choice *B* is correct because the author is trying to demonstrate the main idea, which is that heat loss is proportional to surface area, and so they compare two animals with different surface areas to clarify the main point. Choice *A* is incorrect because the author uses elephants and anteaters to prove a point that heat loss is proportional to surface area, not to express an opinion. Choice *C* is incorrect because though the author does use them to show differences, they do so in order to give examples that prove the above points. Choice *D* is incorrect because there is no language to indicate favoritism between the two animals.

4. C: Since there is an opinion presented along with a fact, *C* is the correct answer. *A* is incorrect—"Not only would you look stupid," is an opinion because there is no way to prove that somebody would look stupid by not wearing a shirt in the cold, even if that may be a popular opinion. However, this opinion is sandwiched inside a factual statement. *B* is incorrect because again, this is a factual statement, but it has been editorialized by interjecting an opinion. Because of the presence of both a fact and an opinion, *D* is the opposite of the correct answer.

5. C: Because of the way the author addresses the reader and the colloquial language the author uses (e.g., "let me explain," "so," "well," didn't," "you would look stupid," etc.), Choice *C* is the best answer because it has a much more casual tone than the usual informative article. Choice *A* may be a tempting choice because the author says the "fact" that most of one's heat is lost through their head is a "lie" and that someone who does not wear a shirt in the cold looks stupid. However, this only happens twice within the passage, and the passage does not give an overall tone of harshness. Choice *B* is incorrect because again, while not necessarily nice, the language does not carry an angry charge. The author is clearly not indifferent to the subject because of the passionate language that they use, so Choice *D* is incorrect.

Essay

Essay Skills

The essay on the FTCE General Knowledge exam will give the test taker the option of choosing between two topics. Fifty minutes is given to plan, write, and edit the essay. Test takers will not be judged on the position they take, but how well they present that position. Raters look at content, ability to support claims, organization, writing style, and mechanics. Essays are scored on a scale from one to six. A score of one is the weakest, while six is a highly effective essay. The list below is a good indicator of what the raters will look for when reading the final essay.

- Consider the audience and purpose of the assignment
- Formulate a clear introduction to the topic
- Conclude the introduction with a clear thesis
- Organize ideas effectively
- Provide support of your claims through proper evidence (may include anecdotal experience)
- Implement effective transitions between paragraphs and sentences
- Use standard written English
- End with a conclusion that summarizes the information appropriately
- Use a variety of sentence structures
- Maintain consistent point of view throughout
- Avoid slang and clichés

Brainstorming

One of the most important steps in writing an essay is prewriting. Before drafting an essay, it's helpful to think about the topic for a moment or two, in order to gain a more solid understanding of the task. Then, spending about five minutes jotting down the immediate ideas that could work for the essay is recommended. It is a way to get some words on the page and offer a reference for ideas when drafting. Scratch paper is provided for writers to use any prewriting techniques such as webbing, free writing, or listing. The goal is to get ideas out of the mind and onto the page.

Considering Opposing Viewpoints

In the planning stage, it's important to consider all aspects of the topic, including different viewpoints on the subject. There are more than two ways to look at a topic, and a strong argument considers those opposing viewpoints. Considering opposing viewpoints can help writers present a fair, balanced, and informed essay that shows consideration for all readers. This approach can also strengthen an argument by recognizing and potentially refuting opposing viewpoint(s).

Drawing from personal experience may help to support ideas. For example, if the goal for writing is a personal narrative, then the story should come from the writer's own life. Many writers find it helpful to draw from personal experience, even in an essay that is not strictly narrative. Personal anecdotes or short stories can help to illustrate a point in other types of essays as well.

Moving from Brainstorming to Planning

Once the ideas are on the page, it's time to turn them into a solid plan for the essay. The best ideas from the brainstorming results can then be developed into a more formal outline. An outline typically has one main point (the thesis) and at least three sub-points that support the main point. Here's an example:

Main Idea
-Point #1
-Point #2
-Point #3

Of course, there will be details under each point, but this approach is the best for dealing with timed writing.

Staying on Track

Basing the essay on the outline aids in both organization and coherence. The goal is to ensure that there is enough time to develop each sub-point in the essay, roughly spending an equal amount of time on each idea. Keeping an eye on the time will help. If there are fifteen minutes left to draft the essay, then it makes sense to spend about 5 minutes on each of the ideas. Staying on task is critical to success and timing out the parts of the essay can help writers avoid feeling overwhelmed.

Parts of the Essay

The introduction should do a few important things:

- Establish the topic of the essay in original wording (i.e., not just repeating the prompt)

- Clarify the significance/importance of the topic or purpose for writing (not too many details, a brief overview)

- Offer a thesis statement that identifies the writer's own viewpoint on the topic (typically one to two brief sentences as a clear, concise explanation of the main point on the topic)

Body paragraphs reflect the ideas developed in the outline. Three-four points is probably sufficient for a short essay, and they should include the following:

- A topic sentence that identifies the sub-point (e.g., a reason why, a way how, a cause or effect)

- A detailed explanation of the point, explaining why the writer thinks this point is valid

- Illustrative examples, such as personal examples or real-world examples, that support and validate the point (i.e., "prove" the point)

- A concluding sentence that connects the examples, reasoning, and analysis to the point being made

The conclusion, or final paragraph, should be brief and should reiterate the focus, clarifying why the discussion is significant or important. It is important to avoid adding specific details or new ideas to this paragraph. The purpose of the conclusion is to sum up what has been said to bring the discussion to a close.

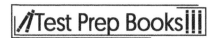

Don't Panic!

Writing an essay can be overwhelming, and performance panic is a natural response. The outline serves as a basis for the writing and helps writers keep focused. Getting stuck can also happen, and it's helpful to remember that brainstorming can be done at any time during the writing process. Following the steps of the writing process is the best defense against writer's block.

Timed essays can be particularly stressful, but assessors are trained to recognize the necessary planning and thinking for these timed efforts. Using the plan above and sticking to it helps with time management. Timing each part of the process helps writers stay on track. Sometimes writers try to cover too much in their essays. If time seems to be running out, this is an opportunity to determine whether all of the ideas in the outline are necessary. Three body paragraphs are sufficient, and more than that is probably too much to cover in a short essay.

More isn't always better in writing. A strong essay will be clear and concise. It will avoid unnecessary or repetitive details. It is better to have a concise, five-paragraph essay that makes a clear point, than a ten-paragraph essay that doesn't. The goal is to write one to two pages of quality writing. Paragraphs should also reflect balance; if the introduction goes to the bottom of the first page, the writing may be going off-track or be repetitive. It's best to fall into the one-two page range, but a complete, well-developed essay is the ultimate goal.

The Final Steps

Leaving a few minutes at the end to revise and proofread offers an opportunity for writers to polish things up. Putting one's self in the reader's shoes and focusing on what the essay actually says helps writers identify problems—it's a movement from the mindset of writer to the mindset of editor. The goal is to have a clean, clear copy of the essay. The following areas should be considered when proofreading:

- Sentence fragments
- Awkward sentence structure
- Run-on sentences
- Incorrect word choice
- Grammatical agreement errors
- Spelling errors
- Punctuation errors
- Capitalization errors

The Short Overview

The essay may seem challenging, but following these steps can help writers focus:

1. Take one or two minutes to think about the topic.
2. Generate some ideas through brainstorming (three-four minutes).
3. Organize ideas into a brief outline, selecting just three-four main points to cover in the essay (eventually the body paragraphs).
4. Develop essay in parts.
5. Introduction paragraph, with intro to topic and main points
6. Viewpoint on the subject at the end of the introduction

119

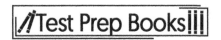

7. Body paragraphs, based on outline
8. Each paragraph: makes a main point, explains the viewpoint, uses examples to support the point
9. Brief conclusion highlighting the main points and closing
10. Read over the essay (last five minutes).
11. Look for any obvious errors, making sure that the writing makes sense.

While this information should be used to help assemble a coherent essay on the FTCE, its use extends beyond the testing date and can be applied to general academic writing. These foundational principles will be helpful in the classroom, while instructing students on the art and science of high-quality writing.

Practice Test #1

English Language Skills

1. DIRECTIONS: Choose the sentence that has an error in capitalization.
   a. The East Coast has experienced very unpredictable weather this year.
   b. My Uncle owns a home in Florida, where he lives in the winter.
   c. I am taking English Composition II on campus this fall.
   d. There are several nice beaches we can visit on our trip to the Jersey Shore this summer.

2. DIRECTIONS: Choose the answer that acts as an adjective in the following sentence.

   Julia Robinson, an avid photographer in her spare time, was able to capture stunning shots of the local wildlife on her last business trip to Australia.

   a. Time
   b. Capture
   c. Avid
   d. Photographer

3. DIRECTIONS: Choose the option that corrects an error in the underlined portion. If no error exists, choose "No change is necessary."

   Every morning <u>we would wake up, eat breakfast, and broke camp.</u>

   a. we are waking up, eating breakfast, and breaking camp.
   b. we would wake up, eat breakfast, and break camp.
   c. would we wake up, eat breakfast, and break camp?
   d. No change is necessary.

4. DIRECTIONS: Choose the answer that acts as a compound sentence.
   a. Alex and Shane spent the morning coloring and later took a walk down to the park.
   b. After coloring all morning, Alex and Shane spent the afternoon at the park.
   c. Alex and Shane spent the morning coloring, and then they took a walk down to the park.
   d. After coloring all morning and spending part of the day at the park, Alex and Shane took a nap.

5. DIRECTIONS: Choose the example that shows incorrect use of subject-verb agreement.
   a. Neither of the cars are parked on the street.
   b. Both of my kids are going to camp this summer.
   c. Any of your friends are welcome to join us on the trip in November.
   d. Each of the clothing options is appropriate for the job interview.

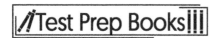

6. DIRECTIONS: Choose the option that corrects an error in the underlined portion. If no error exists, choose "No change is necessary."

Above all, it allowed us to share adventures. While traveling across America, which we could not have experienced in cars and hotels.

    a. Above all, it allowed us to share adventures—while traveling across America
    b. Above all, it allowed us to share adventures while traveling across America
    c. Above all, it allowed us to share adventures; while traveling across America
    d. No change is necessary.

7. DIRECTIONS: Choose the option that corrects an error in the underlined portion. If no error exists, choose "No change is necessary."

Those are also memories that my siblings and me have now shared with our own children.

    a. Those are also memories that I and my siblings
    b. Those are also memories that me and my siblings
    c. Those are also memories that my siblings and I
    d. No change is necessary.

8. DIRECTIONS: Choose the example that uses correct spelling.
    a. Leslie knew that training for the Philadelphia Marathon would take dicsipline and perserverance, but she was up to the challenge.
    b. Leslie knew that training for the Philadelphia Marathon would take discipline and perseverence, but she was up to the challenge.
    c. Leslie knew that training for the Philadelphia Marathon would take disiplin and perservearance, but she was up to the challenge.
    d. Leslie knew that training for the Philadelphia Marathon would take discipline and perseverance, but she was up to the challenge.

9. DIRECTIONS: Choose the option that corrects an error in the underlined portion. If no error exists, choose "No change is necessary."

Hampton was born and raised in Maywood of Chicago, Illinois in 1948.

    a. in Chicago, Illinois of Maywood in 1948.
    b. in Maywood, of Chicago, Illinois in 1948.
    c. in Maywood of Chicago, Illinois, in 1948.
    d. No change is necessary.

10. DIRECTIONS: Choose the example that uses the correct plural form.
    a. Tomatos
    b. Analysis
    c. Cacti
    d. Criterion

11. DIRECTIONS: Choose the example that uses correct punctuation.
   a. The moderator asked the candidates, "Is each of you prepared to discuss your position on global warming?".
   b. The moderator asked the candidates, "Is each of you prepared to discuss your position on global warming?"
   c. The moderator asked the candidates, 'Is each of you prepared to discuss your position on global warming?'
   d. The moderator asked the candidates, "Is each of you prepared to discuss your position on global warming"?

12. DIRECTIONS: Choose the option that corrects an error in the underlined portion. If no error exists, choose "No change is necessary."

Hampton was quickly attracted to the Black Panther Party's approach to the fight for equal rights for African Americans.

   a. Black Panther Parties' approach
   b. Black Panther Parties approach
   c. Black Panther Partys' approach
   d. No change is necessary.

13. DIRECTIONS: Choose the following sentence in which the word *part* functions as an adjective.
   a. The part Brian was asked to play required many hours of research.
   b. She parts ways with the woodsman at the end of the book.
   c. The entire team played a part in the success of the project.
   d. Ronaldo is part Irish on his mother's side of the family.

14. DIRECTIONS: Choose the example that acts as a complete subject of the following sentence.

All of Shannon's family and friends helped her to celebrate her 50th birthday at Café Sorrento.

   a. Family and friends
   b. All
   c. All of Shannon's family and friends
   d. Shannon's family and friends

15. DIRECTIONS: Choose the word that is misspelled in the following sentence.

Hampton's greatest acheivement as the leader of the BPP may be his fight against street gang violence in Chicago.

   a. leader
   b. greatest
   c. acheivement
   d. No change is necessary.

123

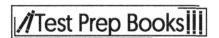
16. DIRECTIONS: Choose the option that corrects an error in the underlined portion. If no error exists, choose "No change is necessary."

In 1969, <u>Hampton was held by a press conference</u> where he made the gangs agree to a nonaggression pact known as the Rainbow Coalition.

a. Hampton to hold a press conference
b. Hampton held a press conference
c. Hampton, holding a press conference
d. No change is necessary.

17. DIRECTIONS: Choose the sentence that correctly uses a hyphen.
a. Last-year, many of the players felt unsure of the coach's methods.
b. Some of the furniture she selected seemed a bit over - the - top for the space.
c. Henry is a beagle-mix and is ready for adoption this weekend.
d. Geena works to maintain a good relationship with her ex-husband to the benefit of their children.

18. DIRECTIONS: Choose the option that corrects an error in the underlined portion. If no error exists, choose "No change is necessary."

<u>In 1976; seven years after the event,</u> it was revealed that William O'Neal, Hampton's trusted bodyguard, was an undercover FBI agent.

a. In 1976. Seven years after the event,
b. In 1976, seven years after the event,
c. In 1976 seven years after the event,
d. No change is necessary.

19. DIRECTIONS: Choose the sentence that shows correct word usage.
a. It's often been said that work is better then rest.
b. Its often been said that work is better then rest.
c. It's often been said that work is better than rest.
d. Its often been said that work is better than rest.

20. DIRECTIONS: Choose the example that correctly identifies the meaning of the suffix -fy as seen in the words below.

Glorify, fortify, gentrify, acidify

a. Marked by, given to
b. Doer, believer
c. Make, cause, cause to have
d. Process, state, rank

124

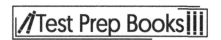

21. DIRECTIONS: Choose the option that corrects an error in the underlined portion. If no error exists, choose "No change is necessary."

Early in my career, <u>a master's teacher shared this thought with me "Education is the last bastion of civility."</u>

    a. a master's teacher shared this thought with me. "Education is the last bastion of civility."
    b. a master's teacher shared this thought with me: "Education is the last bastion of civility."
    c. a master's teacher shared this thought with me: "Education is the last bastion of civility".
    d. No change is necessary.

22. DIRECTIONS: Choose the example that acts as an imperative sentence.
    a. Pennsylvania's state flag includes two draft horses and an eagle.
    b. Go down to the basement and check the hot water heater for signs of a leak.
    c. You must be so excited to have a new baby on the way!
    d. How many countries speak Spanish?

23. DIRECTIONS: Choose which are the transitional words in the following sentence.

    After a long day at work, Tracy had dinner with her family, and then took a walk to the park.

    a. After, then
    b. At, with, to
    c. Had, took
    d. A, the

24. DIRECTIONS: Choose which words are misspelled in the following sentence.

It is really what makes us human and what <u>distinguishes</u> us as <u>civilised</u> <u>creatures.</u>

    a. creatures
    b. distinguishes
    c. civilised
    d. No change is necessary.

25. DIRECTIONS: Choose the words that function as nouns in the following sentence.

    Robert needed to find at least four sources for his final project, so he searched several library databases for reliable academic research.

    a. Robert, sources, project, databases, research
    b. Robert, sources, final, project, databases, academic, research
    c. Robert, sources, project, he, library, databases, research
    d. Sources, project, databases, research

26. DIRECTIONS: Choose the sentence that uses correct subject-verb agreement.
    a. There is two constellations that can be seen from the back of the house.
    b. At least four of the sheep needs to be sheared before the end of summer.
    c. Lots of people were auditioning for the singing competition on Saturday.
    d. Everyone in the group have completed the assignment on time.

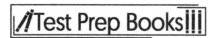

27. DIRECTIONS: Choose the option that corrects an error in the underlined portion. If no error exists, choose "No change is necessary."

Education should never discriminate on any basis, and it should create individuals who are self-sufficient, patriotic, and tolerant of <u>others' ideas.</u>

    a. others's ideas
    b. other's ideas
    c. others ideas
    d. No change is necessary.

28. DIRECTIONS: Choose the option that corrects an error in the underlined portion. If no error exists, choose "No change is necessary."

<u>All children can learn. Although not all children learn in the same manner.</u>

    a. All children can learn, although not all children learn in the same manner.
    b. All children can learn although not all children learn in the same manner.
    c. All children can learn although, not all children learn in the same manner.
    d. No change is necessary.

29. DIRECTIONS: Choose the option that corrects an error in the underlined portion. If no error exists, choose "No change is necessary."

If teachers set high expectations for <u>there students</u>, the students will rise to that high level.

    a. thare students
    b. they're students
    c. their students
    d. No change is necessary.

30. DIRECTIONS: Choose the option that corrects an error in the underlined portion. If no error exists, choose "No change is necessary."

In the modern age of technology, a teacher's focus is no longer the "what" of the content, <u>but more importantly, the 'why.'</u>

    a. but more importantly, the "why".
    b. but more importantly, the "why."
    c. but more importantly, the 'why'.
    d. No change is necessary.

31. DIRECTIONS: Choose the example that acts as a compound sentence.
    a. Shawn and Jerome played soccer in the backyard for two hours.
    b. Marissa last saw Elena and talked to her this morning.
    c. The baby was sick, so I decided to stay home from work.
    d. Denise, Kurt, and Eric went for a run after dinner.

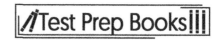

32. DIRECTIONS: Choose the option that corrects an error in the underlined portion. If no error exists, choose "No change is necessary."

Students have to <u>read between the lines, identify bias, and determine</u> who they can trust in the milieu of ads, data, and texts presented to them.

a. reads between the lines, identifies bias, and determines
b. read between the lines, identify bias, and determining
c. read between the lines, identifying bias, and determining
d. No change is necessary.

33. DIRECTIONS: Choose the adjectives in the following sentence.

Philadelphia is home to some excellent walking tours where visitors can learn more about the culture and rich history of the city of brotherly love.

a. Philadelphia, tours, visitors, culture, history, city, love
b. Excellent, walking, rich, brotherly
c. Is, can, learn
d. To, about, of

34. DIRECTIONS: Choose the pronoun pairs to be used in the following sentence.

The realtor showed _____ and _____ a house on Wednesday afternoon.

a. She, I
b. She, me
c. Me, her
d. Her, me

35. DIRECTIONS: Choose the example that uses correct punctuation.
a. Recommended supplies for the hunting trip include the following: rain gear, large backpack, hiking boots, flashlight, and non-perishable foods.
b. I left the store, because I forgot my wallet.
c. As soon as the team checked into the hotel; they met in the lobby for a group photo.
d. None of the furniture came in on time: so they weren't able to move in to the new apartment.

36. DIRECTIONS: Identify the structure of the following sentence.
The restaurant is unconventional because it serves both Chicago style pizza and New York style pizza.

a. Simple
b. Compound
c. Complex
d. Compound-complex

127

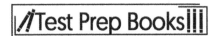

37. DIRECTIONS: Identify the kind of error found in the following sentence.
    This summer, I'm planning to travel to Italy, take a Mediterranean cruise, going to Pompeii, and eat a lot of Italian food.

    a. Parallelism
    b. Sentence fragment
    c. Misplaced modifier
    d. Subject-verb agreement

38. DIRECTIONS: Identify the kind of error found in the following sentence.
    Forgetting that he was supposed to meet his girlfriend for dinner, Anita was mad when Fred showed up late.

    a. Parallelism
    b. Run-on sentence
    c. Misplaced modifier
    d. Subject-verb agreement

39. DIRECTIONS: Choose the example that uses correct punctuation.
    a. Carole is not currently working; her focus is on her children at the moment.
    b. Carole is not currently working and her focus is on her children at the moment.
    c. Carole is not currently working, her focus is on her children at the moment.
    d. Carole is not currently working her focus is on her children at the moment.

40. DIRECTIONS: Identify the kind of error found in the following sentence.
    Some workers use all their sick leave, other workers cash out their leave.

    a. Parallelism
    b. Comma splice
    c. Sentence fragment
    d. Subject-verb agreement

Mathematics

41. Which of the following numbers has the greatest value?
    a. 1.43785
    b. 1.07548
    c. 1.43592
    d. 0.89409

42. The value of 6 x 12 is the same as:
    a. 2 x 4 x 4 x 2
    b. 7 x 4 x 3
    c. 6 x 6 x 3
    d. 3 x 3 x 4 x 2

43. This chart indicates how many sales of CDs, vinyl records, and MP3 downloads occurred over the last year. Approximately what percentage of the total sales was from CDs?

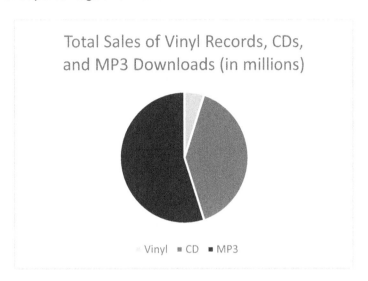

Total Sales of Vinyl Records, CDs, and MP3 Downloads (in millions)

Vinyl ▪ CD ▪ MP3

a. 55%
b. 25%
c. 40%
d. 5%

44. After a 20% sale discount, Frank purchased a new refrigerator for $850. How much did he save from the original price?
a. $170
b. $212.50
c. $105.75
d. $200

45. A student gets an 85% on a test with 20 questions. How many answers did the student solve correctly?
a. 16
b. 17
c. 18
d. 19

46. Alan currently weighs 200 pounds, but he wants to lose weight to get down to 175 pounds. What is this difference in kilograms? (1 pound is approximately equal to 0.45 kilograms.)
a. 9 kg
b. 11.25 kg
c. 78.75 kg
d. 90 kg

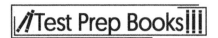

47. Johnny earns $2,334.50 from his job each month. He pays $1,437 for monthly expenses. Johnny is planning a vacation in 3 months that he estimates will cost $1,750 total. How much will Johnny have left over from three months of saving once he pays for his vacation?

    a. $948.50
    b. $584.50
    c. $852.50
    d. $942.50

48. What is $\frac{420}{98}$ rounded to the nearest integer?

    a. 3
    b. 4
    c. 5
    d. 6

49. Dwayne has received the following scores on his math tests: 78, 92, 83, 97. What score must Dwayne get on his next math test to have an overall average of 90?

    a. 89
    b. 98
    c. 95
    d. 100

50. What is the overall median of Dwayne's current scores: 78, 92, 83, 97?

    a. 19
    b. 85
    c. 83
    d. 87.5

51. Solve the following:

$$\left(\sqrt{36} \times \sqrt{16}\right) - 3^2$$

    a. 30
    b. 21
    c. 15
    d. 13

52. In Jim's school, there are 3 girls for every 2 boys. There are 650 students in total. Using this information, how many students are girls?

    a. 260
    b. 130
    c. 65
    d. 390

53. Five of six numbers have a sum of 25. The average of all six numbers is 6. What is the sixth number?

    a. 8
    b. 12
    c. 11
    d. 10

54. Kimberley earns $10 an hour babysitting, and after 10 p.m., she earns $12 an hour, with the amount paid being rounded to the nearest hour accordingly. On her last job, she worked from 5:30 p.m. to 11 p.m. In total, how much did Kimberley earn on her last job?

    a. $45

    b. $57

    c. $62

    d. $42

55. Arrange the following numbers from least to greatest value:

$$0.85, \frac{4}{5}, \frac{2}{3}, \frac{91}{100}$$

    a. $0.85, \frac{4}{5}, \frac{2}{3}, \frac{91}{100}$

    b. $\frac{4}{5}, 0.85, \frac{91}{100}, \frac{2}{3}$

    c. $\frac{2}{3}, \frac{4}{5}, 0.85, \frac{91}{100}$

    d. $0.85, \frac{91}{100}, \frac{4}{5}, \frac{2}{3}$

56. Keith's bakery had 252 customers go through its doors last week. This week, that number increased to 378. Express this increase as a percentage.

    a. 26%

    b. 50%

    c. 35%

    d. 12%

57. The following graph compares the various test scores of the top three students in each of these teacher's classes. Based on the graph, which teacher's students had the lowest range of test scores?

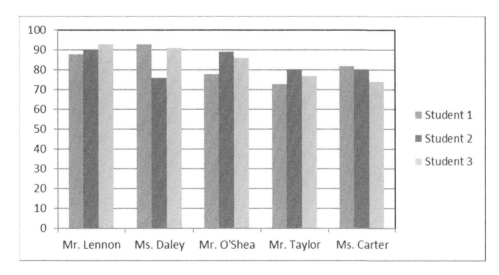

    a. Mr. Lennon

    b. Mr. O'Shea

    c. Mr. Taylor

    d. Ms. Daley

58. Four people split a bill. The first person pays for $\frac{1}{5}$, the second person pays for $\frac{1}{4}$, and the third person pays for $\frac{1}{3}$. What fraction of the bill does the fourth person pay?

    a. $\frac{13}{60}$

    b. $\frac{47}{60}$

    c. $\frac{1}{4}$

    d. $\frac{4}{15}$

59. How is the expression $4\frac{2}{3} - 3\frac{4}{9}$ simplified?

    a. $1\frac{1}{3}$

    b. $1\frac{2}{9}$

    c. 1

    d. $1\frac{2}{3}$

60. A closet is filled with red, blue, and green shirts. If $\frac{1}{3}$ of the shirts are green and $\frac{2}{5}$ are red, what fraction of the shirts are blue?

    a. $\frac{4}{15}$

    b. $\frac{1}{5}$

    c. $\frac{7}{15}$

    d. $\frac{1}{2}$

61. Shawna buys $2\frac{1}{2}$ gallons of paint. If she uses $\frac{1}{3}$ of it on the first day, how much does she have left?

    a. $1\frac{5}{6}$ gallons

    b. $1\frac{1}{2}$ gallons

    c. $1\frac{2}{3}$ gallons

    d. 2 gallons

62. Jessica buys 10 cans of paint. Red paint costs $1 per can and blue paint costs $2 per can. In total, she spends $16. How many red cans did she buy?

    a. 2

    b. 3

    c. 4

    d. 5

63. Six people apply to work for Janice's company, but she only needs four workers. How many different groups of four employees can Janice choose?

 a. 6
 b. 10
 c. 15
 d. 36

64. Which of the following is equivalent to the value of the digit 3 in the number 792.134?

 a. 3×10

 b. 3×100

 c. $\frac{3}{10}$

 d. $\frac{3}{100}$

65. In the following expression, which operation should be completed first? $5 \times 6 + (5 + 4) \div 2 - 1$.

 a. Multiplication
 b. Addition
 c. Division
 d. Parentheses

66. How will the number 847.89632 be written if rounded to the nearest hundredth?

 a. 847.90
 b. 900
 c. 847.89
 d. 847.896

67. The perimeter of a 6-sided polygon is 56 cm. The length of three of the sides are 9 cm each. The length of two other sides are 8 cm each. What is the length of the missing side?

 a. 11 cm
 b. 12 cm
 c. 13 cm
 d. 10 cm

68. Which of the following is a mixed number?

 a. $16\frac{1}{2}$

 b. 16

 c. $\frac{16}{3}$

 d. $\frac{1}{4}$

69. If you were showing your friend how to round 245.2678 to the nearest thousandth, which place value would be used to decide whether to round up or round down?
    a. Ten-thousandth
    b. Thousandth
    c. Hundredth
    d. Thousands

70. What is the value of b in the equation: $5b - 4 = 2b + 17$?
    a. 13
    b. 24
    c. 7
    d. 21

71. What is the solution to $\frac{3}{5} \times \frac{7}{10} \div \frac{1}{2}$ in decimal form?
    a. 0.042
    b. 84%
    c. 0.84
    d. 0.42

72. What is an equivalent measurement for 1.3 cm?
    a. 0.13 m
    b. 0.013 m
    c. 0.13 mm
    d. 0.013 mm

73. Katie works at a clothing company and sold 192 shirts over the weekend. One third of the shirts that were sold were patterned, and the rest were solid. Which mathematical expression would calculate the number of solid shirts Katie sold over the weekend?
    a. $192 \times \frac{1}{3}$
    b. $192 \div \frac{1}{3}$
    c. $192 \times (1 - \frac{1}{3})$
    d. $192 \div 3$

74. Which four-sided shape is always a rectangle?
    a. Rhombus
    b. Square
    c. Parallelogram
    d. Quadrilateral

75. A rectangle was formed out of pipe cleaner. Its length was $\frac{1}{2}$ ft, and its width was $\frac{11}{2}$ inches. What is its area in square inches?
    a. $\frac{11}{4}$ inch^2

    b. $\frac{11}{2}$ inch^2

    c. 22 inches^2

    d. 33 inches^2

76. How will $\frac{4}{5}$ be written as a percent?
   a. 40%
   b. 125%
   c. 90%
   d. 80%

77. If $4x - 3 = 5$, what is the value of x?
   a. 1
   b. 2
   c. 3
   d. 4

78. What is the slope of this line?

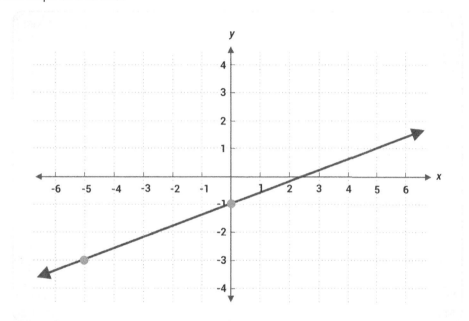

   a. 2
   b. $\frac{5}{2}$
   c. $\frac{1}{2}$
   d. $\frac{2}{5}$

79. 6 is 30% of what number?
   a. 18
   b. 20
   c. 24
   d. 26

80. How will the following algebraic expression be simplified: $(5x^2 - 3x + 4) - (2x^2 - 7)$?
    a. x^5
    b. $3x^2 - 3x + 11$
    c. $3x^2 - 3x - 3$
    d. $x - 3$

Reading Comprehension

Questions 81–93 are based on the following passage.

Christopher Columbus is often credited for discovering America. This is incorrect. First, it is impossible to "discover" something where people already live; however, Christopher Columbus did explore places in the New World that were previously untouched by Europe, so the term "explorer" would be more accurate. Another emendation must be made, as well: Christopher Columbus was not the first European explorer to reach the present-day Americas! Rather, it was Leif Erikson who first came to the New World and contacted the natives, nearly five hundred years before Christopher Columbus.

Leif Erikson, the son of Erik the Red (a famous Viking outlaw and explorer in his own right), was born in either 970 or 980, depending on which historian you seek. His own family, though, did not raise Leif, which was a Viking tradition. Instead, one of Erik's prisoners taught Leif reading and writing, languages, sailing, and weaponry. At age 12, Leif was considered a man and returned to his family. He killed a man during a dispute shortly after his return, and the council banished the Erikson clan to Greenland.

In 999, Leif left Greenland and traveled to Norway where he would serve as a guard to King Olaf Tryggvason. It was there that he became a convert to Christianity. Leif later tried to return home with the intention of taking supplies and spreading Christianity to Greenland, however his ship was blown off course and he arrived in a strange new land: present day Newfoundland, Canada.

When he finally returned to his adopted homeland Greenland, Leif consulted with a merchant who had also seen the shores of this previously unknown land we now know as Canada. The son of the legendary Viking explorer then gathered a crew of 35 men and set sail. Leif became the first European to touch foot in the New World as he explored present-day Baffin Island and Labrador, Canada. His crew called the land Vinland since it was plentiful with grapes.

During their time in present-day Newfoundland, Leif's expedition made contact with the natives whom they referred to as Skraelings (which translates to "wretched ones" in Norse). There are several secondhand accounts of their meetings. Some contemporaries described trade between the peoples. Other accounts describe clashes where the Skraelings defeated the Viking explorers with long spears, while still others claim the Vikings dominated the natives. Regardless of the circumstances, it seems that the Vikings made contact of some kind. This happened around 1000, nearly five hundred years before Columbus famously sailed the ocean blue.

Eventually, in 1003, Leif set sail for home and arrived at Greenland with a ship full of timber.

In 1020, seventeen years later, the legendary Viking died. Many believe that Leif Erikson should receive more credit for his contributions in exploring the New World.

136

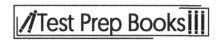

81. Which of the following best describes how the author generally presents the information?
    a. Chronological order
    b. Comparison-contrast
    c. Cause-effect
    d. Conclusion-premises

82. Which of the following is an opinion, rather than historical fact, expressed by the author?
    a. Leif Erikson was definitely the son of Erik the Red; however, historians debate the year of his birth.
    b. Leif Erikson's crew called the land Vinland since it was plentiful with grapes.
    c. Leif Erikson deserves more credit for his contributions in exploring the New World.
    d. Leif Erikson explored the Americas nearly five hundred years before Christopher Columbus.

83. Which of the following most accurately describes the author's main conclusion?
    a. Leif Erikson is a legendary Viking explorer.
    b. Leif Erikson deserves more credit for exploring America hundreds of years before Columbus.
    c. Spreading Christianity motivated Leif Erikson's expeditions more than any other factor.
    d. Leif Erikson contacted the natives nearly five hundred years before Columbus.

84. Which of the following best describes the author's intent in the passage?
    a. To entertain
    b. To inform
    c. To alert
    d. To suggest

85. Which of the following can be logically inferred from the passage?
    a. The Vikings disliked exploring the New World.
    b. Leif Erikson's banishment from Iceland led to his exploration of present-day Canada.
    c. Leif Erikson never shared his stories of exploration with the King of Norway.
    d. Historians have difficulty definitively pinpointing events in the Vikings' history.

86. What is the relationship between these two sentences from the passage?

    Sentence 1: First, it is impossible to "discover" something where people already live; however, Christopher Columbus did explore places in the New World that were previously untouched by Europe, so the term "explorer" would be more accurate.

    Sentence 2: Another emendation must be made, as well: Christopher Columbus was not the first European explorer to reach the present-day Americas!

    a. Sentence 2 adds onto the correction of sentence 1.
    b. Sentence 2 contradicts sentence 1.
    c. Sentence 2 analyzes sentence 1.
    d. Sentence 2 continues the definition begun in sentence 1.

87. All of the following pieces of information relate to Leif's discovery of the New World EXCEPT which of the following?
    a. His crew called the land Vinland since it was plentiful with grapes.
    b. The son of the legendary Viking explorer then gathered a crew of 35 men and set sail.
    c. Christopher Columbus is often credited for discovering America.
    d. Regardless of the circumstances, it seems that the Vikings made contact of some kind.

88. In this context, the word *emendation* (paragraph 1) most nearly means what?
    a. Rationalization
    b. Recidivism
    c. Recompense
    d. Rectification

89. The tone of this passage could best be described as what?
    a. Impartial
    b. Admiring
    c. Evasive
    d. Nostalgic

90. The passage provides information that would answer which of the following questions?
    a. How many other accounts of history have researchers gotten wrong besides Christopher Columbus' "discovery of the New World"?
    b. What percentage of researchers believe that Leif Erikson should receive more credit for his contributions in exploring the New World?
    c. What are some probable examples of accounts of Vikings making contact with Canadian natives?
    d. How is the education system responsible for misinformation trickling down into the minds of our students?

91. The author's attitude toward the idea that Christopher Columbus discovered the New World can be described as what?
    a. Disbelieving and critical
    b. Enraged and vindictive
    c. Envious yet praising
    d. Uncertain but curious

92. Which of the following would the author be most likely to agree with?
    a. To "discover" a land is impossible to do for an outsider coming into a new continent if the land is already inhabited by people.
    b. To "discover" a land, in a sense, means to be the first person to "set out" to do so, and to return with an official report of the newfound continent.
    c. To "discover" a land means to be the first person to step foot on that land from an outside civilization, no matter if that person meant to do so or not.
    d. To "discover" and to "explore" are interchangeable in the context of the Americas.

138

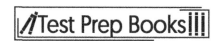

93. According to the passage, how did the Skraelings interact with Leif Erikson and his expedition?

a. The Vikings dominated the Skraelings when they arrived in present-day Newfoundland, but soon the Skraelings fought back with long spears and defeated the Vikings, sending them back home soon afterwards.

b. When the Vikings arrived on the new continent, they found that the Skraelings were hostile. Eventually they defeated the Vikings with long spears.

c. As soon as the Vikings arrived in present-day Newfoundland, the Vikings and the Skraelings began a trade route that lasted for centuries.

d. It is impossible to say. Some accounts say the Vikings fought with the Skraelings, and some accounts say that they traded amongst each other, but we do not know for sure.

Questions 94–101 are based on the following passages.

Passage I

Lethal force, or deadly force, is defined as the physical means to cause death or serious harm to another individual. The law holds that lethal force is only accepted when you or another person are in immediate and unavoidable danger of death or severe bodily harm. For example, a person could be beating a weaker person in such a way that they are suffering severe enough trauma that could result in death or serious harm. This would be an instance where lethal force would be acceptable and possibly the only way to save that person from irrevocable damage.

Another example of when to use lethal force would be when someone enters your home with a deadly weapon. The intruder's presence and possession of the weapon indicate mal-intent and the ability to inflict death or severe injury to you and your loved ones. Again, lethal force can be used in this situation. Lethal force can also be applied to prevent the harm of another individual. If a woman is being brutally assaulted and is unable to fend off an attacker, lethal force can be used to defend her as a last-ditch effort. If she is in immediate jeopardy of rape, harm, and/or death, lethal force could be the only response that could effectively deter the assailant.

The key to understanding the concept of lethal force is the term *last resort*. Deadly force cannot be taken back; it should be used only to prevent severe harm or death. The law does distinguish whether the means of one's self-defense is fully warranted, or if the individual goes out of control in the process. If you continually attack the assailant after they are rendered incapacitated, this would be causing unnecessary harm, and the law can bring charges against you. Likewise, if you kill an attacker unnecessarily after defending yourself, you can be charged with murder. This would move lethal force beyond necessary defense, making it no longer a last resort but rather a use of excessive force.

Passage II

Assault is the unlawful attempt of one person to apply apprehension on another individual by an imminent threat or by initiating offensive contact. Assaults can vary, encompassing physical strikes, threatening body language, and even provocative language. In the case of the latter, even if a hand has not been laid, it is still considered an assault because of its threatening nature.

Let's look at an example: A homeowner is angered because his neighbor blows fallen leaves into his freshly mowed lawn. Irate, the homeowner gestures a fist to his fellow neighbor and

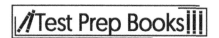

threatens to bash his head in for littering on his lawn. The homeowner's physical motions and verbal threat heralds a physical threat against the other neighbor. These factors classify the homeowner's reaction as an assault. If the angry neighbor hits the threatening homeowner in retaliation, that would constitute an assault as well because he physically hit the homeowner.

Assault also centers on the involvement of weapons in a conflict. If someone fires a gun at another person, it could be interpreted as an assault unless the shooter acted in self-defense. If an individual drew a gun or a knife on someone with the intent to harm them, it would be considered assault. However, it's also considered an assault if someone simply aimed a weapon, loaded or not, at another person in a threatening manner.

94. What is the purpose of the second passage?
   a. To inform the reader about what assault is and how it is committed
   b. To inform the reader about how assault is a minor example of lethal force
   c. To argue that the use of assault is more common than the use of lethal force
   d. To recount an incident in which the author was assaulted

95. Which of the following situations, according to the passages, would not constitute an illegal use of lethal force?
   a. A disgruntled cashier yells obscenities at a customer.
   b. A thief is seen running away with stolen cash.
   c. A man is attacked in an alley by another man with a knife.
   d. A woman punches another woman in a bar.

96. Given the information in the passages, which of the following must be true about assault?
   a. All assault is considered an expression of lethal force.
   b. There are various forms of assault.
   c. Assault is justified only as a last resort.
   d. Assault charges are more severe than unnecessary use of force charges.

97. Which of the following, if true, would most seriously undermine the explanation proposed by the author in the third paragraph of Passage I?
   a. An instance of lethal force in self-defense is not absolutely absolved from blame. The law takes into account the necessary use of force at the time it is committed.
   b. An individual who uses necessary defense under lethal force is in direct compliance of the law under most circumstances.
   c. Lethal force in self-defense should be forgiven in all cases for the peace of mind of the primary victim.
   d. The use of lethal force is not evaluated on the intent of the user but rather the severity of the primary attack that warranted self-defense.

98. Based on the passages, what can we infer about the relationship between assault and lethal force?
   a. An act of lethal force always leads to a type of assault.
   b. Assault and lethal force have no conceivable connection.
   c. An assault with deadly intent can lead to an individual using lethal force to preserve their well-being.
   d. If someone uses self-defense in a conflict, it is called deadly force; if actions or threats are intended, it is called assault.

140

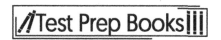
99. Which of the following best describes the way the passages are structured?
    a. Both passages open by defining a legal concept and then continue to describe situations in order to further explain the concept.
    b. Both passages begin with situations, introduce accepted definitions, and then cite legal ramifications.
    c. Both cite specific legal doctrines, then proceed to explain the rulings.
    d. The first passage explains both concepts and then focuses on lethal force. The second passage picks up with assault and explains the concept in depth.

100. What can we infer about the role of intent in lethal force and assault?
    a. Intent is very important for determining both lethal force and assault; intent is examined in both parties and helps determine the severity of the issue.
    b. Intent is vital for determining the lawfulness of using lethal force.
    c. Intent is only taken into account for assault charges.
    d. The intent of the assailant is the main focus for determining legal ramifications; it is used to determine if the defender was justified in using force to respond.

101. The author uses the example in the second paragraph of Passage II in order to do what?
    a. To demonstrate two different types of assault by showing how each specifically relates to the other.
    b. To demonstrate a single example of two different types of assault, then adding in the third type of assault in the example's conclusion.
    c. To prove that the definition of lethal force is altered when the victim in question is a homeowner and his property is threatened.
    d. To suggest that verbal assault can be an exaggerated crime by the law and does not necessarily lead to physical violence.
    e. To demonstrate that threatening body language is only considered a type of assault if it leads to physical violence.

Questions 102–108 are based on the following passage.

In the quest to understand existence, modern philosophers must question if humans can fully comprehend the world. Classical western approaches to philosophy tend to hold that one can understand something, be it an event or object, by standing outside of the phenomena and observing it. It is then by unbiased observation that one can grasp the details of the world. This seems to hold true for many things. Scientists conduct experiments and record their findings, and thus many natural phenomena become comprehendible. However, several of these observations were possible because humans used tools in order to make these discoveries.

This may seem like an extraneous matter. After all, people invented things like microscopes and telescopes in order to enhance their capacity to view cells or the movement of stars. While humans are still capable of seeing things, the question remains if human beings have the capacity to fully observe and see the world in order to understand it. It would not be an impossible stretch to argue that what humans see through a microscope is not the exact thing itself, but a human interpretation of it.

This would seem to be the case in the "Business of the Holes" experiment conducted by Richard Feynman. To study the way electrons behave, Feynman set up a barrier with two holes and a plate. The plate was there to indicate how many times the electrons would pass through the

141

hole(s). Rather than casually observe the electrons acting under normal circumstances, Feynman discovered that electrons behave in two totally different ways depending on whether or not they are observed. The electrons that were observed had passed through either one of the holes or were caught on the plate as particles. However, electrons that weren't observed acted as waves instead of particles and passed through both holes. This indicated that electrons have a dual nature. Electrons seen by the human eye act like particles, while unseen electrons act like waves of energy.

This dual nature of the electrons presents a conundrum. While humans now have a better understanding of electrons, the fact remains that people cannot entirely perceive how electrons behave without the use of instruments. We can only observe one of the mentioned behaviors, which only provides a partial understanding of the entire function of electrons. Therefore, we're forced to ask ourselves whether the world we observe is objective or if it is subjectively perceived by humans. Or, an alternative question: can man understand the world only through machines that will allow them to observe natural phenomena?

Both questions humble man's capacity to grasp the world. However, those ideas don't take into account that many phenomena have been proven by human beings without the use of machines, such as the discovery of gravity. Like all philosophical questions, whether man's reason and observation alone can understand the universe can be approached from many angles.

102. What is the author's motivation for writing the passage?
  a. Bring to light an alternative view on human perception by examining the role of technology in human understanding.
  b. Educate the reader on the latest astroparticle physics discovery and offer terms that may be unfamiliar to the reader.
  c. Argue that humans are totally blind to the realities of the world by presenting an experiment that proves that electrons are not what they seem on the surface.
  d. Reflect on opposing views of human understanding.

103. Which of the following most closely resembles the way in which paragraph four is structured?
  a. It offers one solution, questions the solution, and then ends with an alternative solution.
  b. It presents an inquiry, explains the detail of that inquiry, and then offers a solution.
  c. It presents a problem, explains the details of that problem, and then ends with more inquiry.
  d. It gives a definition, offers an explanation, and then ends with an inquiry.

104. For the classical approach to understanding to hold true, which of the following must be required?
  a. A telescope.
  b. The person observing must prove their theory beyond a doubt.
  c. Multiple witnesses present.
  d. The person observing must be unbiased.

105. Which best describes how the electrons in the experiment behaved like waves?
  a. The electrons moved up and down like actual waves.
  b. The electrons passed through both holes and then onto the plate.
  c. The electrons converted to photons upon touching the plate.
  d. Electrons were seen passing through one hole or the other.

142

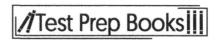

106. The author mentions "gravity" in the last paragraph in order to do what?
   a. In order to show that different natural phenomena test man's ability to grasp the world.
   b. To prove that since man has not measured it with the use of tools or machines, humans cannot know the true nature of gravity.
   c. To demonstrate an example of natural phenomena humans discovered and understood without the use of tools or machines.
   d. To show an alternative solution to the nature of electrons that humans have not thought of yet.

107. Which situation best parallels the revelation of the dual nature of electrons discovered in Feynman's experiment?
   a. A man is born color-blind and grows up observing everything in lighter or darker shades. With the invention of special goggles he puts on, he discovers that there are other colors in addition to different shades.
   b. The coelacanth was thought to be extinct, but a live specimen was just recently discovered. There are now two living species of coelacanth known to man, and both are believed to be endangered.
   c. In the Middle Ages, blacksmiths added carbon to iron, thus inventing steel. The consequences of this important discovery would have its biggest effects during the industrial revolution.
   d. In order to better examine and treat broken bones, the x-ray machine was invented and put to use in hospitals and medical centers.

108. Which statement about technology would the author likely disagree with?
   a. Technology can help expand the field of human vision.
   b. Technology renders human observation irrelevant.
   c. Developing tools used in observation and research indicates growing understanding of our world in itself.
   d. Studying certain phenomena necessitates the use of tools and machines.

Questions 109–114 are based upon the following passage:

This excerpt is an adaptation of Jonathan Swift's *Gulliver's Travels into Several Remote Nations of the World*.

My gentleness and good behaviour had gained so far on the emperor and his court, and indeed upon the army and people in general, that I began to conceive hopes of getting my liberty in a short time. I took all possible methods to cultivate this favourable disposition. The natives came, by degrees, to be less apprehensive of any danger from me. I would sometimes lie down, and let five or six of them dance on my hand; and at last the boys and girls would venture to come and play at hide-and-seek in my hair. I had now made a good progress in understanding and speaking the language. The emperor had a mind one day to entertain me with several of the country shows, wherein they exceed all nations I have known, both for dexterity and magnificence. I was diverted with none so much as that of the rope-dancers, performed upon a slender white thread, extended about two feet, and twelve inches from the ground. Upon which I shall desire liberty, with the reader's patience, to enlarge a little.

This diversion is only practised by those persons who are candidates for great employments, and high favour at court. They are trained in this art from their youth, and are not always of noble birth, or liberal education. When a great office is vacant, either by death or disgrace (which often happens,) five or six of those candidates

143

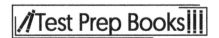

petition the emperor to entertain his majesty and the court with a dance on the rope; and whoever jumps the highest, without falling, succeeds in the office. Very often the chief ministers themselves are commanded to show their skill, and to convince the emperor that they have not lost their faculty. Flimnap, the treasurer, is allowed to cut a caper on the straight rope, at least an inch higher than any other lord in the whole empire. I have seen him do the summerset several times together, upon a trencher fixed on a rope which is no thicker than a common packthread in England. My friend Reldresal, principal secretary for private affairs, is, in my opinion, if I am not partial, the second after the treasurer; the rest of the great officers are much upon a par.

109. Which of the following statements best summarizes the central purpose of this text?
   a. Gulliver details his fondness for the archaic yet interesting practices of his captors.
   b. Gulliver conjectures about the intentions of the aristocratic sector of society.
   c. Gulliver becomes acquainted with the people and practices of his new surroundings.
   d. Gulliver's differences cause him to become penitent around new acquaintances.

110. What is the word *principal* referring to in the following text?
   My friend Reldresal, principal secretary for private affairs, is, in my opinion, if I am not partial, the second after the treasurer; the rest of the great officers are much upon a par.

   a. Primary or chief
   b. An acolyte
   c. An individual who provides nurturing
   d. One in a subordinate position

111. What can the reader infer from this passage?
   I would sometimes lie down, and let five or six of them dance on my hand; and at last the boys and girls would venture to come and play at hide-and-seek in my hair.

   a. The children tortured Gulliver.
   b. Gulliver traveled because he wanted to meet new people.
   c. Gulliver is considerably larger than the children who are playing around him.
   d. Gulliver has a genuine love and enthusiasm for people of all sizes.

112. What is the significance of the word *mind* in the following passage?
   The emperor had a mind one day to entertain me with several of the country shows, wherein they exceed all nations I have known, both for dexterity and magnificence.

   a. The ability to think
   b. A collective vote
   c. A definitive decision
   d. A mythological question

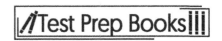
113. Which of the following assertions does NOT support the fact that games are a commonplace event in this culture?
    a. My gentleness and good behavior . . . short time.
    b. They are trained in this art from their youth . . . liberal education.
    c. Very often the chief ministers themselves are commanded to show their skill . . . not lost their faculty.
    d. Flimnap, the treasurer, is allowed to cut a caper on the straight rope . . . higher than any other lord in the whole empire.

114. How do Flimnap and Reldresal demonstrate the community's emphasis on physical strength and leadership abilities?
    a. Only children used Gulliver's hands as a playground.
    b. The two men who exhibited superior abilities held prominent positions in the community.
    c. Only common townspeople, not leaders, walk the straight rope.
    d. No one could jump higher than Gulliver.

Questions 115–120 are based upon the following passage:

This excerpt is an adaptation of Robert Louis Stevenson's *The Strange Case of Dr. Jekyll and Mr. Hyde.*

"Did you ever come across a protégé of his—one Hyde?" He asked.

"Hyde?" repeated Lanyon. "No. Never heard of him. Since my time."

That was the amount of information that the lawyer carried back with him to the great, dark bed on which he tossed to and fro until the small hours of the morning began to grow large. It was a night of little ease to his toiling mind, toiling in mere darkness and besieged by questions.

Six o'clock struck on the bells of the church that was so conveniently near to Mr. Utterson's dwelling, and still he was digging at the problem. Hitherto it had touched him on the intellectual side alone; but now his imagination also was engaged, or rather enslaved; and as he lay and tossed in the gross darkness of the night in the curtained room, Mr. Enfield's tale went by before his mind in a scroll of lighted pictures. He would be aware of the great field of lamps in a nocturnal city; then of the figure of a man walking swiftly; then of a child running from the doctor's; and then these met, and that human Juggernaut trod the child down and passed on regardless of her screams. Or else he would see a room in a rich house, where his friend lay asleep, dreaming and smiling at his dreams; and then the door of that room would be opened, the curtains of the bed plucked apart, the sleeper recalled, and, lo! There would stand by his side a figure to whom power was given, and even at that dead hour he must rise and do its bidding. The figure in these two phrases haunted the lawyer all night; and if at anytime he dozed over, it was but to see it glide more stealthily through sleeping houses, or move the more swiftly, and still the more smoothly, even to dizziness, through wider labyrinths of lamplighted city, and at every street corner crush a child and leave her screaming. And still the figure had no face by which he might know it; even in his dreams it had no face, or one that baffled him and melted before his eyes; and thus there it was that there sprung up and grew apace in the lawyer's mind a singularly strong, almost an inordinate, curiosity to behold the features of the real Mr. Hyde. If he

145

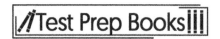

could but once set eyes on him, he thought the mystery would lighten and perhaps roll altogether away, as was the habit of mysterious things when well examined. He might see a reason for his friend's strange preference or bondage, and even for the startling clauses of the will. And at least it would be a face worth seeing: the face of a man who was without bowels of mercy: a face which had but to show itself to raise up, in the mind of the unimpressionable Enfield, a spirit of enduring hatred.

From that time forward, Mr. Utterson began to haunt the door in the by-street of shops. In the morning before office hours, at noon when business was plenty of time scarce, at night under the face of the full city moon, by all lights and at all hours of solitude or concourse, the lawyer was to be found on his chosen post.

"If he be Mr. Hyde," he had thought, "I should be Mr. Seek."

115. What is the purpose of the use of repetition in the following passage?
It was a night of little ease to his toiling mind, toiling in mere darkness and besieged by questions.

    a. It serves as a demonstration of the mental state of Mr. Lanyon.
    b. It is reminiscent of the church bells that are mentioned in the story.
    c. It mimics Mr. Utterson's ambivalence.
    d. It emphasizes Mr. Utterson's anguish in failing to identify Hyde's whereabouts.

116. What is the setting of the story in this passage?
    a. In the city
    b. On the countryside
    c. In a jail
    d. In a mental health facility

117. What can one infer about the meaning of the word "Juggernaut" from the author's use of it in the passage?
    a. It is an apparition that appears at daybreak.
    b. It scares children.
    c. It is associated with space travel.
    d. Mr. Utterson finds it soothing.

118. What is the definition of the word *haunt* in the following passage?
From that time forward, Mr. Utterson began to haunt the door in the by-street of shops. In the morning before office hours, at noon when business was plenty of time scarce, at night under the face of the full city moon, by all lights and at all hours of solitude or concourse, the lawyer was to be found on his chosen post.

    a. To levitate
    b. To constantly visit
    c. To terrorize
    d. To daunt

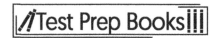

119. The phrase *labyrinths of lamplighted city* contains an example of what?

    a. Hyperbole
    b. Simile
    c. Juxtaposition
    d. Alliteration

120. What can one reasonably conclude from the final comment of this passage?
    "If he be Mr. Hyde," he had thought, "I should be Mr. Seek."

    a. The speaker is considering a name change.
    b. The speaker is experiencing an identity crisis.
    c. The speaker has mistakenly been looking for the wrong person.
    d. The speaker intends to continue to look for Hyde.

Essay

Read the two topics presented below. Select one of the topics to write your essay. Prepare an essay of about 300 to 600 words on the essay you choose.

Topic 1

Some people feel that sharing their lives on social media sites such as Facebook, Instagram, and Snapchat is fine. They share every aspect of their lives, including pictures of themselves and their families, what they ate for lunch, and when they are going on vacation. Other people believe that sharing so much personal information is an invasion of privacy. Write an essay to someone who is considering whether to participate in social media. Take a side on the issue and argue whether or not they should join a social media network. Use specific examples to support your argument.

Topic 2

Substance abuse is becoming an increasing problem in our schools. More than 17 percent of middle schoolers were reported using drugs in the year 2015. Some people think that drug testing should become regulatory in middle schools, and that the consequences for drug use should be stringent. Other people believe that students should be encouraged to attend school regardless of drug use, and that help should be afforded to students in alternate ways. Take a side on the issue and argue whether or not middle schoolers should be drug tested, and what to do about it if they are. Use specific examples to support your argument.

147

Answer Explanations #1

English Language Skills

1. B: In choice *B*, the word *Uncle* should not be capitalized, because it is not functioning as a proper noun. If the word named a specific uncle, such as *Uncle Jerry*, then it would be considered a proper noun and should be capitalized. Choice A correctly capitalizes the proper noun East Coast. Choice C correctly capitalizes the name of a specific college course, which is considered a proper noun. Choice D correctly capitalizes the proper noun *Jersey Shore*.

2. C: In Choice C, *avid* is functioning as an adjective that modifies the word photographer. *Avid* describes the photographer Julia Robinson's style. The words *time* and *photographer* are functioning as nouns, and the word *capture* is functioning as a verb in the sentence. Other words functioning as adjectives in the sentence include, *local*, *business*, and *spare*, as they all describe the nouns they precede.

3. B: This sentence calls for parallel structure. Choice B is correct because the verbs "wake," "eat," and "break" are consistent in tense and parts of speech. Choice A is incorrect because it breaks tense with the rest of the passage. "Waking," "eating," and "breaking" are all present participles, and the context around the sentence is in past tense. Choice C is incorrect because this turns the sentence into a question, which doesn't make sense within the context. Choice D is incorrect because the words "wake" and "eat" are present tense while the word "broke" is in past tense.

4. C: Choice C is a compound sentence because it joins two independent clauses with a comma and the coordinating conjunction *and*. The sentences in Choices B and D include one independent clause and one dependent clause, so they are complex sentences, not compound sentences. The sentence in Choice A has both a compound subject, *Alex and Shane*, and a compound verb, *spent and took*, but the entire sentence itself is one independent clause.

5. A: Choice A uses incorrect subject-verb agreement because the indefinite pronoun *neither* is singular and must use the singular verb form *is*. The pronoun *both* is plural and uses the plural verb form of *are*. The pronoun *any* can be either singular or plural. In this example, it is used as a plural, so the plural verb form *are* is used. The pronoun *each* is singular and uses the singular verb form *is*.

6. B: Choice B is correct because there is no punctuation needed if a dependent clause ("while traveling across America") is located behind the independent clause ("it allowed us to share adventures"). Choice A is incorrect because the dash simply interrupts the complete sentence. Choice C is incorrect because of the same reason as Choice A. Semicolons have the same function as periods: there must be an independent clause on either side of the semicolon. Choice D is incorrect because there are two dependent clauses connected and no independent clause, and a complete sentence requires at least one independent clause.

7. C: The rules for "me" and "I" is that one should use "I" when it is the subject pronoun of a sentence, and "me" when it is the object pronoun of the sentence. Break the sentence up to see if "I" or "me" should be used. To say "Those are memories that I have now shared" is correct, rather than "Those are memories that me have now shared." Choice A is incorrect because "my siblings" should come before "I."

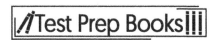

8. D: *Discipline* and *perseverance* are both spelled correctly in Choice *D*. These are both considered commonly misspelled words. One or both words are spelled incorrectly in Choices *A, B,* and *C*.

9. D: Choice *D* is correct because there should be a comma between the city and state. Choice *A* is incorrect because the order of the sentence designates that Chicago, Illinois is in Maywood, which is incorrect. Choice *B* is incorrect because the comma after "Maywood" interrupts the phrase "Maywood of Chicago." Choice *C* is incorrect because a comma after "Illinois" is unnecessary.

10. C: Cacti is the correct plural form of the word *cactus*. Choice *A* (*tomatos*) includes an incorrect spelling of the plural of *tomato*. Both *B* (*analysis*) and *D* (*criterion*) are incorrect because they are in singular form. The correct plural form for these choices would be *criteria* and *analyses*.

11. B: Quotation marks are used to indicate something someone said. The example sentences feature a direct quotation that requires the use of double quotation marks. Also, the end punctuation, in this case a question mark, should always be contained within the quotation marks. Choice *A* is incorrect because there is an unnecessary period after the quotation mark. Choice *C* is incorrect because it uses single quotation marks, which are used for a quote within a quote. Choice *D* is incorrect because it places the punctuation outside of the quotation marks.

12. D: Choice *D* is correct because the Black Panther Party is one entity, therefore the possession should show the "Party's approach" with the apostrophe between the "y" and the "s." Choice *A* is incorrect because the word "parties" should not be plural; instead, it is one unified party. Choice *B* is incorrect because, again, the word "Parties" should not be plural. Choice *C* is incorrect because the apostrophe indicates that the word "Partys" is plural. The plural of "party" is "parties."

13. D: In Choice *D*, the word *part* functions as an adjective that modifies the word *Irish*. Choices *A* and *C* are incorrect because the word *part* functions as a noun in these sentences. Choice *B* is incorrect because the word *part* functions as a verb.

14. C: *All of Shannon's family and friends* is the complete subject because it includes who or what is doing the action in the sentence as well as the modifiers that go with it. Choice *A* is incorrect because it only includes the simple subject of the sentence. Choices *B* and *D* are incorrect because they only include part of the complete subject.

15. C: The word "acheivement" is misspelled. Remember the rules for "*i* before *e* except after *c*." Choices *B* and *D*, "greatest" and "leader," are both spelled correctly.

16. B: Choice *B* is correct because it provides the correct verb tense and also makes sense within the context of the passage. Choice *A* is incorrect because it adds an infinitive ("to hold") where a past tense form of a verb should be. Choice *C* is incorrect because, with this use of the sentence, it would create a fragment because the verb "holding" has no helping verb in front of it. Choice *D* is incorrect because it doesn't make sense for someone to be "held by a press conference."

17. D: Choice *D* correctly places a hyphen after the prefix *ex* to join it to the word *husband*. Words that begin with the prefixes *great, trans, ex, all,* and *self*, require a hyphen. Choices *A* and *C* place hyphens in words where they are not needed. *Beagle mix* would only require a hyphen if coming before the word *Henry*, since it would be serving as a compound adjective in that instance. Choice *B* contains hyphens that are in the correct place but are formatted incorrectly since they include spaces between the hyphens and the surrounding words.

18. B: Choice *B* is correct. Choice *A* is incorrect because the sentence "In 1976." is a fragment. Choice *C* is incorrect because there should be a comma after introductory phrases in general, such as "In 1976," and Choice *C* omits a comma. Choice *D* is incorrect because there should be an independent clause on either side of a semicolon, and the phrase "In 1976" is not an independent clause.

19. C: This question focuses on the correct usage of the commonly confused word pairs of *it's/its* and *then/than*. *It's* is a contraction for *it is* or *it has*. *Its* is a possessive pronoun. The word *than* shows comparison between two things. *Then* is an adverb that conveys time. Choice *C* correctly uses *it's* and *than*. *It's* is a contraction for *it has* in this sentence, and *than* shows comparison between *work* and *rest*. None of the other answer choices use both of the correct words.

20. C: The suffix *-fy* means to make, cause, or cause to have. Choices *A*, *B*, and *D* are incorrect because they show meanings of other suffixes. Choice *A* shows the meaning of the suffix *-ous*. Choice *B* shows the meaning of the suffix *–ist*, and *D* shows the meaning of the suffix *-age*.

21. B: Choice *B* is correct. Here, a colon is used to introduce an explanation. Colons either introduce explanations or lists. Additionally, the quote ends with the punctuation inside the quotes, unlike Choice *C*.

22. B: Choice *B* is an imperative sentence because it issues a command. In addition, it ends with a period, and an imperative sentence must end in a period or exclamation mark. Choice *A* is a declarative sentence that states a fact and ends with a period. Choice *C* is an exclamatory sentence that shows strong emotion and ends with an exclamation point. Choice *D* is an interrogative sentence that asks a question and ends with a question mark.

23. A: *After* and *then* are transitional words that indicate time or position. Choice *B* is incorrect because the words *at, with,* and *to* are used as prepositions in this sentence, not transitions. Choice *C* is incorrect because the words *had* and *took* are used as verbs in this sentence. In Choice *D*, *a* and *the* are used as articles in the sentence.

24. C: The word *civilised* should be spelled *civilized.* The words "distinguishes" and "creatures" are both spelled correctly.

25. A: Choice *A* includes all of the words functioning as nouns in the sentence. Choice *B* is incorrect because it includes the words *final* and *academic,* which are functioning as adjectives in this sentence. The word *he* makes Choice *C* incorrect because it is a pronoun. This example also includes the word *library*, which can function as a noun, but is functioning as an adjective modifying the word *databases* in this sentence. Choice *D* is incorrect because it leaves out the proper noun *Robert*.

26. C: The simple subject of this sentence, the word *lots*, is plural. It agrees with the plural verb form *were*. Choice *A* is incorrect, because the simple subject *there*, referring to the two constellations, is considered plural. It does not agree with the singular verb form *is*. In Choice *B*, the singular subject *four*, does not agree with the plural verb form *needs*. In Choice *D,* the plural subject *everyone* does not agree with the singular verb form *have*.

27. D: Choice *D* is correct because the phrase "others' ideas" is both plural and indicates possession. Choice *A* is incorrect because the word "other" does not end in *s*. Others's is not a correct form of the plural possessive word. Choice *B* is incorrect because "other's" indicates only one "other" that's in possession of "ideas," which is incorrect. Choice *C* is incorrect because no possession is indicated.

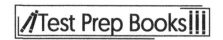

28. A: This sentence must have a comma before "although" because the word "although" is connecting two independent clauses. Thus, Choices *B* and *C* are incorrect. Choice *D* is incorrect because the second sentence in the underlined section is a fragment.

29. C: Choice *C* is the correct choice because the word "their" indicates possession, and the text is talking about "their students," or the students of someone. Choice *A* is not a word. Choice *B*, "they're," is a contraction and means "they are." Choice *D*, "there," means at a certain place and is incorrect.

30. B: Choice *B* uses all punctuation correctly in this sentence. In American English, single quotes should only be used if they are quotes within a quote, making Choices *D* and *C* incorrect. Additionally, punctuation here should go inside the quotes, making Choice *A* incorrect.

31. C: Choice *C* is a compound sentence because it joins two independent clauses—*The baby was sick* and *I decided to stay home from work*—with a comma and the coordinating conjunction *so*. Choices *A, B,* and *D*, are all simple sentences, each containing one independent clause with a complete subject and predicate. Choices *A* and *D* each contain a compound subject, or more than one subject, but they are still simple sentences that only contain one independent clause. Choice *B* contains a compound verb (more than one verb), but it's still a simple sentence.

32. D: Choice *D* has consistent parallel structure with the verbs "read," "identify," and "determine." Choices *B* and *C* have faulty parallel structure with the words "determining" and "identifying." Choice *A* has incorrect subject/verb agreement. The sentence should read, "Students have to read . . . identify . . . and determine."

33. B: *Excellent* and *walking* are adjectives modifying the noun *tours*. *Rich* is an adjective modifying the noun *history*, and *brotherly* is an adjective modifying the noun *love*. Choice *A* is incorrect because all of these words are functioning as nouns in the sentence. Choice *C* is incorrect because all of these words are functioning as verbs in the sentence. Choice *D* is incorrect because all of these words are considered prepositions, not adjectives.

34. D: The object pronouns *her* and *me* act as the indirect objects of the sentence. If *me* is in a series of object pronouns, it should always come last in the series. Choice *A* is incorrect because it uses subject pronouns *she* and *I*. Choice *B* is incorrect because it uses the subject pronoun *she*. Choice *C* uses the correct object pronouns, but they are in the wrong order.

35. A: In this example, a colon is correctly used to introduce a series of items. Choice *B* places an unnecessary comma before the word *because*. A comma is not needed before the word *because* when it introduces a dependent clause at the end of a sentence and provides necessary information to understand the sentence. Choice *C* is incorrect because it uses a semi-colon instead of a comma to join a dependent clause and an independent clause. Choice *D* is incorrect because it uses a colon in place of a comma and coordinating conjunction to join two independent clauses.

36. C: A complex sentence joins an independent or main clause with a dependent or subordinate clause. In this case, the main clause is "The restaurant is unconventional." This is a clause with one subject-verb combination that can stand alone as a grammatically-complete sentence. The dependent clause is "because it serves both Chicago style pizza and New York style pizza." This clause begins with the subordinating conjunction *because* and also consists of only one subject-verb combination. *A* is incorrect because a simple sentence consists of only one verb-subject combination—one independent clause. *B* is incorrect because a compound sentence contains two independent clauses connected by a conjunction.

D is incorrect because a complex-compound sentence consists of two or more independent clauses and one or more dependent clauses.

37. A: Parallelism refers to consistent use of sentence structure or word form. In this case, the list within the sentence does not utilize parallelism; three of the verbs appear in their base form—*travel*, *take*, and *eat*—but one appears as a gerund—*going*. A parallel version of this sentence would be "This summer, I'm planning to travel to Italy, take a Mediterranean cruise, go to Pompeii, and eat a lot of Italian food." *B* is incorrect because this description is a complete sentence. *C* is incorrect as a misplaced modifier is a modifier that is not located appropriately in relation to the word or words they modify. *D* is incorrect because subject-verb agreement refers to the appropriate conjugation of a verb in relation to its subject.

38. C: In this sentence, the modifier is the phrase "Forgetting that he was supposed to meet his girlfriend for dinner." This phrase offers information about Fred's actions, but the noun that immediately follows it is Anita, creating some confusion about the "do-er" of the phrase. A more appropriate sentence arrangement would be "Forgetting that he was supposed to meet his girlfriend for dinner, Fred made Anita mad when he showed up late." *A* is incorrect as parallelism refers to the consistent use of sentence structure and verb tense, and this sentence is appropriately consistent. *B* is incorrect as a run-on sentence does not contain appropriate punctuation for the number of independent clauses presented, which is not true of this description. *D* is incorrect because subject-verb agreement refers to the appropriate conjugation of a verb relative to the subject, and all verbs have been properly conjugated.

39. A: Choice *A* is correctly punctuated because it uses a semicolon to join two independent clauses that are related in meaning. Each of these clauses could function as an independent sentence. Choice *B* is incorrect because the conjunction is not preceded by a comma. A comma and conjunction should be used together to join independent clauses. Choice *C* is incorrect because a comma should only be used to join independent sentences when it also includes a coordinating conjunction such as *and* or *so*. Choice *D* does not use punctuation to join the independent clauses, so it is considered a fused (same as a run-on) sentence.

40. B: A comma splice occurs when a comma is used to join two independent clauses together without the additional use of an appropriate conjunction. One way to remedy this problem is to replace the comma with a semicolon. Another solution is to add a conjunction: "Some workers use all their sick leave, but other workers cash out their leave." *A* is incorrect as parallelism refers to the consistent use of sentence structure and verb tense; all tenses and structures in this sentence are consistent. *C* is incorrect because a sentence fragment is a phrase or clause that cannot stand alone—this sentence contains two independent clauses. *D* is incorrect because subject-verb agreement refers to the proper conjugation of a verb relative to the subject, and all verbs have been properly conjugated.

Mathematics

41. A: Compare each number after the decimal point to figure out which overall number is greatest. In Choices *A* (1.43785) and *C* (1.43592), both have the same tenths place (4) and hundredths place (3). However, the thousandths place is greater in Choice *A* (7), so *A* has the greatest value overall.

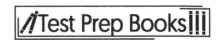

42. D: By grouping the four numbers in the answer into factors of the two numbers of the question (6 and 12), it can be determined that:

$$(3 \times 2) \times (4 \times 3) = 6 \times 12$$

Alternatively, you could find the prime factorization of each answer choices and compare it to the original value. The product of 6×12 is 72 and has a prime factorization of $2^3 \times 3^2$. The answer choices respectively have values of 64, 84, 108, and 72 and prime factorizations of 2^6, $2^2 \times 3 \times 7$, $2^2 \times 3^3$, and $2^3 \times 3^2$, so Choice *D* is the correct choice.

43. C: The sum total percentage of a pie chart must equal 100%. Since the CD sales take up less than half of the chart (50%) and more than a quarter (25%), it can be determined to be 40% overall. This can also be measured with a protractor. The angle of a circle is 360°. Since 25% of 360° would be 90° and 50% would be 180°, the angle percentage of CD sales falls in between; therefore, it would be Choice *C*.

44. B: Since $850 is the price *after* a 20% discount, $850 represents 80% of the original price. To determine the original price, set up a proportion with the ratio of the sale price (850) to original price (unknown) equal to the ratio of sale percentage (where x represents the unknown original price):

$$\frac{850}{x} = \frac{80}{100}$$

To solve a proportion, cross multiply and set the products equal to each other:

$$(850)(100) = (80)(x)$$

Multiplying each side results in the equation:

$$85,000 = 80x$$

To solve for x, divide both sides by 80:

$$\frac{85,000}{80} = \frac{80x}{80}$$

$$x = 1,062.5$$

Remember that x represents the original price. Subtracting the sale price from the original price ($\$1,062.50 - \$850$) indicates that Frank saved $212.50.

45. B: 85% of a number means that number should be multiplied by 0.85: $0.85 \times 20 = \frac{85}{100} \times \frac{20}{1}$, which can be simplified to $\frac{17}{20} \times \frac{20}{1} = 17$.

46. B: Using the conversion rate, multiply the projected weight loss of 25 lb. by $0.45 \frac{\text{kg}}{\text{lb}}$ to get the amount in kilograms (11.25 kg).

47. D: First, subtract $1437 from $2334.50 to find Johnny's monthly savings; this equals $897.50. Then, multiply this amount by 3 to find out how much he will have in three months before he pays for his vacation; this equals $2692.50. Finally, subtract the cost of the vacation ($1750) from this amount to find how much Johnny will have left: $942.50.

48. B: Dividing by 98 can be approximated by dividing by 100, which would mean shifting the decimal point of the numerator to the left by 2. The result is 4.2, which rounds to 4.

49. D: To find the average of a set of values, add the values together and then divide by the total number of values. In this case, include the unknown value of what Dwayne needs to score on his next test, in order to solve it.

$$\frac{78 + 92 + 83 + 97 + x}{5} = 90$$

Add the unknown value to the new average total, which is 5. Then multiply each side by 5 to simplify the equation, resulting in:

78 + 92 + 83 + 97 + x = 450
350 + x = 450
x = 100

Dwayne would need to get a perfect score of 100 in order to get an average of at least 90.

Test this answer by substituting back into the original formula.

$$\frac{78 + 92 + 83 + 97 + 100}{5} = 90$$

50. D: For an even number of total values, the median is calculated by finding the mean, or average, of the two middle values once all values have been arranged in ascending order from least to greatest. In this case, $(92 + 83) \div 2$ would equal the median 87.5, Choice *D*.

51. C: Follow the order of operations in order to solve this problem. Solve the parentheses first, being sure to follow the order of operations inside the parentheses as well. First, simplify the square roots:

$$(6 \times 4) - 3^2$$

Then, multiply inside the parentheses:

$$24 - 3^2$$

Next, simplify the exponents:

$$24 - 9$$

Finally, subtract to get 15, Choice *C*.

52. D: Three girls for every two boys can be expressed as a ratio: 3:2. This can be visualized as splitting the school into 5 groups: 3 girl groups and 2 boy groups. The number of students that are in each group can be found by dividing the total number of students by 5:

$$\frac{650 \text{ students}}{5 \text{ groups}} = \frac{130 \text{ students}}{\text{group}}$$

To find the total number of girls, multiply the number of students per group (130) by the number of girl groups in the school (3). This equals 390, Choice *D*.

154

53. C: If the average of all six numbers is 6, that means:

$$\frac{a + b + c + d + e + x}{6} = 6$$

The sum of the first five numbers is 25, so this equation can be simplified to $\frac{25+x}{6} = 6$. Multiplying both sides by 6 gives $25 + x = 36$, and x, or the sixth number, can be solved to equal 11.

54. C: Kimberley worked 4.5 hours at the rate of $10 / h and 1 hour at the rate of $12 / h. The problem states that her pay is rounded to the nearest hour, so the 4.5 hours would round up to 5 hours at the rate of $10 / h.

$$(5h) \times \left(\frac{\$10}{h}\right) + (1h) \times \left(\frac{\$12}{h}\right) = \$50 + \$12 = \$62$$

55. C: The first step is to depict each number using decimals:

$$\frac{91}{100} = 0.91$$

Dividing the numerator by denominator of $\frac{4}{5}$ to convert it to a decimal yields 0.80, while $\frac{2}{3}$ becomes 0.66 recurring. Rearrange each expression in ascending order, as found in Choice C.

56. B: First, calculate the difference between the larger value and the smaller value:

$$378 - 252 = 126$$

To calculate this difference as a percentage of the original value, and thus calculate the percentage *increase*, divide 126 by 252, then multiply by 100 to reach the percentage 50%, Choice B.

57. A: To calculate the range in a set of data, subtract the highest value with the lowest value. In this graph, the range of Mr. Lennon's students is 5, which can be seen physically in the graph as having the smallest difference compared with the other teachers between the highest value and the lowest value.

58. A: To find the fraction of the bill that the first three people pay, the fractions need to be added, which means finding the common denominator. The common denominator will be 60.

$$\frac{1}{5} + \frac{1}{4} + \frac{1}{3} = \frac{12}{60} + \frac{15}{60} + \frac{20}{60} = \frac{47}{60}$$

The remainder of the bill is:

$$1 - \frac{47}{60} = \frac{60}{60} - \frac{47}{60} = \frac{13}{60}$$

59. B: Simplify each mixed number of the problem into a fraction by multiplying the denominator by the whole number and adding the numerator:

$$\frac{14}{3} - \frac{31}{9}$$

155

Since the first denominator is a multiple of the second, simplify it further by multiplying both the numerator and denominator of the first expression by 3 so that the denominators of the fractions are equal.

$$\frac{42}{9} - \frac{31}{9} = \frac{11}{9}$$

Simplifying this further, divide the numerator 11 by the denominator 9; this leaves 1 with a remainder of 2. To write this as a mixed number, place the remainder over the denominator, resulting in $1\frac{2}{9}$.

60. A: The total fraction taken up by green and red shirts will be:

$$\frac{1}{3} + \frac{2}{5} = \frac{5}{15} + \frac{6}{15} = \frac{11}{15}$$

The remaining fraction is:

$$1 - \frac{11}{15} = \frac{15}{15} - \frac{11}{15} = \frac{4}{15}$$

61. C: If she has used $\frac{1}{3}$ of the paint, she has $\frac{2}{3}$ remaining. The mixed fraction can be converted because $2\frac{1}{2}$ gallons is the same as $\frac{5}{2}$ gallons. The calculation is:

$$\frac{2}{3} \times \frac{5}{2} = \frac{5}{3} = 1\frac{2}{3} \text{ gal}$$

62. C: We are trying to find x, the number of red cans. The equation can be set up like this:

$$x + 2(10 - x) = 16$$

The left x is actually multiplied by \$1, the price per red can. Since we know Jessica bought 10 total cans, $10 - x$ is the number blue cans that she bought. We multiply the number of blue cans by \$2, the price per blue can.

That should all equal \$16, the total amount of money that Jessica spent. Working that out gives us:

$$x + 20 - 2x = 16$$

$$20 - x = 16$$

$$x = 4$$

63. C: Janice will be choosing 4 employees out of a set of 6 applicants, so this will be given by the choice function. The following equation shows the choice function worked out:

$$\binom{6}{4} = \frac{6!}{4!\,(6-4)!} = \frac{6!}{4!\,(2)!}$$

$$\frac{6 \times 5 \times 4 \times 3 \times 2 \times 1}{4 \times 3 \times 2 \times 1 \times 2 \times 1} = \frac{6 \times 5}{2} = 15$$

64. D: $\frac{3}{100}$. Each digit to the left of the decimal point represents a higher multiple of 10 and each digit to the right of the decimal point represents a quotient of a higher multiple of 10 for the divisor. The first digit to the right of the decimal point is equal to the value ÷ 10. The second digit to the right of the decimal point is equal to the value ÷ (10 × 10), or the value ÷ 100.

65. D: Using the order of operations, multiplication and division are computed first from left to right. Multiplication is on the left; therefore, multiplication should be performed first.

66. A: 847.90. The hundredths place value is located two digits to the right of the decimal point (the digit 9 in the original number). The digit to the right of the place value is examined to decide whether to round up or keep the digit. In this case, the digit 6 is 5 or greater so the hundredth place is rounded up. When rounding up, if the digit to be increased is a 9, the digit to its left is increased by one and the digit in the desired place value is made a zero. Therefore, the number is rounded to 847.90.

67. C: The perimeter is found by calculating the sum of all sides of the polygon:

$$9 + 9 + 9 + 8 + 8 + s = 56$$

where s is the missing side length. Therefore, $43 + s = 56$. The missing side length is 13 cm.

68. A: $16\frac{1}{2}$. A mixed number contains both a whole number and either a fraction or a decimal. Therefore, the mixed number is $16\frac{1}{2}$.

69. A: The place value to the right of the thousandth place, which would be the ten-thousandth place, is what gets utilized. The value in the thousandth place is 7. The number in the place value to its right is greater than 4, so the 7 gets bumped up to 8. Everything to its right turns to a zero, to get 245.2680. The zero is dropped because it is part of the decimal.

70. C: To solve for the value of b, isolate the variable b on one side of the equation.

Start by moving the lower value of -4 to the other side by adding 4 to both sides:

$$5b - 4 = 2b + 17$$

$$5b - 4 + 4 = 2b + 17 + 4$$

$$5b = 2b + 21$$

Then subtract $2b$ from both sides:

$$5b - 2b = 2b + 21 - 2b$$

$$3b = 21$$

Then divide both sides by 3 to get the value of b:

$$\frac{3b}{3} = \frac{21}{3}$$

$$b = 7$$

71. C: The first step in solving this problem is expressing the result in fraction form. Separate this problem first by solving the division operation of the last two fractions. When dividing one fraction by another, invert or flip the second fraction and then multiply the numerator and denominator.

$$\frac{7}{10} \times \frac{2}{1} = \frac{14}{10}$$

Next, multiply the first fraction with this value:

$$\frac{3}{5} \times \frac{14}{10} = \frac{42}{50}$$

In this instance, you can find the decimal form by converting the fraction into $\frac{x}{100}$, where x is the number from which the final decimal is found. Multiply both the numerator and denominator by 2 to get the fraction as an expression of $\frac{x}{100}$.

$$\frac{42}{50} \times \frac{2}{2} = \frac{84}{100}$$

In decimal form, this would be expressed as 0.84.

72. B: 100 cm is equal to 1 m. 1.3 divided by 100 is 0.013. Therefore, 1.3 cm is equal to 0.013 m. Because 1 cm is equal to 10 mm, 1.3 cm is equal to 13 mm.

73. C: $\frac{1}{3}$ of the shirts sold were patterned. Therefore, $1 - \frac{1}{3} = \frac{2}{3}$ of the shirts sold were solid. Anytime "of" a quantity appears in a word problem, multiplication needs to be used. Therefore:

$$192 \times \frac{2}{3} = 192 \times \frac{2}{3} = \frac{384}{3} = 128 \text{ solid shirts were sold}$$

The entire expression is $192 \times \left(1 - \frac{1}{3}\right)$.

74. B: A rectangle is a specific type of parallelogram. It has 4 right angles. A square is a rhombus that has 4 right angles. Therefore, a square is always a rectangle because it has two sets of parallel lines and 4 right angles.

75. D: Recall the formula for area, area = length × width. The answer must be in square inches, so all values must be converted to inches. Half of a foot is equal to 6 inches. Therefore, the area of the rectangle is equal to:

$$6 \text{ in} \times \frac{11}{2} \text{ in} = \frac{66}{2} \text{in}^2 = 33 \text{ in}^2$$

76. D: 80%. To convert a fraction to a percent, the fraction is first converted to a decimal. To do so, the numerator is divided by the denominator: $4 \div 5 = 0.8$. To convert a decimal to a percent, the number is multiplied by 100:

$$0.8 \times 10 = 80\%$$

77. B: Add 3 to both sides to get $4x = 8$. Then divide both sides by 4 to get $x = 2$.

78. D: The slope is given by the change in y divided by the change in x. Specifically, it's:

$$slope = \frac{y_2 - y_1}{x_2 - x_1}$$

The first point is $(-5, -3)$, and the second point is $(0, -1)$. Work from left to right when identifying coordinates. Thus, the point on the left is point 1 $(-5, -3)$ and the point on the right is point 2 $(0, -1)$.

Now we need to just plug those numbers into the equation:

$$slope = \frac{-1 - (-3)}{0 - (-5)}$$

It can be simplified to:

$$slope = \frac{-1 + 3}{0 + 5}$$

$$slope = \frac{2}{5}$$

79. B: 30% is 3/10. The number itself must be 10/3 of 6, or $\frac{10}{3} \times 6 = 10 \times 2 = 20$.

80. B: $3x^2 - 3x + 11$. By distributing the implied one in front of the first set of parentheses and the -1 in front of the second set of parentheses, the parentheses can be eliminated:

$$1(5x^2 - 3x + 4) - 1(2x^2 - 7) = 5x^2 - 3x + 4 - 2x^2 + 7$$

Next, like terms (same variables with same exponents) are combined by adding the coefficients and keeping the variables and their powers the same:

$$5x^2 - 3x + 4 - 2x^2 + 7 = 3x^2 - 3x + 11$$

Reading Comprehension

81. D: The passage does not proceed in chronological order since it begins by pointing out Christopher Columbus's explorations in America, so Choice A does not work. Although the author compares and contrasts Erikson with Christopher Columbus, this is not the main way the information is presented; therefore, Choice B does not work. Neither does Choice C because there is no mention of or reference to cause and effect in the passage. However, the passage does offer a conclusion (Leif Erikson deserves more credit) and premises (first European to set foot in the New World and first to contact the natives) to substantiate Erikson's historical importance. Thus, Choice D is correct.

82. C: Choice A is incorrect because it describes facts: Leif Erikson was the son of Erik the Red and historians debate Leif's date of birth. These are not opinions. Choice B is incorrect; that Erikson called the land Vinland is a verifiable fact as is Choice D because he did contact the natives almost 500 years before Columbus. Choice C is the correct answer because it is the author's opinion that Erikson deserves more credit. That, in fact, is his conclusion in the piece, but another person could argue that Columbus

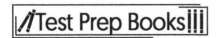

or another explorer deserves more credit for opening up the New World to exploration. Rather than being an incontrovertible fact, it is a subjective value claim.

83. B: Choice A is incorrect because the author aims to go beyond describing Erikson as merely a legendary Viking. Choice C is incorrect because the author does not focus on Erikson's motivations, let alone name the spreading of Christianity as his primary objective. Choice D is incorrect because it is a premise that Erikson contacted the natives 500 years before Columbus, which is simply a part of supporting the author's conclusion. Choice B is correct because, as stated in the previous answer, it accurately identifies the author's statement that Erikson deserves more credit than he has received for being the first European to explore the New World.

84. B: Choice B is correct because the author wants the reader to be informed about Leif Erikson's contribution to exploring the new world. While several other answers are possible options, Choice B is the strongest. Choice A is incorrect because the author is not in any way trying to entertain the reader. Choice C is incorrect because the nature of the writing does not indicate the author would be satisfied with the reader merely being alerted to Erikson's exploration; instead, the author is making an argument about the credit he should receive. Choice D is incorrect because the author goes beyond merely a suggestion; "suggest" is too vague.

85. D: Choice A is incorrect because the author never addresses the Vikings' state of mind or emotions. Choice B is incorrect because the author does not elaborate on Erikson's exile and whether he would have become an explorer if not for his banishment. Choice C is incorrect because there is not enough information to support this premise. It is unclear whether Erikson informed the King of Norway of his finding. Although it is true that the King did not send a follow-up expedition, he could have simply chosen not to expend the resources after receiving Erikson's news. It is not possible to logically infer whether Erikson told him. Choice D is correct because there are two examples—Leif Erikson's date of birth and what happened during the encounter with the natives—of historians having trouble pinning down important details in Viking history.

86. A: Sentence 2 adds onto the correction of sentence 1. Sentence 1 is meant to be a correction of the sentiment that Christopher Columbus discovered America. Sentence 1 gives proof to why this is untrue: it is "impossible to discover something where people already live." Sentence 2 adds onto the correction by saying that Columbus was not even the first explorer to reach the present-day Americas. Sentence 2 does not contradict or analyze sentence 1, which makes Choices B and C incorrect. There is also no definition in either of these sentences, which makes Choice D incorrect.

87. C: Christopher Columbus is often credited for discovering America. This piece of information from the passage does not relate to Leif's discovery of the New World. This has to do with the misinformation that Columbus discovered America. Choice A mentions that when Leif and his crew landed in present-day Newfoundland, they called the land Vinland since it was plentiful with grapes. This information *does* relate to Leif's discovery of the New World. Choice B talks about the size of Leif's crew when they set sail back to "Vinland." Finally, Choice D talks about the contact the Vikings made with the natives of present-day Newfoundland, whom they called the "Skraelings."

88. D: Rectification. The sentence says "Another emendation must be made," meaning another correction or revision must be made to the story of Columbus. *Rectification* is the closest word to correction or revision. Choice A, *rationalization*, means to explain something in a reasonable manner; this is not the best answer choice. Choice B, *recidivism*, means to relapse into criminal activity, and does

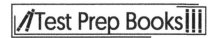

not make sense in this context. Choice *C*, *recompense*, means to return or pay something back, and is also incorrect in this context.

89. B: Admiring. This is the best choice among the others. In the middle of the passage, we see the author recounting a narrative about Leif Erikson and how he overcame the obstacles of learning to read and write. The passage is also bookended by praise for the Viking and his accomplishments. The author says in the beginning that "it was Leif Erikson who first came to the New World" and at the end that "[m]any believe that Leif Erikson should receive more credit for his contributions in exploring the New World. Choice *A*, *impartial*, means non-biased, but we see the author showing bias toward Leif Erikson in this passage. Choice *C*, *evasive*, means ambiguous or unclear, and the author seems pretty straightforward in their writing. Choice *D*, nostalgic, means to wish for something from the past. Although we see the author recounting a story from the past, the author does not seem to display nostalgia for this era. This is not the best answer choice.

90. C: What are some probable examples of accounts of Vikings making contact with Canadian natives? The passage could answer this question with the accounts of contact in paragraph 5. Choice *A* is incorrect; we could not know from the passage how many other accounts of history researchers have gotten wrong, because we are only told of one account. Choice *B* is incorrect; we are told that many believe Leif Erikson should receive more credit, but we are not told a specific percentage. Choice *D* is incorrect; the passage does not talk about *how* the education system presents misinformation in any way.

91. A: The author's attitude is best described as disbelieving and critical. We see this in the very first paragraph, where the author debunks the idea that Columbus was a "discoverer" rather than an "explorer," and informs us that Columbus was not the first European to reach the present-day Americas. Choice *B* is incorrect because, although the author might seem a bit frustrated, the author does not display vindictiveness, so this is not the best answer. Choice *C* is incorrect—there is no display of envy or praise on behalf of the author. Choice *D* is incorrect, because the author seems fairly certain from the very beginning of the passage that Columbus did not "discover" the New World.

92. A: To "discover" a land is impossible to do for an outsider coming into a new continent if the land is already inhabited by people. The author makes this sentiment in the first paragraph, and even calls Leif Erikson an "explorer" rather than a "discoverer." Choice *B* is incorrect; the author makes no comment that someone who discovers something is the one who makes it official. Choice *C* is incorrect; Erikson was from an outside civilization and may have been the first to step foot on this new continent, but the author does not name Erikson a "discoverer." Choice *D* is incorrect; "discover" and "explore" mean two very different things for the author as seen in paragraph one.

93. D: The passage says that there "are several secondhand accounts of their meetings"—some accounts say that there was fighting, and some accounts say that there was trading, but the accounts differ from one another. Choices *A, B,* and *C,* are all mentioned in the passage as one type of account of the interactions between the Vikings and the Skraelings, but they leave out the contradicting information that concludes we do not know for sure what the outcome of their meeting was.

94. A: The purpose is to inform the reader about what assault is and how it is committed. Choice *B* is incorrect because the passage does not state that assault is a lesser form of lethal force, only that an assault can use lethal force, or alternatively, lethal force can be utilized to counter a dangerous assault. Choice *C* is incorrect because the passage is informative and does not have a set agenda. Finally, Choice

D is incorrect because although the author uses an example in order to explain assault, it is not indicated that this is the author's personal account.

95. C: The situation of the man who is attacked in an alley by another man with a knife would most merit the use of lethal force. If the man being attacked used self-defense by lethal force, it would not be considered illegal. The presence of a deadly weapon indicates mal-intent and because the individual is isolated in an alley, lethal force in self-defense may be the only way to preserve his life. Choices *A* and *B* can be ruled out because in these situations, no one is in danger of immediate death or bodily harm by someone else. Choice *D* is an assault that does exhibit intent to harm, but this situation isn't severe enough to merit lethal force; there is no intent to kill.

96. B: As discussed in the second passage, there are several forms of assault, like assault with a deadly weapon, verbal assault, or threatening posture or language. Choice *A* is incorrect because lethal force and assault are separate as indicated by the passages. Choice *C* is incorrect because assault is never justified. Self-defense resulting in lethal force can be justified. Choice *D* is incorrect because the author does mention what the charges are on assaults; therefore, we cannot assume that they are more or less than unnecessary use of force charges.

97. D: The use of lethal force is not evaluated on the intent of the user but rather the severity of the primary attack that warranted self-defense. This statement most undermines the last part of the passage because it directly contradicts how the law evaluates the use of lethal force. Choices *A* and *B* are stated in the paragraph, and therefore do not undermine the explanation from the author. Choice *C* does not necessarily undermine the passage, but it does not support the passage either. It is more of an opinion that does not strengthen or weaken the explanation.

98. C: An assault with deadly intent can lead to an individual using lethal force to preserve their well-being. Choice *C* is correct because it clearly establishes what both assault and lethal force are and gives the specific way in which the two concepts meet. Choice *A* is incorrect because lethal force doesn't necessarily result in assault. Choice *B* is incorrect because it contradicts the information in the passage (that assault with deadly intent can lead to an individual using lethal force). Choice *D* is compelling but ultimately too vague; the statement touches on aspects of the two ideas but fails to present the concrete way in which the two are connected to each other.

99. A: Both passages open by defining a legal concept and then describing situations in order to further explain the concept. Choice *C* is incorrect because while the passages utilize examples to help explain the concepts discussed, the author doesn't indicate that they are specific court cases. It's also clear that the passages don't open with examples, but instead, begin by defining the terms addressed in each passage. This eliminates Choice *B* and ultimately reveals Choice *A* to be the correct answer. Choice *A* accurately outlines the way both passages are structured. Because the passages follow a near identical structure, the rest of the choices can easily be ruled out.

100. A: Intent is very important for determining both lethal force and assault; intent is examined in both parties and helps determine the severity of the issue. Choices *B* and *C* are incorrect because it is clear in both passages that intent is a prevailing theme in both lethal force and assault. Choice *D* is compelling, but if a person uses lethal force to defend themselves, the intent of the defender is also examined in order to help determine if there was excessive force used. Choice *A* is correct because it states that intent is important for determining both lethal force and assault, and that intent is used to gauge the severity of the issues. Remember, just as lethal force can escalate to excessive use of force, there are different kinds of assault. Intent dictates several different forms of assault.

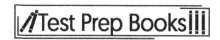

101. B: To demonstrate a single example of two different types of assault, then adding in a third type of assault to the example's conclusion. The example mainly serves to show an instance of "threatening body language" and "provocative language" with the homeowner gesturing threats to his neighbor. It ends the example by adding a third type of assault: physical strikes. This example is used to show the variant nature of assaults. Choice A is incorrect because it doesn't mention the "physical strike" assault at the end and is not specific enough. Choice C is incorrect because the example does not say anything about the definition of lethal force or how it might be altered. Choice D is incorrect, as the example mentions nothing of cause and effect.

102. A: Bring to light an alternative view on human perception by examining the role of technology in human understanding. This is a challenging question because the author's purpose is somewhat open-ended. The author concludes by stating that the questions regarding human perception and observation can be approached from many angles. Thus they do not seem to be attempting to prove one thing or another. Choice B is incorrect because we cannot know for certain whether the electron experiment is the latest discovery in astroparticle physics because no date is given. Choice C is a broad generalization that does not reflect accurately on the writer's views. While the author does appear to reflect on opposing views of human understanding (Choice D), the best answer is Choice A.

103. C: It presents a problem, explains the details of that problem, and then ends with more inquiry. The beginning of this paragraph literally "presents a conundrum," explains the problem of partial understanding, and then ends with more questions, or inquiry. There is no solution offered in this paragraph, making Choices A and B incorrect. Choice D is incorrect because the paragraph does not begin with a definition.

104. D: Looking back in the text, the author describes that classical philosophy holds that understanding can be reached by careful observation. This will not work if they are overly invested or biased in their pursuit. Choices A and C are in no way related and are completely unnecessary. A specific theory is not necessary to understanding, according to classical philosophy mentioned by the author. Again, the key to understanding is observing the phenomena outside of it, without bias or predisposition. Thus, Choice B is wrong.

105. B: The electrons passed through both holes and then onto the plate. Choices A and C are incorrect because such movement is not mentioned at all in the text. In the passage, the author says that electrons that were physically observed appeared to pass through one hole or another. Remember, the electrons that were observed doing this were described as acting like particles. Therefore, Choice D is incorrect. Recall that the plate actually recorded electrons passing through both holes simultaneously and hitting the plate. This behavior, the electron activity that wasn't seen by humans, was characteristic of waves. Thus, Choice B is the correct answer.

106. C: To demonstrate an example of natural phenomena humans discovered and understood without the use of tools or machines. Choice A mirrors the language in the beginning of the paragraph but is incorrect in its intent. Choice B is incorrect; the paragraph mentions nothing of "not knowing the true nature of gravity." Choice D is incorrect as well. There is no mention of an "alternative solution" in this paragraph.

107. A: The important thing to keep in mind is that we must choose a scenario that best parallels, or is most similar to, the discovery of the experiment mentioned in the passage. The important aspects of the experiment can be summed up like so: humans directly observed one behavior of electrons and then through analyzing a tool (the plate that recorded electron hits), discovered that there was another

163

electron behavior that could not be physically seen by human eyes. This best parallels the scenario in Choice *A*. Like Feynman, the colorblind person is able to observe one aspect of the world but through the special goggles (a tool) he is able to see a natural phenomenon that he could not physically see on his own. While Choice *D* is compelling, the x-ray helps humans see the broken bone, not necessarily revealing that the bone is broken in the first place. The other choices do not parallel the scenario in question. Therefore, Choice *A* is the best choice.

108. B: The author would not agree that technology renders human observation irrelevant. Choice *A* is incorrect because much of the passage discusses how technology helps humans observe what cannot be seen with the naked eye, therefore the author would agree with this statement. This line of reasoning is also why the author would agree with Choice *D*, making it incorrect as well. As indicated in the second paragraph, the author seems to think that humans create inventions and tools with the goal of studying phenomena more precisely. This indicates increased understanding as people recognize limitations and develop items to help bypass the limitations and learn. Therefore, Choice *C* is incorrect as well. Again, the author doesn't attempt to disprove or dismiss classical philosophy.

109. C: Gulliver becomes acquainted with the people and practices of his new surroundings. Choice *C* is the correct answer because it most extensively summarizes the entire passage. While Choices *A* and *B* are reasonable possibilities, they reference portions of Gulliver's experiences, not the whole. Choice *D* is incorrect because Gulliver doesn't express repentance or sorrow in this particular passage.

110. A: Principal refers to *chief* or *primary* within the context of this text. Choice *A* is the answer that most closely aligns with this definition. Choices *B* and *D* make reference to a helper or followers while Choice *C* doesn't meet the description of Reldresal from the passage.

111. C: One can reasonably infer that Gulliver is considerably larger than the children who were playing around him because multiple children could fit into his hand. Choice *B* is incorrect because there is no indication of stress in Gulliver's tone. Choices *A* and *D* aren't the best answer because though Gulliver seems fond of his new acquaintances, he didn't travel there with the intentions of meeting new people or to express a definite love for them in this particular portion of the text.

112. C: The emperor made a *definitive decision* to expose Gulliver to their native customs. In this instance, the word *mind* was not related to a vote, question, or cognitive ability.

113. A: Choice *A* is correct. This assertion does *not* support the fact that games are a commonplace event in this culture because it mentions conduct, not games. Choices *B*, *C*, and *D* are incorrect because these do support the fact that games were a commonplace event.

114. B: Choice *B* is the only option that mentions the correlation between physical ability and leadership positions. Choices *A* and *D* are unrelated to physical strength and leadership abilities. Choice *C* does not make a deduction that would lead to the correct answer—it only comments upon the abilities of common townspeople.

115. D: It emphasizes Mr. Utterson's anguish in failing to identify Hyde's whereabouts. Context clues indicate that Choice *D* is correct because the passage provides great detail of Mr. Utterson's feelings about locating Hyde. Choice *A* does not fit because there is no mention of Mr. Lanyon's mental state. Choice *B* is incorrect; although the text does make mention of bells, Choice *B* is not the *best* answer overall. Choice *C* is incorrect because the passage clearly states that Mr. Utterson was determined, not unsure.

116. A: In the city. The word *city* appears in the passage several times, thus establishing the location for the reader.

117. B: It scares children. The passage states that the Juggernaut causes the children to scream. Choices *A* and *D* don't apply because the text doesn't mention either of these instances specifically. Choice *C* is incorrect because there is nothing in the text that mentions space travel.

118. B: To constantly visit. The mention of *morning, noon,* and *night* make it clear that the word *haunt* refers to frequent appearances at various times. Choice *A* doesn't work because the text makes no mention of levitating. Choices *C* and *D* are not correct because the text makes mention of Mr. Utterson's anguish and disheartenment because of his failure to find Hyde but does not make mention of Mr. Utterson's feelings negatively affecting anyone else.

119. D: This is an example of alliteration. Choice *D* is the correct answer because of the repetition of the *L*-words. Hyperbole is an exaggeration, so Choice *A* doesn't work. No comparison is being made, so no simile or juxtaposition is being used, thus eliminating Choices *B* and *C*.

120. D: The speaker intends to continue to look for Hyde. Choices *A* and *B* are not possible answers because the text doesn't refer to any name changes or an identity crisis, despite Mr. Utterson's extreme obsession with finding Hyde. The text also makes no mention of a mistaken identity when referring to Hyde, so Choice *C* is also incorrect.

Practice Test #2

English Language Skills

1. DIRECTIONS: Choose the appropriately punctuated correction for the following sentence
   Protestors filled the streets of the city. Because they were dissatisfied with the government's leadership.

   a. Protestors filled the streets of the city, because they were dissatisfied with the government's leadership.
   b. Protesters, filled the streets of the city, because they were dissatisfied with the government's leadership.
   c. Because they were dissatisfied with the government's leadership protestors filled the streets of the city.
   d. Protestors filled the streets of the city because they were dissatisfied with the government's leadership.

2. DIRECTIONS: Choose the correct part of speech for the underlined word in the following sentence.
   We need to come up with a fresh <u>approach</u> to this problem.

   a. Noun
   b. Verb
   c. Adverb
   d. Adjective

3. DIRECTIONS: Choose the correct part of speech for the underlined word in the following sentence.
   Investigators conducted an <u>exhaustive</u> inquiry into the accusations of corruption.

   a. Noun
   b. Verb
   c. Adverb
   d. Adjective

4. DIRECTIONS: Choose the sentence component that describes the underlined phrase.
   New students should report <u>to the student center</u>.

   a. Dependent clause
   b. Adverbial phrase
   c. Adjective clause
   d. Noun phrase

5. DIRECTIONS: Choose the noun phrase in the following sentence.
   Charlotte's new German shepherd puppy is energetic.

   a. Puppy
   b. Charlotte
   c. German shepherd puppy
   d. Charlotte's new German shepherd puppy

6. DIRECTIONS: Choose the word that will correctly complete the sentence.
>   Increasing the price of bus fares has had a greater [affect / effect] on ridership [then / than] expected.

a. affect; then
b. affect; than
c. effect; then
d. effect; than

7. DIRECTIONS: While studying vocabulary, a student notices that the words *circumference*, *circumnavigate*, and *circumstance* all begin with the prefix *circum–*. The student uses her knowledge of affixes to infer that all of these words share what related meaning?
a. Around, surrounding
b. Travel, transport
c. Size, measurement
d. Area, location

8. DIRECTIONS: A student wants to rewrite the following sentence:
>   Entrepreneurs use their ideas to make money.

He wants to use the word *money* as a verb, but he isn't sure which word ending to use. What is the appropriate suffix to add to *money* to complete the following sentence?

>   *Entrepreneurs _____ their ideas.*

a. –ize
b. –ical
c. –en
d. –ful

9. DIRECTIONS: Choose the context clue that is essential to decipher the meaning of *ubiquitous* in the following sentence.
>   A hundred years ago, automobiles were rare, but now cars are ubiquitous.

a. Ago
b. Cars
c. Now
d. Rare

10. DIRECTIONS: Choose the correct word forms to complete the following sentence.
>   The student at a high school, after witnessing some wrongdoing on behalf of others, needed to talk to several _____ based on his _____ .

a. principals; principles
b. principles; principals
c. princapals; princaples
d. princaples; princapals

167

11. DIRECTIONS: Choose the correct word(s) to complete the following sentence.
Each patient, having gone through rehabilitative therapy, needed _____ file returned to the nursing station.

    a. their
    b. there
    c. his or her
    d. the people's

12. DIRECTIONS: Choose the correct word to complete the following sentence.
A man decided not to take his family to the zoo after hearing about a bomb threat on the news. The man believed the threat to be real and _____ .

    a. eminent
    b. imminent
    c. emanate
    d. amanita

13. DIRECTIONS: Choose the sentence that is punctuated correctly.
    a. Martha expertly read and analyzed a copy of *Taming of the Shrew*: she presented her findings to the class.
    b. Martha expertly read and analyzed a copy of *Taming of the Shrew*, she presented her findings to the class.
    c. Martha expertly read and analyzed a copy of *Taming of the Shrew*; she presented her findings to the class.
    d. Martha expertly read and analyzed a copy of *Taming of the Shrew* she presented her findings to the class.

14. DIRECTIONS: Choose the compound sentence.
    a. Tod and Elissa went to the movies, got some dessert, and slept.
    b. Though Tod and Elissa decided to go to the movies, Marge stayed home.
    c. Tod and Elissa decided to go to the movies, and Marge read a book.
    d. Tod and Elissa went to the movies while Marge slept.

15. DIRECTIONS: Choose the verb in the following sentence.
The professor's engaging lecture, though not his best, ran over thirty minutes late.

    a. Engaging
    b. Though
    c. Ran
    d. Over

16. DIRECTIONS: Choose the adverb in the following sentences.
Dave arrived at work almost thirty minutes late. His boss, who was irritated, lectured him. Dave was inconsolable the rest of the shift.

    a. Arrived
    b. Almost
    c. Irritated
    d. Rest

17. DIRECTIONS: Choose the sentences that are capitalized correctly.
a. History 220 is taught by one of my favorite professors. He used to teach an entry-level sociology class but decided he likes teaching Advanced History better.
b. History 220, taught by Mr. Hart, the Professor, focuses on the conflicts that transformed America: The Revolution, The Civil War, The Korean War, World War I, World War II, and Vietnam.
c. In particular, he likes to discuss how Yankee ingenuity helped overcome the British army and navy, the world's most formidable world power at the time.
d. Mr. Hart is scheduled to retire in the summer of 2018. President Williams already said he'll be in charge of retirement party planning.

18. DIRECTIONS: Choose the sentences that are capitalized correctly.
a. After reading *Frankenstein*, Daisy turned to her sister and said, "You told me this book wasn't 'all that bad.' You scare me as much as the book!"
b. After reading "Frankenstein," Daisy turned to her sister and said, "You told me this book wasn't 'all that bad.' You scare me as much as the book!"
c. After reading *Frankenstein*, Daisy turned to her sister and said, 'You told me this book wasn't "all that bad." You scare me as much as the book!'
d. After reading *Frankenstein*, Daisy turned to her sister, and said "You told me this book wasn't 'all that bad'. You scare me as much as the book!"

19. DIRECTIONS: Choose the sentence that contains correct subject-verb agreement.
a. Each of the members of the chess club, who have been successful before on their own, struggled to unite as a team.
b. Everyone who has ever owned a pet and hasn't had help knows it's difficult.
c. Neither of the boys, after a long day of slumber, have cleaned their bedrooms.
d. One of the very applauded and commended lecturers are coming to our campus!

20. DIRECTIONS: Choose the adjective from the following passage.
Sara, who is never late, showed up today ten minutes after Mr. Gray's class had begun. Her hair was a mess, and she looked distraught. Everybody wondered what had happened.

a. Never
b. After
c. Mess
d. Distraught

21. DIRECTIONS: Choose which point(s) of view is/are represented in the following passage.
When giving a presentation, one should have three to five bullet points per slide. It is impossible for a presenter to memorize an entire speech, but if you can memorize the main ideas connected to the bullet points, then your speech will be more natural and fluid.

a. First person only
b. Third person only
c. Second person and third person
d. First person and third person

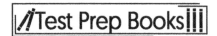

22. DIRECTIONS: Choose the word that correctly completes the sentence.
Even though Ralph knew it was wrong to steal, he had still taken a grape from the vegetable stand. He stood there, befuddled, wrestling with his _____ , trying decide whether to put it back or pop it in his mouth.

    a. Conscious
    b. Conscience
    c. Consensus
    d. Census

23. DIRECTIONS: Choose the example that demonstrates a simple sentence.
    a. Ted loves to rock climb even though he tore his rotator cuff.
    b. Ted, who is not yet sixty, still easily fishes and camps, too.
    c. Ted loves the outdoors, but, strangely enough, his wife is a homebody.
    d. Ted will also be retired soon; nevertheless, he likes to stay busy.

24. DIRECTIONS: Choose the example that displays correct use of the possessive.
    a. The womens' portfolios are available for the teacher's review.
    b. A well-trained dog always returns to it's master.
    c. The visitor center is a good place to start the tour.
    d. The businesses' clients had a great time at the convention.

25. DIRECTIONS: Choose the meaning of the Latin prefix *anti-* based on the following definitions.
An antibiotic is prescribed to eliminate bacterial infections; someone who is antisocial ignores society and laws.

    a. Reduce
    b. Revolt
    c. Oppose
    d. Without

26. DIRECTIONS: Choose the meaning of the Latin suffix *-form* based on the following definitions.
Conform means to adjust one's behavior to better fit in with social norms. Inform means to communicate new knowledge to another.

    a. Match
    b. Relay
    c. Negate
    d. Shape

27. DIRECTIONS: Choose the best substitute for *curmudgeon* based on the context in this passage.
Every week, Cindy volunteers time at the local shelter. She always has a smile on her face, and she always talks to others with kindness and patience. Considering that her current job is very taxing, that two of her three children are still in diapers, and that her husband, Steve, the old curmudgeon, is the opposite of her in temperament, it's amazing that no one has ever seen her angry.

    a. Stingy
    b. Surly
    c. Scared
    d. Shy

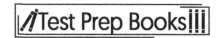

28. DIRECTIONS: Choose which point(s) of view is/are represented in the following passage.
We went on vacation this summer to Arizona. Mom had always wanted to see the Grand Canyon. Dad, on the other hand, wanted to see Saguaro National Park and Hoover Dam. Other than the flat tire our car got, it was a fantastic time.

    a. First person only
    b. Third person only
    c. Second person and third person
    d. First person and third person

29. DIRECTIONS: Choose the complex sentence.
    a. To make your fruit last longer, keep it out of the sunlight.
    b. Make sure to clock out after your shift is through.
    c. Making a good fire requires using the proper wood and stacking it properly.
    d. Whenever possible, make sure to yield to oncoming traffic.

30. DIRECTIONS: Choose the correct word forms to complete the following sentence.
The people of Scotland are known not only for their unique _____ but also the taxing ____ they make to villages nestled high in the mountains.

    a. ascents; accents
    b. accents; ascents
    c. accents; assents
    d. assents; accents

31. DIRECTIONS: Choose the sentence that does not contain an error in comma usage.
    a. My niece arrives from Australia on Monday, February 4, 2016.
    b. My cousin's wedding this Saturday June 9, conflicts with my best friend's birthday party.
    c. The project is due on Tuesday, May, 17, 2016.
    d. I can't get a flight home until Thursday September 21.

32. DIRECTIONS: Choose the sentence that shows correct usage of a defining clause.
    a. The ball that was red had low air pressure.
    b. The dog, that needed to eat, was whimpering.
    c. I looked at the second boat which was very old.
    d. If this is a problem which you are concerned about, you should tell the teacher.

33. DIRECTIONS: Choose the sentence with an incorrect use of a proper noun.
    a. Bob's dog, Gill, was 12 years old.
    b. I went to San Antonio, Texas, on vacation.
    c. I talked to senator Greene about his stance on the new bill.
    d. Have you heard of that new restaurant in town, Lotus Sushi?

34. DIRECTIONS: Choose the sentence that does NOT contain a spelling error.
    a. He recieved word that construction would begin on Monday.
    b. The advertisement lead her to believe she would save money.
    c. The plaintiff felt that his attorney missrepresented him.
    d. Since the woman was crying, I gave her some tissues.

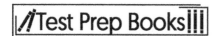

35. DIRECTIONS: Choose the sentence with correct comma usage.
   a. My friends Joe, Steve, and Ryan joined me for dinner.
   b. Why did the damage that was mild, cost so much to fix?
   c. Sometimes it rains, the garden gets flooded.
   d. On Wednesday March 3, at 12:00 p.m. I have a job interview.

36. DIRECTIONS: Choose the option that corrects an error in the underlined portion of the sentence below. If no error exists, choose "No change is necessary."
   While speeding on the way to work, the car crashed.

   a. the car crashed badly.
   b. I crashed my car.
   c. the accident happened.
   d. No change is necessary.

37. DIRECTIONS: Choose the sentence with the correct use of a compound modifier.
   a. The farmer was frustrated at the quickly-fluctuating weather this season.
   b. My boss's email follow-up was somewhat curt.
   c. Rachel proposed a shortterm fix to the project.
   d. The high-tech smartwatch looked very impressive.

38. DIRECTIONS: Choose the sentence with correct usage of past tense.
   a. I drunk the milkshake.
   b. The girls have took the bracelets.
   c. The paper was full of errors.
   d. Whenever the bear hibernated, it would store its fat for winter.

39. DIRECTIONS: Identify the adverb in the following sentence:
   The wind briskly blew the soggy newspapers.

   a. Soggy
   b. Briskly
   c. Blew
   d. Wind

40. DIRECTIONS: Choose the option that corrects an error in the underlined portion of the sentence below. If no error exists, choose "No change is necessary."
   None of the student's grades were strong enough to pass the course.

   a. None of the students
   b. None of the students's
   c. None of the students'
   d. No change is necessary.

Mathematics

41. What's the probability of rolling a 6 exactly once in two rolls of a die?

    a. $1/3$

    b. $1/36$

    c. $1/6$

    d. $11/36$

42. A rectangle has a length that is 5 feet longer than three times its width. If the perimeter is 90 feet, what is the length in feet?

    a. 10

    b. 20

    c. 25

    d. 35

43. What is the value of the sum of $\frac{1}{3}$ and $\frac{2}{5}$?

    a. $\frac{3}{8}$

    b. $\frac{11}{15}$

    c. $\frac{11}{30}$

    d. $\frac{4}{5}$

44. What is the value of the expression: $7^2 - 3 \times (4 + 2) + 15 \div 5$?

    a. 12.2

    b. 40.2

    c. 34

    d. 58.2

45. What are all the factors of 12?

    a. 12, 24, 36

    b. 1, 2, 4, 6, 12

    c. 12, 24, 36, 48

    d. 1, 2, 3, 4, 6, 12

46. A construction company is building a new housing development with the property of each house measuring 30 feet wide. If the length of the street is zoned off at 345 feet, how many houses can be built on the street?

    a. 11

    b. 115

    c. 11.5

    d. 12

47. Kassidy drove for 3 hours at a speed of 60 miles per hour. Using the distance formula, $d = r \times t$ ($distance = rate \times time$), how far did Kassidy travel?
   a. 20 miles
   b. 180 miles
   c. 65 miles
   d. 120 miles

48. Which of the following is the definition of a prime number?
   a. A number that factors only into itself and one
   b. A number greater than one that factors only into itself and one
   c. A number less than 10
   d. A number divisible by 10

49. Determine the next number in the following series: $1, 3, 6, 10, 15, 21, \ldots$
   a. 26
   b. 27
   c. 28
   d. 29

50. Which of the following is the correct order of operations?
   a. Parentheses, Exponents, Multiplication, Division, Addition, Subtraction
   b. Exponents, Parentheses, Multiplication, Division, Addition, Subtraction
   c. Parentheses, Exponents, Addition, Multiplication, Division, Subtraction
   d. Parentheses, Exponents, Division, Addition, Subtraction, Multiplication

51. Carey bought 184 pounds of fertilizer to use on her lawn. Each segment of her lawn required $11\frac{1}{2}$ pounds of fertilizer to do a sufficient job. If asked to determine how many segments could be fertilized with the amount purchased, what operation would be necessary to solve this problem?
   a. Multiplication
   b. Division
   c. Addition
   d. Subtraction

52. It is necessary to line up decimal places within the given numbers before performing which of the following operations?
   a. Multiplication
   b. Division
   c. Subtraction
   d. Fractions

53. Which of the following expressions best exemplifies the additive and subtractive identity?
   a. $5 + 2 - 0 = 5 + 2 + 0$
   b. $6 + x = 6 - 6$
   c. $9 - 9 = 0$
   d. $8 + 2 = 10$

54. Which of the following represents one hundred eighty-two million, thirty-six thousand, four hundred twenty-one and three hundred fifty-six thousandths?
- a. 182,036,421.356
- b. 182,036,421.0356
- c. 182,000,036,421.0356
- d. 182,000,036,421.356

55. Which of the following is NOT a way to write 40 percent of N?
- a. $(0.4)N$
- b. $\frac{2}{5}N$
- c. $40N$
- d. $\frac{4N}{10}$

56. $3\frac{2}{3} - 1\frac{4}{5} =$
- a. $1\frac{13}{15}$
- b. $\frac{14}{15}$
- c. $2\frac{2}{3}$
- d. $\frac{4}{5}$

57. The total perimeter of a rectangle is 36 cm. If the length is 12 cm, what is the width?
- a. 3 cm
- b. 12 cm
- c. 6 cm
- d. 8 cm

58. If Sarah reads at an average rate of 21 pages in four nights, how long will it take her to read 140 pages?
- a. 6 nights
- b. 26 nights
- c. 8 nights
- d. 27 nights

59. Twenty is 40% of what number?
- a. 50
- b. 8
- c. 200
- d. 5000

60. Divide and reduce: $4/13 \div 27/169$.
    a. 52/27
    b. 51/27
    c. 52/29
    d. 51/29

61. Which of the following shows a line of symmetry?

a.

b.

c.

d.

62. Convert 0.351 to a percentage.
    a. 3.51%

    b. 35.1%

    c. $\frac{351}{100}$

    d. 0.00351%

63. Convert $\frac{2}{9}$ to a percentage.
    a. 22%
    b. 4.5%
    c. 450%
    d. 0.22%

64. Convert 57% to a decimal.
    a. 570
    b. 5.70
    c. 0.06
    d. 0.57

65. What is 3 out of 8 expressed as a percent?
    a. 37.5%
    b. 37%
    c. 26.7%
    d. 2.67%

66. What is 39% of 164?
    a. 63.96
    b. 23.78
    c. 6,396
    d. 2.38

67. 32 is 25% of what number?
    a. 64
    b. 128
    c. 12.65
    d. 8

68. Convert $\frac{5}{8}$ to a decimal to the nearest hundredth.
    a. 0.62
    b. 1.05
    c. 0.63
    d. 1.60

69. Change $3\frac{3}{5}$ to a decimal.
    a. 3.6
    b. 4.67
    c. 5.3
    d. 0.28

70. Change 0.56 to a fraction.
    a. $\frac{5.6}{100}$

    b. $\frac{14}{25}$

    c. $\frac{56}{1000}$

    d. $\frac{56}{10}$

71. Change 9.3 to a fraction.
    a. $9\frac{3}{7}$

    b. $\frac{903}{1000}$

    c. $\frac{9.03}{100}$

    d. $9\frac{3}{10}$

72. The hospital has a nurse-to-patient ratio of 1:25. If there is a maximum of 325 patients admitted at a time, how many nurses are there?
    a. 13 nurses
    b. 25 nurses
    c. 325 nurses
    d. 12 nurses

73. A hospital has a bed-to-room ratio of 2:1. If there are 145 rooms, how many beds are there?
    a. 145 beds
    b. 2 beds
    c. 90 beds
    d. 290 beds

74. Store brand coffee beans cost $1.23 per pound. A local coffee bean roaster charges $1.98 per 1 ½ pounds. How much more would 5 pounds from the local roaster cost than 5 pounds of the store brand?
    a. $0.55
    b. $1.55
    c. $1.45
    d. $0.45

75. Paint Inc. charges $2000 for painting the first 1,800 feet of trim on a house and $1.00 per foot for each foot after. How much would it cost to paint a house with 3,125 feet of trim?
    a. $3,125
    b. $2,000
    c. $5,125
    d. $3,325

76. Which inequality represents the values displayed on the number line?

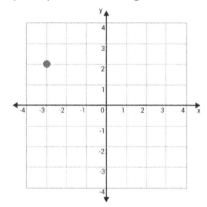

   a. $x < 1$
   b. $x \leq 1$
   c. $x > 1$
   d. $x \geq 1$

77. What are the coordinates of the point plotted on the grid?

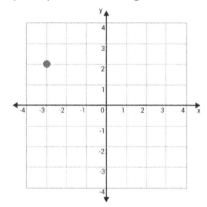

   a. $(-3, 2)$
   b. $(2, -3)$
   c. $(-3, -2)$
   d. $(2, 3)$

78. The graph of which function has an x-intercept of -2?
   a. $y = 2x - 3$
   b. $y = 4x + 2$
   c. $y = x^2 + 5x + 6$
   d. $y = -\frac{1}{2} \times 2^x$

79. If $-3(x + 4) \geq x + 8$, what is the value of x?
   a. $x = 4$
   b. $x \geq 2$
   c. $x \geq -5$
   d. $x \leq -5$

80. Karen gets paid a weekly salary and a commission for every sale that she makes. The table below shows the number of sales and her pay for different weeks.

Sales	2	7	4	8
Pay	$380	$580	$460	$620

Which of the following equations represents Karen's weekly pay?

a. $y = 90x + 200$

b. $y = 90x - 200$

c. $y = 40x + 300$

d. $y = 40x - 300$

Reading Comprehension

Questions 81–93 are based on the following passage:

Knowing that Mrs. Mallard was afflicted with heart trouble, great care was taken to break to her as gently as possible the news of her husband's death.

It was her sister Josephine who told her, in broken sentences; veiled hints that revealed in half concealing. Her husband's friend Richards was there, too, near her. It was he who had been in the newspaper office when intelligence of the railroad disaster was received, with Brently Mallard's name leading the list of "killed." He had only taken the time to assure himself of its truth by a second telegram, and had hastened to forestall any less careful, less tender friend in bearing the sad message.

She did not hear the story as many women have heard the same, with a paralyzed inability to accept its significance. She wept at once, with sudden, wild abandonment, in her sister's arms. When the storm of grief had spent itself she went away to her room alone. She would have no one follow her.

There stood, facing the open window, a comfortable, roomy armchair. Into this she sank, pressed down by a physical exhaustion that haunted her body and seemed to reach into her soul.

She could see in the open square before her house the tops of trees that were all aquiver with the new spring life. The delicious breath of rain was in the air. In the street below a peddler was crying his wares. The notes of a distant song which some one was singing reached her faintly, and countless sparrows were twittering in the eaves.

There were patches of blue sky showing here and there through the clouds that had met and piled one above the other in the west facing her window.

She sat with her head thrown back upon the cushion of the chair, quite motionless, except when a sob came up into her throat and shook her, as a child who has cried itself to sleep continues to sob in its dreams.

She was young, with a fair, calm face, whose lines bespoke repression and even a certain strength. But now here was a dull stare in her eyes, whose gaze was fixed away off yonder on one of those patches of blue sky. It was not a glance of reflection, but rather indicated a suspension of intelligent thought.

180

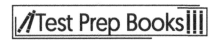

There was something coming to her and she was waiting for it, fearfully. What was it? She did not know; it was too subtle and elusive to name. But she felt it, creeping out of the sky, reaching toward her through the sounds, the scents, and color that filled the air.

Now her bosom rose and fell tumultuously. She was beginning to recognize this thing that was approaching to possess her, and she was striving to beat it back with her will—as powerless as her two white slender hands would have been. When she abandoned herself a little whispered word escaped her slightly parted lips. She said it over and over under her breath: "free, free, free!" The vacant stare and the look of terror that had followed it went from her eyes. They stayed keen and bright. Her pulses beat fast, and the coursing blood warmed and relaxed every inch of her body.

She did not stop to ask if it were or were not a monstrous joy that held her. A clear and exalted perception enabled her to dismiss the suggestion as trivial. She knew that she would weep again when she saw the kind, tender hands folded in death; the face that had never looked save with love upon her, fixed and gray and dead. But she saw beyond that bitter moment a long procession of years to come that would belong to her absolutely. And she opened and spread her arms out to them in welcome.

Excerpt from "The Story of An Hour," Kate Chopin, 1894

81. What point of view is the above passage told in?
    a. First person
    b. Second person
    c. Third person omniscient
    d. Third person limited

82. What kind of irony are we presented with in this story?
    a. The way Mrs. Mallard reacted to her husband's death.
    b. The way in which Mr. Mallard died.
    c. The way in which the news of her husband's death was presented to Mrs. Mallard.
    d. The way in which nature is compared with death in the story.

83. What is the meaning of the word *elusive* in paragraph 9?
    a. Horrible
    b. Indefinable
    c. Quiet
    d. Joyful

84. What is the best summary of the passage above?
    a. Mr. Mallard, a soldier during World War I, is killed in the field of battle and leaves his wife widowed.
    b. Mrs. Mallard understands the value of friendship when her friends show up for her after her husband's death.
    c. Mrs. Mallard combats mental illness daily and will perhaps be sent to a mental institution soon.
    d. Mrs. Mallard, a newly widowed woman, finds unexpected relief in her husband's death.

85. What is the tone of this story?
    a. Confused
    b. Joyful
    c. Depressive
    d. All of the above

86. What is the meaning of the word *tumultuously* in paragraph 10?
    a. Orderly
    b. Unashamedly
    c. Violently
    d. Calmly

87. What is the relationship between these two sentences from the passage?

    Sentence 1: But now here was a dull stare in her eyes, whose gaze was fixed away off yonder on one of those patches of blue sky.

    Sentence 2: It was not a glance of reflection, but rather indicated a suspension of intelligent thought.

    a. Sentence 2 provides a continued description of sentence 1.
    b. Sentence 2 analyzes a comment in sentence 1.
    c. Sentence 2 explains a solution to the problem in sentence 1.
    d. Sentence 2 continues the definition begun in sentence 1.

88. The suggestion in the passage that Mrs. Mallard's husband was not unkind arises from the author's statement that
    a. "She wept at once, with sudden, wild abandonment, in her sister's arms."
    b. "She said it over and over under her breath: 'free, free, free!'"
    c. "She knew that she would weep again when she saw the kind, tender hands folded in death"
    d. "It was he who had been in the newspaper office when intelligence of the railroad disaster was received, with Brently Mallard's name leading the list of 'killed.'"

89. With which of the following questions would critics most likely dispute in this passage?
    a. The news in which we receive Mr. Mallard's death is not credible enough to satisfy the fact that Mr. Mallard is actually dead. The crux of the story is the questionable death of a soldier.
    b. The question of Mrs. Mallard's state of mind is the core issue of the passage. Some critics will say Mrs. Mallard is ecstatic that her husband is dead; others will say she is in the throes of grief, and her behavior is unpredictable.
    c. The main question of the passage is whether or not Mrs. Mallard was abused or neglected by her husband. Judged on her reaction of denial, repression, and freedom, many critics will assert that domestic abuse was part of her past.
    d. Something critics dispute in this passage is whether or not Mrs. Mallard is experiencing a heart attack. Her whispering "free" is possibly a testament to her own freedom in death, and her altered breathing and blank staring may be signs of heart failure.

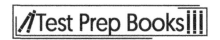

90. Which of the following can we infer after reading this passage?
    a. Mrs. Mallard's sister, Josephine, was horrified by Mrs. Mallard's reaction to her husband's death.
    b. Mrs. Mallard had a bedroom window that faced toward the west.
    c. There was no funeral held for Mr. Mallard, as he was disliked by many people in the community.
    d. Mrs. Mallard finds out the news of her husband's death during the wintertime.

91. What is the primary purpose of paragraph 5?
    a. To objectively describe the setting of the narrative.
    b. To explain to the audience how Mr. Mallard died.
    c. To present to the reader the depths of Mrs. Mallard's grief.
    d. To show the reader the present state of mind of Mrs. Mallard.

92. The author's attitude toward Mrs. Mallard can be best described as which of the following?
    a. Harsh and judging
    b. Sympathetic and understanding
    c. Regretful and fearful
    d. Joyous and carefree

93. What does the word "it" refer to in the following sentence in the context of the passage?

    But she felt it, creeping out of the sky, reaching toward her through the sounds, the scents, and color that filled the air.

    a. Incompetence
    b. Consternation
    c. Uninhibitedness
    d. Merriment

Questions 94-100 are based upon the following passage:

The Global Water Crisis

For decades, the world's water supply has been decreasing. At least ten percent of the world population, or over 780 million people, do not have access to potable water. They have to walk for miles, carrying heavy buckets in intense heat in order to obtain the essential life source that comes freely from our faucets.

We are in a global water crisis. Only 2.5% of the water on Earth is suitable for drinking, and over seventy percent of this water is frozen in the polar ice caps, while much of the rest is located deep underground. This leaves a very small percentage available for drinking, yet we see millions of gallons of water wasted on watering huge lawns in deserts like Arizona, or on running dishwashers that are only half-full, or on filling all the personal pools in Los Angeles, meanwhile people in Africa are dying of thirst.

In order to reduce water waste, Americans and citizens of other first world countries should adhere to the following guidelines: run the dishwasher only when it is full, do only full loads of laundry, wash the car with a bucket and not with a hose, take showers only when necessary, swim in public pools, and just be <u>cognizant</u> of how much water they are using in general. Our planet is getting thirstier by the year, and if we do not solve this problem, our species will surely perish.

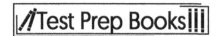

94. Which of the following best supports the assertion that we need to limit our water usage?
    a. People are wasting water on superfluous things.
    b. There is very little water on earth suitable for drinking.
    c. At least ten percent of the world population does not have access to drinking water.
    d. There is plenty of drinking water in first world countries, but not anywhere else.

95. How is the content in the selection organized?
    a. In chronological order
    b. Compare and contrast
    c. As a set of problems and solutions
    d. As a series of descriptions

96. Which of the following, if true, would challenge the assertion that we are in a global water crisis?
    a. There are abundant water stores on earth that scientists are not reporting.
    b. Much of the water we drink comes from rain.
    c. People in Africa only have to walk less than a mile to get water.
    d. Most Americans only run the dishwasher when it is full.

97. The selection is written in which of the following styles?
    a. As a narrative
    b. In a persuasive manner
    c. As an informative piece
    d. As a series of descriptions

98. Which of the following is implicitly stated within the following sentence? "This leaves a very small percentage available for drinking, yet we see millions of gallons of water wasted on watering huge lawns in deserts like Arizona, or on running dishwashers that are only half-full, or on filling all the personal pools in Los Angeles, meanwhile people in Africa are dying of thirst."
    a. People run dishwashers that are not full.
    b. People in Africa are dying of thirst.
    c. People take water for granted.
    d. People should stop watering their lawns.

99. Why does the author mention that people have to walk for miles in intense heat to get water?
    a. To inform the reader on the hardships of living in a third world country.
    b. To inspire compassion in the reader.
    c. To show that water is only available in first world countries.
    d. To persuade the reader to reduce their water usage.

100. What is the main idea of the passage?
    a. People should reduce their water usage.
    b. There is very little drinking water on earth.
    c. People take their access to water for granted.
    d. People should swim in public pools.

Questions 101–106 are based upon the following passage:

This excerpt is adapted from "What to the Slave is the Fourth of July?" Rochester, New York July 5, 1852

Fellow-citizens, pardon me, allow me to ask, why am I called upon to speak here to-day? What have I, or those I represent, to do with your national independence? Are the great principles of political freedom and of natural justice, embodied in that Declaration of Independence, extended to us? and am I, therefore, called upon to bring our humble offering to the national altar, and to confess the benefits and express devout gratitude for the blessings resulting from your independence to us?

Would to God, both for your sakes and ours, ours that an affirmative answer could be truthfully returned to these questions! Then would my task be light, and my burden easy and delightful. For who is there so cold, that a nation's sympathy could not warm him? Who so obdurate and dead to the claims of gratitude, that would not thankfully acknowledge such priceless benefits? Who so stolid and selfish, that would not give his voice to swell the hallelujahs of a nation's jubilee, when the chains of servitude had been torn from his limbs? I am not that man. In a case like that, the dumb may eloquently speak, and the lame man leap as an hart.

But, such is not the state of the case. I say it with a sad sense of the disparity between us. I am not included within the pale of this glorious anniversary. Oh pity! Your high independence only reveals the immeasurable distance between us. The blessings in which you, this day, rejoice, are not enjoyed in common. – The rich inheritance of justice, liberty, prosperity and independence, bequeathed by your fathers, is shared by you, not by me. The sunlight that brought life and healing to you, as brought stripes and death to me. This Fourth [of] July is yours, not mine. You may rejoice, I must mourn. To drag a man in fetters into the grand illuminated temple of liberty, and call upon him to join you in joyous anthems, were inhuman mockery and sacrilegious irony. Do you mean, citizens, to mock me, by asking me to speak to-day? If so, there is a parallel to your conduct. And let me warn you that it is dangerous to copy the example of a nation whose crimes, lowering up to heaven, were thrown down by the breath of the Almighty, burying that nation in irrecoverable ruin! I can to-day take up the plaintive lament of a peeled and woe-smitten people!

"By the rivers of Babylon, there we sat down. Yea! we wept when we remembered Zion. We hanged our harps upon the willows in the midst thereof. For there, they that carried us away captive, required of us a song; and they who wasted us required of us mirth, saying, 'Sing us one of the songs of Zion.' How can we sing the Lord's song in a strange land? If I forget thee, O Jerusalem, let my right hand forget her cunning. If I do not remember thee, let my tongue cleave to the roof of my mouth."

101. What is the tone of the first paragraph of this passage?
    a. Incredulous
    b. Inclusive
    c. Contemplative
    d. Nonchalant

185

Test Prep Books

The

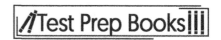
rookeries from the attacks of money-hungry desperadoes to whom the accursed plumes were worth their weight in gold, is a very chancy proceeding. There is now one warden in Florida who says that "before they get my rookery they will first have to get me."

Thus far the protective work of the Audubon Association has been successful. Now there are twenty colonies, which contain all told, about 5,000 egrets and about 120,000 herons and ibises which are guarded by the Audubon wardens. One of the most important is on Bird Island, a mile out in Orange Lake, central Florida, and it is ably defended by Oscar E. Baynard. To-day, the plume hunters who do not dare to raid the guarded rookeries are trying to study out the lines of flight of the birds, to and from their feeding-grounds, and shoot them in transit. Their motto is—"Anything to beat the law, and get the plumes." It is there that the state of Florida should take part in the war.

The success of this campaign is attested by the fact that last year a number of egrets were seen in eastern Massachusetts—for the first time in many years. And so to-day the question is, can the wardens continue to hold the plume-hunters at bay?

107. The author's use of first-person pronouns in the following text does NOT have which of the following effects?

Three years ago, I think there were not many bird-lovers in the United States who believed it possible to prevent the total extinction of both egrets from our fauna.

a. The phrase *I think* acts as a sort of hedging, where the author's tone is less direct and/or absolute.
b. It allows the reader to more easily connect with the author.
c. It encourages the reader to empathize with the egrets.
d. It distances the reader from the text by overemphasizing the story.

108. What purpose does the quote serve at the end of the first paragraph?
a. The quote shows proof of a hunter threatening one of the wardens.
b. The quote lightens the mood by illustrating the colloquial language of the region.
c. The quote provides an example of a warden protecting one of the colonies.
d. The quote provides much needed comic relief in the form of a joke.

109. What is the meaning of the word *rookeries* in the following text?

To-day, the plume hunters who do not dare to raid the guarded rookeries are trying to study out the lines of flight of the birds, to and from their feeding-grounds, and shoot them in transit.

a. Houses in a slum area
b. A place where hunters gather to trade tools
c. A place where wardens go to trade stories
d. A colony of breeding birds

110. What is on Bird Island?
a. Hunters selling plumes
b. An important bird colony
c. Bird Island Battle between the hunters and the wardens
d. An important egret with unique plumes

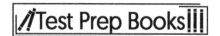

111. What is the main purpose of the passage?
  a. To persuade the audience to act in preservation of the bird colonies
  b. To show the effect hunting egrets has had on the environment
  c. To argue that the preservation of bird colonies has had a negative impact on the environment
  d. To demonstrate the success of the protective work of the Audubon Association

112. Why are hunters trying to study the lines of flight of the birds?
  a. To study ornithology, one must know the lines of flight that birds take.
  b. To help wardens preserve the lives of the birds
  c. To have a better opportunity to hunt the birds
  d. To build their homes under the lines of flight because they believe it brings good luck

Questions 113–116 are based on the following passage:

> Four score and seven years ago our fathers brought forth on this continent, a new nation, conceived in Liberty, and dedicated to the proposition that all men are created equal.
>
> Now we are engaged in a great civil war, testing whether that nation, or any nation so conceived and so dedicated, can long endure. We are met on a great battle-field of that war. We have come to dedicate a portion of that field, as a final resting place for those who here gave their lives that that nation might live. It is altogether fitting and proper that we should do this.
>
> But, in a larger sense, we cannot dedicate --- we cannot consecrate that we cannot hallow --- this ground. The brave men, living and dead, who struggled here, have consecrated it, far above our poor power to add or detract. The world will little note, nor long remember what we say here, but it can never forget what they did here. It is for us the living, rather, to be dedicated here to the unfinished work which they who fought here have thus far so nobly advanced. It is rather for us to be here dedicated to the great task remaining before us--- that from these honored dead we take increased devotion to that cause for which they gave the last full measure of devotion --- that we here highly resolve that these dead shall not have died in vain --- that this nation, under God, shall have a new birth of freedom --- and that government of the people, by the people, for the people, shall not perish from the earth.

Abraham Lincoln's Address Delivered at the Dedication of the Cemetery at Gettysburg, 1863

113. The best description for the phrase "Four score and seven years ago" is?
  a. A unit of measurement
  b. A period of time
  c. A literary movement
  d. A statement of political reform

114. Which war is Abraham Lincoln referring to in the following passage? "Now we are engaged in a great civil war, testing whether that nation, or any nation so conceived and so dedicated, can long endure."
  a. World War I
  b. The War of Spanish Succession
  c. World War II
  d. The American Civil War

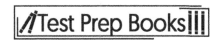

115. What message is the author trying to convey through this address?
    a. The audience should consider the death of the people that fought in the war as an example.
    b. The audience should honor the dead by establishing an annual memorial service.
    c. The audience should form a militia that would overturn the current political structure.
    d. The audience should forget the lives that were lost and discredit the soldiers.

116. What is the effect of Lincoln's statement in the following passage? "But, in a larger sense, we cannot dedicate --- we cannot consecrate that we cannot hallow --- this ground. The brave men, living and dead, who struggled here, have consecrated it, far above our poor power to add or detract."
    a. His comparison emphasizes the great sacrifice of the soldiers who fought in the war.
    b. His comparison serves as a remainder of the inadequacies of his audience.
    c. His comparison serves as a catalyst for guilt and shame among audience members.
    d. His comparison attempts to illuminate the great differences between soldiers and civilians.

Questions 117-120 are based upon the following passage, which is an adaptation from Mineralogy --- Encyclopedia International, Grolier

Mineralogy is the science of minerals, which are the naturally occurring elements and compounds that make up the solid parts of the universe. Mineralogy is usually considered in terms of materials in the Earth, but meteorites provide samples of minerals from outside the Earth.

A mineral may be defined as a naturally occurring, homogeneous solid, inorganically formed, with a definite chemical composition and an ordered atomic arrangement. The qualification *naturally occurring* is essential because it is possible to reproduce most minerals in the laboratory. For example, evaporating a solution of sodium chloride produces crystal indistinguishable from those of the mineral halite, but such laboratory-produced crystals are not minerals.

A *homogeneous solid* is one consisting of a single kind of material that cannot be separated into simpler compounds by any physical method. The requirement that a mineral be solid eliminates gases and liquids from consideration. Thus, ice is a mineral (a very common one, especially at high altitudes and latitudes) but water is not. Some mineralogists dispute this restriction and would consider both water and native mercury (also a liquid) as minerals.

The restriction of minerals to *inorganically formed* substances eliminates those homogenous solids produced by animals and plants. Thus, the shell of an oyster and the pearl inside, though both consist of calcium carbonate indistinguishable chemically or physically from the mineral aragonite, are not usually considered minerals.

The requirement of a *definite chemical composition* implies that a mineral is a chemical compound, and the composition of a chemical compound is readily expressed by a formula. Mineral formulas may be simple or complex, depending upon the number of elements present and the proportions in which they are combined.

Minerals are crystalline solids, and the presence of an *ordered atomic arrangement* is the criterion of the crystalline state. Under favorable conditions of formation, the ordered atomic arrangement is expressed in the external crystal form. In fact, the presence of an ordered atomic arrangement and crystalline solids was deduced from the external regularity of crystals by a French mineralogist, Abbé R. Haüy, early in the 19th century.

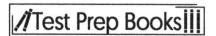

117. According to the text, an object or substance must have all of the following criteria to be considered a mineral except for?
  a. Be naturally occurring
  b. Be a homogeneous solid
  c. Be organically formed
  d. Have a definite chemical composition

118. One can deduce that French mineralogist Abbé R. Haüy specialized in what field of study?
  a. Geology
  b. Psychology
  c. Biology
  d. Botany

119. What is the definition of the word "homogeneous" as it appears in the following passage?

"A homogeneous solid is one consisting of a single kind of material that cannot be separated into simpler compounds by any physical method."
  a. Made of similar substances
  b. Differing in some areas
  c. Having a higher atomic mass
  d. Lacking necessary properties

120. The suffix -logy refers to:
  a. The properties of
  b. The chemical makeup of
  c. The study of
  d. The classification of

Essay

Read the two topics presented below. Select one of the topics to write your essay. Prepare an essay of about 300 to 600 words on the essay you choose.

Topic 1
Some parents choose to give their children a monetary allowance. Parents in favor of this idea may argue that a consistent allowance of a set amount can help children learn the value of saving money at a young age and teach them healthy spending habits. Other parents disagree with the concept of an allowance and ask their children to do chores to earn money instead, wanting to motivate their children to work hard. Take a side on the issue and argue whether or not children should be given an allowance. Use specific examples to support your argument.

Topic 2
Many companies are trying out a four-day work week with ten-hour workdays instead of the traditional five-day work week with eight-hour workdays. Proponents of the four-day work week believe that a shorter week offers employees better work-life balance, decreasing burnout in the long run. Those against it say that it can complicate business with companies that don't follow the same schedule, and it can rush employees to complete time-sensitive tasks. Take a side on the issue and argue whether or not a four-day work week is beneficial or harmful. Use specific examples to support your argument.

Answer Explanations #2

English Language Skills

1. D: The problem in the original passage is that the second sentence is a dependent clause that cannot stand alone as a sentence; it must be attached to the main clause found in the first sentence. Because the main clause comes first, it does not need to be separated by a comma. However, if the dependent clause came first, then a comma would be necessary, which is why Choice C is incorrect. A and B also insert unnecessary commas into the sentence.

2. A: A noun refers to a person, place, thing, or idea. Although the word *approach* can also be used as a verb, in the sentence it functions as a noun within the noun phrase "a fresh approach," so B is incorrect. An adverb is a word or phrase that provides additional information of the verb, but because the verb is *need* and not *approach*, then C is false. An adjective is a word that describes a noun, used here as the word *fresh*, but it is not the noun itself. Thus, D is also incorrect.

3. D: An adjective modifies a noun, answering the question "Which one?" or "What kind?" In this sentence, the word *exhaustive* is an adjective that modifies the noun investigation. Another clue that this word is an adjective is the suffix –ive, which means "having the quality of." The nouns in this sentence are investigators, inquiry, accusations, and corruption; therefore, A is incorrect. The verb in this sentence is conducted because this was the action taken by the subject the investigators; therefore, B is incorrect. C is incorrect because an adverb is a word or phrase that provides additional information about the verb, expressing how, when, where, or in what manner.

4. B: In this case, the phrase functions as an adverb modifying the verb *report*, so B is the correct answer. "To the student center" does not consist of a subject-verb combination, so it is not a clause; thus, Choices A and C can be eliminated. This group of words is a phrase. Phrases are classified by either the controlling word in the phrase or its function in the sentence. D is incorrect because a noun phrase is a series of words that describe or modify a noun.

5. D: A noun phrase consists of the noun and all of its modifiers. In this case, the subject of the sentence is the noun *puppy*, but it is preceded by several modifiers—adjectives that give more information about what kind of puppy, which are also part of the noun phrase. Thus, A is incorrect. Charlotte is the owner of the puppy and a modifier of the puppy, so B is false. C is incorrect because it contains some, but not all, of the modifiers pertaining to the puppy. D is correct because it contains all of them.

6. D: In this sentence, the first answer choice requires a noun meaning *impact* or *influence*, so *effect* is the correct answer. For the second answer choice, the sentence is drawing a comparison. *Than* shows a comparative relationship whereas *then* shows sequence or consequence. A and C can be eliminated because they contain the choice *then*. B is incorrect because *affect* is a verb while this sentence requires a noun.

7. A: The affix *circum–* originates from Latin and means *around or surrounding*. It is also related to other words that indicate something round, such as circle and circus. The rest of the choices do not relate to the affix *circum–* and are therefore incorrect.

8. A: Only two of these suffixes, –ize and –en, can be used to form verbs, so B and D are incorrect. Those choices create adjectives. The suffix –ize means "to convert or turn into." The suffix –en means "to

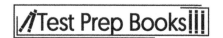

become." Because this sentence is about converting ideas into money, money + –ize or *monetize* is the most appropriate word to complete the sentence, so *C* is incorrect.

9. D: Students can use context clues to make a careful guess about the meaning of unfamiliar words. Although all of the words in a sentence can help contribute to the overall sentence, in this case, the adjective that pairs with *ubiquitous* gives the most important hint to the student—cars were first *rare*, but now they are *ubiquitous.* The inversion of *rare* is what gives meaning to the rest of the sentence and *ubiquitous* means "existing everywhere" or "not rare." *A* is incorrect because *ago* only indicates a time frame. *B* is incorrect because *cars* does not indicate a contrasting relationship to the word *ubiquitous* to provide a good context clue. *C* is incorrect because it also only indicates a time frame, but used together with *rare*, it provides the contrasting relationship needed to identify the meaning of the unknown word.

10. A: *Principals* are the leaders of a school. *Principles* indicate values, morals, or ideology. For Choice *B*, the words are reversed. For Choices *C* and *D*, both answers are misspelled, regardless of position.

11. C: *His* or *her* is correct. *Each* indicates the need for a singular pronoun, and because the charts belong to the patients, they must be possessive as well. To indicate that the group of patients could include males and females, *his* and *her* must be included. For Choice *A*, *their* is plural. For Choice *B*, *there* is an adverb, not a pronoun. For Choice *D*, *the people's* is collective plural, not singular.

12. B: *Imminent* means impending or happening soon. The man fears going to the zoo because a bomb might soon be detonated. For Choice *A*, *eminent* means of a high rank or status. For Choice *C*, *emanate* means to originate from. For Choice *D*, *amanita* is a type of fungus.

13. C: Semicolons can function as conjunctions. When used thus, they take the place of *and*, joining two independent clauses together. Choice *A* is incorrect because colons introduce lists or a final, emphasized idea. The independent clauses in this example carry equal emphasis. Choice *B* is an example of a run-on sentence. Commas may not be used to join two independent clauses. Choice *D* is also a run-on sentence. There's not punctuation of any type to indicate two separate clauses that can stand on their own.

14. C: This answer includes two independent clauses that could stand on their own. To test this, try separating each sentence and putting a period at the end. For Choice *C*, since each clause includes its own noun and verb, they each could stand independently of one another. For Choice *A*, there are two nouns, Tod and Elissa, and three verbs: went, got, and slept. This sentence cannot be separated into independent clauses. Choice *B* begins with a subordinate conjunction, making one sentence rely on the other. The same goes for Choice *D*; *while Marge slept* is a dependent clause.

15. C: *Ran* functions as a verb and is conjugated with the noun *lecture*. For Choice *A*, *engaging* acts as a gerund and an adjective, describing what type of lecture. For Choice *B*, *though* can act as a conjunction or adverb, but not a verb. For Choice *D*, *over* is an adverb that describes *ran*.

16. B: Adverbs describe verbs or adjectives. In this instance, *almost* describes *arrived*, the verb. Adverbs answer questions like *how* or *where* and here *almost* describes *how* he arrived. For *A*, *arrived* is a past-tense verb. For *C*, *irritated* functions as an adjective, describing Dave's boss. *Rest* (Choice *D*) is a noun, evidenced by the article, *the*, before it.

17. D: Summer is generic, so it doesn't require capitalization. Titles (*President*) are capitalized when they're specific and precede the person's name. It's similar to saying *Mr.* or *Mrs.*, followed by a person's name. Choice *A* is incorrect because *advanced history* should not be capitalized. It's already been established that *History 220* is the official name of the class, and *advanced* is indicating that the class is

192

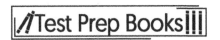

rigorous, especially in contrast to *entry-level*. Choice *B* is incorrect because *professor* should not be capitalized. It follows the name of the individual, and, therefore, does not qualify as a title. Choice *C* is incorrect because *army* and *navy* are specific to the British Empire, and, therefore, function as proper nouns.

18. A: Books are italicized, like *Frankenstein*, and smaller works are put in quotation marks. A direct quotation takes a single set of quotation marks (" ") and a quote within a quote take a single set (' '). Choice *B* is incorrect because *Frankenstein* should be italicized, not put in quotation marks. In Choice *C*, the double and single-set quotation marks should be reversed. In Choice *D*, the comma is missing before the first quotation mark, and the period for the quote within a quote is on the outside of the quotation mark, not the inside. Punctuation belongs inside the quotation marks, regardless of whether it a single or double set.

19. B: Indefinite pronouns such as *everyone* always take the singular. The key is to delete unnecessary language mentally ("who has ever owned a pet and hasn't had help"), which allows one to better test the conjugation between noun and verb. In this case, *everyone* and *knows* are joined. Choice *A* is incorrect because *each* (another indefinite pronoun) is singular while the verb *have* is plural. In Choice *C*, *neither* is indefinite, so *is* should be *has*, not *have*. In Choice *D*, *One*, which is indefinite, is the noun. The prepositional phrase "of the very applauded and commended lecturers" can be removed from the sentence. Therefore, the singular *is* is needed, not *are*.

20. D: *Distraught* is an adjective because it describes *what* Sara (the noun) looks like. In Choice *A*, *never* is an adverb that modifies *is*. In Choice *B*, *after* is a preposition because it occurs before a noun, *class*, and establishes a relationship with the rest of the sentence. *Mess* (Choice *D*) is a noun.

21. C: Both second and third person points of view are represented. The phrases *one should have* and *it is* are in the third person. Typical third-person subjects include *he, she, him, her, they, one, person, people*, and *someone*. Second person voice is indicated in the second half of the passage by the words *you* and *your*. Second person is simple to identify because it is the *you* voice, in which the reader is directly addressed.

22. B: The word *conscience* means a sense of right and wrong. *Conscious* (Choice *A*) refers to a state of being awake and alert. *Consensus* (Choice *C*) means an opinion shared by many, and a *census* (Choice *D*) is a count of an area's population.

23. B: A simple sentence must contain three things: the subject, the verb, and the completed idea or thought. Once the nonessential clause "who is not yet sixty" is removed, one is left with, "Ted still easily fishes and camps, too." The combination of the verbs *fishes* and *camps* are known as compound verbs, but because there are no independent or dependent clauses combined, it is still considered simple. For Choice *A*, there's an independent clause ("Ted loves to rock climb") and a dependent clause ("even though he tore his rotator cuff.") *Even though* functions as a subordinate conjunction. For Choice *C*, there's two independent clauses ("Ted loves the outdoors" and "his wife is a homebody") joined by the compound conjunction *but*. For Choice *D*, there's two independent clauses ("Ted will also be retired soon" and "he likes to stay busy") joined with the conjunctive adverb *nevertheless*.

24. D: Here, the rules of plural possessive are followed, placing the apostrophe outside the *s*. The outside apostrophe confirms that there are multiple *businesses*, not just one, entertaining many *clients*. In Choice *A*, the word *women* is plural, so the apostrophe belongs before the added *s*; the correct usage

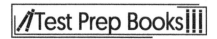
is *women's*. For Choice *B*, knowing how to use *it's* versus *its* is critical. *It's* is always a contraction while *its* always shows ownership. In Choice *C*, the possessive is not in use at all.

25. C: For the prefix *anti-* to work in both situations, it must have the same meaning, one that generalizes to any word in the English language. *Oppose* makes sense in both instances. Antibiotics *oppose* bacteria, and antisocials *oppose* society. Choice *A* is illogical. *Reducing* the number of bacteria is somewhat logical, but *reducing* society doesn't make sense when considering the definition of antisocial. Choice *B* is not the best match for bacteria. *Revolt*, a word normally reserved for human opposition, sounds odd when paired with bacteria. Choice *D* might work for antibiotic (without bacteria) but doesn't work for antisocial (without society).

26. D: Shape is the best answer. If *conform* means to adjust behavior, *shape* could replace *conform*, as in the behavior was *re-shaped* or modified. The same goes for *inform*. New information *re-shapes* how one thinks about the world. Also, the word *shape* gives rise to the abstract idea that both behavior and information are malleable, like modeling clay, and can be molded into new forms. Choice *A* (*match*) works for *conform* (matching to society), but it doesn't work for *inform* (one cannot *match* information to a person). Choice *B* (*relay*) doesn't work for *conform* (there's no way to pass on new behavior), but it does work for *inform*, as to pass on new information. Choice *C* (*negate*) works for neither *conform* (the behavior is not being completely cancelled out) nor *inform* (the information is not being rescinded).

27. B: To arrive at the best answer (*surly*), all the character traits for Cindy must be analyzed. She's described as *happy* ("always has a smile on her face"), *kind* ("volunteers at the local shelter"), and *patient* ("no one has ever seen her angry"). Since Cindy's husband is the *opposite* of her, these adjectives must be converted to antonyms. Someone who is *surly* is *unhappy*, *rude*, and *impatient*. Choice *A* (*stingy*) is too narrow of a word. Someone could be *happy* and *kind*, for instance, but still be *stingy*. For Choice *C*, *scared*, to be plausible, the rest of the passage would need instances of Cindy being *bold* or *courageous*. Though she's certainly *kind* and *helpful*, none of those traits are modeled. Choice *D* (*shy*) also doesn't match. Someone who is *shy* could still be *happy*, *kind*, and *patient*.

28. A: First person is the point of view represented. First person is known as the "I" voice. There are no "I's" in this passage, but the words *we* and *our* indicate first person plural. *We*, rationally, includes *I* and *other people*. *Our*, plural possessive, includes *mine* and *other's*. There is no evidence of second person (*you* voice), or third person (he, she, they). The narrator here is the "I," which means they are writing in first person.

29. B: "Make sure to clock out after your shift is through," includes both an independent and dependent clause. "Make sure to clock out" is the independent clause while "after your shift is through" is the dependent clause. *After* is the subordinate conjunction in this instance. Choice *A* is incorrect because "To make your fruit last longer" is a prepositional phrase, not a clause. "Keep it out of the sunlight" is an independent clause as well as an imperative command. For Choice *C*, "making a good fire" is considered a gerund phrase and is followed by the compound verbs *using* and *stacking*. Since there are no compound or complex sentences joined, it's considered a simple sentence. "Whenever possible," is an adverbial clause, not a dependent clause, so it's not classified as a complex sentence when paired with an independent clause ("Make sure to yield to oncoming traffic"). It, too, is a simple sentence.

30. B: *Accent* refers to the regional manner or style in which one speaks. *Ascent* refers to the act of rising or climbing. *Assent* means consensus or agreement. The people of Scotland have unique *accents* or dialects, and they're used to lofty *ascents* or climbs.

194

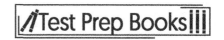

31. A: It is necessary to put a comma between the date and the year and between the day of the week and the month. Choice *B* is incorrect because it is missing the comma between the day of the week and the month. Choice *C* is incorrect because it adds an unnecessary comma between the month and date. Choice *D* is missing the necessary comma between day of the week and month.

32. A: In Choice *A*, the defining clause, *that was red*, describes the ball in the sentence. The defining clause is necessary and correct because it specifies that the red ball is the ball that has low air pressure. In Choice *B*, the defining clause, *that needed to eat*, is necessary because it gives context to the sentence and describes why the dog is whimpering. However, it incorrectly sets off the defining clause with commas. Choice *C* contains the non-defining clause, *which was very old*. The non-defining clause is not necessary to include to clarify meaning, so it should be set off with a comma. In Choice *D*, the clause *which you are concerned about* gives important context to the sentence, so it is a defining clause. However, the word *that* should be used instead of *which* since *which* only describes non-defining clauses.

33. C: Choice *C* is the correct answer because titles should be capitalized when they precede proper nouns, so the lowercase use of the word *senator* is incorrect. Choices *A*, *B*, and *C* are not the right answer because all proper nouns in these sentences are capitalized correctly.

34. D: Choice *D* is correct because all the words in the sentence are spelled correctly. In Choice *A*, the word *received* is spelled incorrectly. In Choice *B*, the word *led* is spelled incorrectly. In Choice *C*, the word *misrepresented* is spelled incorrectly.

35. A: Choice *A* is correct because the sentence contains a list of more than two names, and commas are needed to separate each element in the list. The comma before the word *and* is an example of an Oxford or serial comma. Usage of the Oxford comma is grammatically correct; whether to include it is typically a style preference. In Choice *B*, the defining clause, *that was mild*, is necessary to give context to the sentence, so a comma should not be included after the clause. Choice *C* is an example of a comma splice. The clauses *sometimes it rains* and *the garden gets flooded* can stand alone independently, so they should be punctuated as two separate sentences or linked by a semicolon or a conjunction. Choice *D* should have a comma after the day of the week and after the time to precede the independent clause: "On Wednesday, March 3, at 12:00 p.m., I have a job interview."

36. B: Choice *B* is correct because it avoids a dangling modifier. The car did not crash itself, so the sentence correctly identifies the subject. Choices *A*, *C*, and *D* are incorrect because they don't identify the correct subject that the introductory phrase is modifying.

37. D: Choice *D* is correct because the hyphen combines the two adjectives *high* and *tech* into a compound adjective. Choice *A* is incorrect because a hyphen should not be used to combine the adverb *quickly* with the adjective *fluctuating*. Choice *B* is incorrect because *follow-up* is not being used as an adjective before the word *email*, and it should instead be written as two words when used as a noun. Choice *C* is incorrect because *shortterm* is being used as an adjective to modify the noun *fix*, so it should include a hyphen between the words *short* and *term*.

38. C: Choice *C* is correct because the word *was* is the correct past tense form of the verb *to be*. Choice *A* is incorrect because the word *drank* is the correct simple past tense form, instead of *drunk*. Choice *B* is incorrect because *have took* should be corrected to *have taken*. Choice *D* is incorrect because the sentence has incorrect verb tense agreement. Because the first clause uses the simple past tense verb *hibernated* and is not a conditional statement, the second dependent clause should use the simple past tense verb *stored* instead of *would store.*

39. B: Choice *B* is correct because the word *briskly* is an adverb. It is modifying and describing the verb *blew.* Choice *A* is incorrect because *soggy* is an adjective. Choice *C* is incorrect because *blew* is a verb. Choice *D* is incorrect because *wind* is a noun.

40. C: Choice *C* is correct because the apostrophe after the *s* in *students* is describing plural possession of the students as a group. The sentence refers to the grades of all the students, not just one student. Choice *A* is incorrect because the word *students* requires an apostrophe to show possession of the noun *grades.* Choice *B* is incorrect because the word *students* is the incorrect plural form. Choice *D* is incorrect because the sentence is referring to all the students 'grades, not one student's grades.

Mathematics

41. D: The addition rule is necessary to determine the probability because a 6 can be rolled on either roll of the die but not both. The rule used is:

$$P(A \text{ or } B) = P(A) + P(B) - P(A \text{ and } B)$$

The probability of a 6 being individually rolled is $\frac{1}{6}$ and the probability of a 6 being rolled twice is:

$$\frac{1}{6} \times \frac{1}{6} = \frac{1}{36}$$

Therefore, the probability that a 6 is rolled at least once is:

$$\frac{1}{6} + \frac{1}{6} - \frac{1}{36} = \frac{11}{36}$$

42. D: Denote the width as w and the length as l. Then,

$$l = 3w + 5$$

The perimeter is:

$$2w + 2l = 90$$

Substituting the first expression for l into the second equation yields:

$$2(3w + 5) + 2w = 90$$

$$6w + 10 + 2w = 90$$

$$8w = 80$$

$$w = 10$$

Putting this into the first equation, it yields:

$$l = 3(10) + 5 = 35$$

196

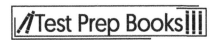

43. B: $\frac{11}{15}$. Fractions must have like denominators to be added. We are trying to add a fraction with a denominator of 3 to a fraction with a denominator of 5, so we have to convert both fractions to their respective equivalent fractions that have a common denominator. The common denominator is the least common multiple (LCM) of the two original denominators. In this case, the LCM is 15, so both fractions should be changed to equivalent fractions with a denominator of 15.

To determine the numerator of the new fraction, the old numerator is multiplied by the same number by which the old denominator is multiplied to obtain the new denominator.

For the fraction $\frac{1}{3}$, 3 multiplied by 5 will produce 15.

Therefore, the numerator is multiplied by 5 to produce the new numerator:

$$\frac{1 \times 5}{3 \times 5} = \frac{5}{15}$$

For the fraction $\frac{2}{5}$, multiplying both the numerator and denominator by 3 produces $\frac{6}{15}$. When fractions have like denominators, they are added by adding the numerators and keeping the denominator the same:

$$\frac{5}{15} + \frac{6}{15} = \frac{11}{15}$$

44. C: When performing calculations consisting of more than one operation, the order of operations should be followed: Parentheses, Exponents, Multiplication/Division, Addition/Subtraction.

Parentheses:

$$7^2 - 3 \times (4 + 2) + 15 \div 5$$

$$7^2 - 3 \times (6) + 15 \div 5$$

Exponents:

$$49 - 3 \times 6 + 15 \div 5$$

Multiplication/Division (from left to right):

$$49 - 18 + 3$$

Addition/Subtraction (from left to right):

$$49 - 18 + 3 = 34$$

45. D: 1, 2, 3, 4, 6, 12. A given number divides evenly by each of its factors to produce an integer (no decimals). The number 5, 7, 8, 9, 10, 11 (and their opposites) do not divide evenly into 12. Therefore, these numbers are not factors.

46. A: 11. To determine the number of houses that can fit on the street, the length of the street is divided by the width of each house:
$$345 \div 30 = 11.5$$

Answer Explanations #2 | Mathematics

Although the mathematical calculation of 11.5 is correct, this answer is not reasonable. Half of a house cannot be built, so the company will need to either build 11 or 12 houses. Since the width of 12 houses (360 feet) will extend past the length of the street, only 11 houses can be built.

47. B: 180 miles. The rate, 60 miles per hour, and time, 3 hours, are given for the scenario. To determine the distance traveled, the given values for the rate (r) and time (t) are substituted into the distance formula and evaluated:

$$d = r \times t \rightarrow d = \left(\frac{60 \text{ mi}}{\text{h}}\right) \times (3 \text{ h}) \rightarrow d = 180 \text{ mi}$$

48. B: A number is prime because its only factors are itself and one. Positive numbers (greater than zero) can be prime numbers.

49. C: Each number in the sequence is adding one more than the difference between the previous two. For example,

$$10 - 6 = 4, 4 + 1 = 5$$

Therefore, the next number after 10 is:
$$10 + 5 = 15$$

Going forward,
$$21 - 15 = 6, 6 + 1 = 7$$

The next number is:

$$21 + 7 = 28$$

Therefore, the difference between numbers is the set of whole numbers starting at 2: 2, 3, 4, 5, 6, 7, ….

50. A: Order of operations follows PEMDAS—Parentheses, Exponents, Multiplication and Division from left to right, and Addition and Subtraction from left to right.

51. B: This is a division problem because the original amount needs to be split up into equal amounts. The mixed number $11\frac{1}{2}$ should be converted to an improper fraction first:

$$11\frac{1}{2} = \frac{(11 \times 2) + 1}{2} = \frac{23}{2}$$

Carey needs to determine how many times $\frac{23}{2}$ goes into 184. This is a division problem:

$$184 \div \frac{23}{2} = ?$$

The fraction can be flipped, and the problem turns into the multiplication:

$$184 \times \frac{2}{23} = \frac{368}{23}$$

This improper fraction can be simplified into 16 because $368 \div 23 = 16$. The answer is 16 lawn segments.

198

52. C: Numbers should be lined up by decimal places before subtraction is performed. This is because subtraction is performed within each place value. The other operations, such as multiplication, division, and exponents (which is a form of multiplication), involve ignoring the decimal places at first and then including them at the end.

53. A: The additive and subtractive identity is zero. When added or subtracted to any number, zero does not change the original number.

54. A: 182 is in the millions, 36 is in the thousands, 421 is in the hundreds, and 356 is the decimal.

55. C: $40N$ would be 4,000% of N. All of the other coefficients are equivalent to $\frac{40}{100}$ or 40%.

56. A: First, convert the mixed numbers to improper fractions: $\frac{11}{3} - \frac{9}{5}$. Then, use 15 as a common denominator:

$$\frac{11}{3} - \frac{9}{5} = \frac{55}{15} - \frac{27}{15} = \frac{28}{15} = 1\frac{13}{15}$$

57. C: The formula for the perimeter of a rectangle is $P = 2L + 2W$, where P is the perimeter, L is the length, and W is the width. The first step is to substitute all of the data into the formula:

$$36 = 2(12) + 2W$$

Simplify by multiplying 2×12:

$$36 = 24 + 2W$$

Simplifying this further by subtracting 24 on each side gives:

$$36 - 24 = 24 - 24 + 2W$$

$$12 = 2W$$

Divide by 2:

$$6 = W$$

The width is 6 cm. Remember to test this answer by substituting this value into the original formula:

$$36 = 2(12) + 2(6)$$

58. D: This problem can be solved by setting up a proportion involving the given information and the unknown value. The proportion is:

$$\frac{21 \text{ pages}}{4 \text{ nights}} = \frac{140 \text{ pages}}{x \text{ nights}}$$

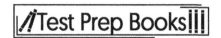

Solving the proportion by cross-multiplying, the equation becomes $21x = 4 \times 140$, where $x = 26.67$. Since it is not an exact number of nights, the answer is rounded up to 27 nights. Twenty-six nights would not give Sarah enough time.

59. A: Setting up a proportion is the easiest way to represent this situation. The proportion becomes $\frac{20}{x} = \frac{40}{100}$, where cross-multiplication can be used to solve for x. The answer can also be found by observing the two fractions as equivalent, knowing that twenty is half of forty, and fifty is half of one-hundred.

60. A: $\frac{52}{27}$

Set up the division problem.

$$\frac{4}{13} \div \frac{27}{169}$$

Flip the second fraction and multiply.

$$\frac{4}{13} \times \frac{169}{27}$$

Simplify the fractions before multiplying to make numbers simpler to work with.

$$\frac{4}{1} \times \frac{13}{27}$$

Multiply across the top and across the bottom to solve.

$$\frac{4 \times 13}{1 \times 27} = \frac{52}{27}$$

61. C: The triangle in Choice B doesn't contain a line of symmetry. The figures in Choices A and D do contain a line of symmetry but it is not the line that is shown here. Choice C is the only one with a correct line of symmetry shown, such that the figure is mirrored on each side of the line.

62. B: 35.1%

To convert from a decimal to a percentage, the decimal needs to be moved two places to right. In this case, that makes 0.351 become 35.1%.

63. A: 22%

Converting from a fraction to a percentage generally involves two steps. First, the fraction needs to be converted to a decimal.

Divide 2 by 9 which results in $0.\overline{22}$. The top line indicates that the decimal actually goes on forever with an endless amount of 2's.

Second, the decimal needs to be moved two places to the right:

$$22\%$$

200

64. D: 0.57

To convert from a percentage to a decimal, or vice versa, you always need to move the decimal two places. A percentage like 57% has an invisible decimal after the 7, like this:

$$57.\%$$

That decimal then needs to be moved two places to the left to get:

$$0.57$$

65. A: 37.5%

Solve this by setting up the percent formula:

$$\frac{3}{8} = \frac{\%}{100}$$

Multiply 3 by 100 to get 300. Then divide 300 by 8:

$$300 \div 8 = 37.5\%$$

Note that with the percent formula, 37.5 is automatically a percentage and does not need to have any further conversions.

66. A: 63.96

This question involves the percent formula. Since we're beginning with a percent, also known as a number over 100, we'll put 39 on the right side of the equation:

$$\frac{x}{164} = \frac{39}{100}$$

Now, multiply 164 and 39 to get 6,396, which then needs to be divided by 100.

$$6,396 \div 100 = 63.96$$

67. B: 128

This question involves the percent formula.

$$\frac{32}{x} = \frac{25}{100}$$

We multiply the diagonal numbers, 32 and 100, to get 3,200. Dividing by the remaining number, 25, gives us 128.

The percent formula does not have to be used for a question like this. Since 25% is ¼ of 100, you know that 32 needs to be multiplied by 4, which yields 128.

68. C: 0.63

Divide 5 by 8, which results in 0.625. This rounds up to 0.63.

69. A: 3.6

Divide 3 by 5 to get 0.6 and add that to the whole number 3, to get 3.6. An alternative is to incorporate the whole number 3 earlier on by creating an improper fraction: $\frac{18}{5}$. Then dividing 18 by 5 to get 3.6.

70. B: $\frac{14}{25}$

Since 0.56 goes to the hundredths place, it can be placed over 100:

$$\frac{56}{100}$$

Essentially, the way we got there is by multiplying the numerator and denominator by 100:

$$\frac{0.56}{1} \times \frac{100}{100} = \frac{56}{100}$$

Then, the fraction can be simplified down to $\frac{14}{25}$:

$$\frac{56}{100} \div \frac{4}{4} = \frac{14}{25}$$

71. D: $9\frac{3}{10}$

To convert a decimal to a fraction, remember that any number to the left of the decimal point will be a whole number. Then, since 0.3 goes to the tenths place, it can be placed over 10.

72. A: 13 nurses

Using the given information of 1 nurse to 25 patients and 325 patients, set up an equation to solve for number of nurses (*N*):

$$\frac{N}{325} = \frac{1}{25}$$

Multiply both sides by 325 to get *N* by itself on one side.

$$\frac{N}{1} = \frac{325}{25} = 13 \text{ nurses}$$

73. D: 290 beds

Using the given information of 2 beds to 1 room and 145 rooms, set up an equation to solve for number of beds (B):

$$\frac{B}{145} = \frac{2}{1}$$

Multiply both sides by 145 to get B by itself on one side.

$$\frac{B}{1} = \frac{290}{1} = 290 \text{ beds}$$

202

74. D: $0.45

List the givens.

$$\text{Store coffee} = \$1.23/\text{lb}$$

$$\text{Local roaster coffee} = \$1.98/1.5 \text{ lb}$$

Calculate the cost for 5 pounds of store brand.

$$\frac{\$1.23}{1 \text{ lb}} \times 5 \text{ lb} = \$6.15$$

Calculate the cost for 5 pounds of the local roaster.

$$\frac{\$1.98}{1.5 \text{ lb}} \times 5 \text{ lb} = \$6.60$$

Subtract to find the difference in price for 5 pounds.

```
 $6.60
-$6.15
 $0.45
```

75. D: $3,325

List the givens.

$$1,800 \text{ ft} = \$2,000$$

$$\text{Cost after } 1,800 \text{ ft} = \$1.00/\text{ft.}$$

Find how many feet left after the first 1,800 feet.

```
 3,125 ft
-1,800 ft
 1,325 ft
```

Calculate the cost for the feet over 1,800 feet.

$$1,325 \text{ ft} \times \frac{\$1.00}{1 \text{ ft}} = \$1,325$$

Add these together to find the total for the entire cost.

$$\$2,000 + \$1,325 = \$3,325$$

76. D: $x \geq 1$. The closed dot on one indicates that the value is included in the set. The arrow pointing right indicates that numbers greater than one (numbers get larger to the right) are included in the set. Therefore, the set includes numbers greater than or equal to one, which can be written as $x \geq 1$.

77. A: $(-3, 2)$. The coordinates of a point are written as an ordered pair (x, y). To determine the x-coordinate, a line is traced directly above or below the point until reaching the x-axis. This step notes

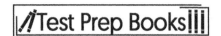

the value on the x-axis. In this case, the x-coordinate is -3. To determine the y-coordinate, a line is traced directly to the right or left of the point until reaching the y-axis, which notes the value on the y-axis. In this case, the y-coordinate is 2. Therefore, the ordered pair is written $(-3, 2)$.

78. C: An x-intercept is the point where the graph crosses the x-axis. At this point, the value of y is 0. To determine if an equation has an x-intercept of -2, substitute -2 for x, and calculate the value of y. If the value of -2 for x corresponds with a y-value of 0, then the equation has an x-intercept of -2. The only answer choice that produces this result is Choice C:

$$0 = (-2)^2 + 5(-2) + 6$$

79. D: Solve a linear inequality in a similar way to solving a linear equation. First, start by distributing the -3 on the left side of the inequality.

$$-3x - 12 \geq x + 8$$

Then, add 12 to both sides.

$$-3x \geq x + 20$$

Next, subtract x from both sides.

$$-4x \geq 20$$

Finally, divide both sides of the inequality by -4. Don't forget to flip the inequality sign because you are dividing by a negative.

$$x \leq -5$$

80. C: $y = 40x + 300$. In this scenario, the variables are the number of sales and Karen's weekly pay. The weekly pay depends on the number of sales. Therefore, weekly pay is the dependent variable (y), and the number of sales is the independent variable (x). Each pair of values from the table can be written as an ordered pair (x, y): $(2, 380)$, $(7, 580)$, $(4, 460)$, $(8, 620)$. The ordered pairs can be substituted into the equations to see which creates true statements (both sides equal) for each pair. Even if one ordered pair produces equal values for a given equation, the other three ordered pairs must be checked. The only equation which is true for all four ordered pairs is $y = 40x + 300$:

$$380 = 40(2) + 300 \rightarrow 380 = 380$$

$$580 = 40(7) + 300 \rightarrow 580 = 580$$

$$460 = 40(4) + 300 \rightarrow 460 = 460$$

$$620 = 40(8) + 300 \rightarrow 620 = 620$$

Reading Comprehension

81. C: The point of view is told in third-person omniscient. We know this because the story starts out with us knowing something that the character does not know: that her husband has died. Mrs. Mallard eventually comes to know this, but we as readers know this information before it is revealed to her. In third person limited, Choice D, we would only see and know what Mrs. Mallard herself knew, and we would find out the news of her husband's death when she found out the news, not before.

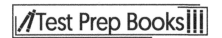

82. A: The way Mrs. Mallard reacted to her husband's death. The irony in this story is called situational irony, which means the situation that takes place is different than what the audience anticipated. At the beginning of the story, we see Mrs. Mallard react with a burst of grief to her husband's death. However, once she's alone, she begins to contemplate her future and says the word "free" over and over. This is quite a different reaction from Mrs. Mallard than what readers expected from the first of the story.

83. B: The word "elusive" most closely means "indefinable." Horrible, Choice *A*, doesn't quite fit with the tone of the word "subtle" that comes before it. Choice *C*, "quiet," is more closely related to the word "subtle." Choice *D*, "joyful," also doesn't quite fit the context here. "Indefinable" is the best option.

84. D: Mrs. Mallard, a newly widowed woman, finds unexpected relief in her husband's death. A summary is a brief explanation of the main point of a story. The story mostly focuses on Mrs. Mallard and her reaction to her husband's death, especially in the room when she's alone and contemplating the present and future. Choice B is briefly mentioned in the story; however it is not.

85. D: The interesting thing about this story is that feelings that are confused, joyful, and depressive all play a unique and almost equal part of this story. There is no one right answer here, because the author seems to display all of these emotions through the character of Mrs. Mallard. She displays feelings of depressiveness by her grief at the beginning; then when she receives feelings of joy, she feels moments of confusion. We as readers cannot help but go through these feelings with the character. Thus, the author creates a tone of depression, joy, and confusion, all in one story.

86. C: The word "tumultuously" most nearly means "violently." Even if you don't know the word "tumultuously," look at the surrounding context to figure it out. The next few sentences we see Mrs. Mallard striving to "beat back" the "thing that was approaching to possess her." We see a fearful and almost violent reaction to the emotion that she's having. Thus, her chest would rise and fall tumultuously, or violently.

87. A: Sentence 2 provides a continued description of sentence 1. We see the author describing Mrs. Mallard's stare in sentence 1, and then continuing the description of the stare ("It was not a glance of reflection") in sentence 2. Choice *B* is incorrect because there is no analysis of the author's comment in sentence 2, only a continued description. Choice *C* is incorrect because there is no problem/solution structure that can be found in either of these sentences. Choice *D* is incorrect because there is also no definition in sentence 1, just the description of Mrs. Mallard's stare.

88. C: "She knew that she would weep again when she saw the kind, tender hands folded in death." This is the first sentence we see where the author suggests that Mrs. Mallard's husband was not unkind, because we see Mrs. Mallard anticipating grieving his "kind, tender hands" again. Choice *A* is incorrect because, while this may suggest Mrs. Mallard's husband was kind, it's not the *best* answer, because Mrs. Mallard could have just been pretending to mourn in front of her sister. Choice *B* is incorrect; this is when Mrs. Mallard rejoices at the possibility of being free and does not suggest that the husband is kind. Choice *D* is incorrect; this is a sentence that tells us that the husband's friend, Richards, was the first one who received the news of the death.

89. B: Critics would most likely dispute Mrs. Mallard's state of mind in relation to her dead husband. That is, is she happy that he is dead, or is she devastated? This is the central question of the passage. Choice *A* is not a viable question—of course, Mrs. Mallard did not see her husband die herself, but we as the audience are not meant to question whether Mr. Mallard is or isn't truly dead. Choice *C* is incorrect; this is a possible answer, as we may wonder why Mrs. Mallard is somewhat relieved at her husband's death. But this is not the *best* answer, as we learn that Mr. Mallard was kind, and he had "the face that had never looked save with love upon her." Choice *D* is incorrect, though this is a good alternative; we are told at the beginning of the passage that Mrs. Mallard has heart trouble, so these could be signs of a heart attack. However, we do not have enough evidence of a heart attack at this point in the story, as we only see Mrs. Mallard display symptoms of shock and grief.

90. B: An inference is making a conclusion based on evidence in the passage. We can conclude that Mrs. Mallard had a bedroom window that faced toward the west, because of this sentence: "There were patches of blue sky showing here and there through the clouds that had met and piled one above the other in the west facing her window. Choice *A* is incorrect; Josephine did not know Mrs. Mallard's true reaction to her husband's death, because Mrs. Mallard goes upstairs by herself. Choice *C* is incorrect; we do not know if Mr. Mallard was disliked by people in the community—he seems to be well-liked by his friends and family. Choice *D* is incorrect. It is springtime when Mrs. Mallard finds out the news of her husband's death.

91. D: The primary purpose of paragraph 5 is to show the reader the present state of mind of Mrs. Mallard. Choice *A* is incorrect. We are not "objectively" told the setting, because the author says "She could see in the open square before her," denoting that this scene is from Mrs. Mallard's point of view, not an objective entity. Choice *B* is incorrect. We do not know the specifics of how Mr. Mallard died. Choice *C* is incorrect. Mrs. Mallard is not lost in her grieving thoughts in this paragraph; in fact, she is totally present, enjoying the gifts of springtime.

92. B: Sympathetic and understanding. We see the author approach Mrs. Mallard's character with gentleness, especially with her description in paragraph 8, and the way the author describes her joy in the last paragraph. Choice *A* is incorrect; Mrs. Mallard may judge herself when she represses her joy, but the author never does, nor is there any harshness towards her. Choice *C* is incorrect; there does not seem to be any regret or fear coming from the author, although Mrs. Mallard does experience fear in the passage. Finally, Choice *D* is incorrect. The author seems to share a bit in Mrs. Mallard's joy, but there is no feeling of being carefree in this passage.

93. C: The word "it" in the sentence refers to "uninhibitedness," which means to be free from inhabitation, to feel unrestrained, to feel free. Mrs. Mallard begins to feel freedom in these moments of self-exploration in her room. Choice *A* is incorrect; *incompetence* is the opposite of what Mrs. Mallard feels, as this means a lack of freedom or ability. Choice *B* is incorrect; *consternation* means dread or dismay, so this is also incorrect. Choice *D* is incorrect; *merriment* is a bit of a stretch, although the author does attribute a kind of joy to Mrs. Mallard. However, the best answer is Choice *C*—uninhibitedness.

94. B: Choice *B* is correct because having very little drinking water on earth is a very good reason that one should limit their water usage so that the human population does not run out of drinking water and die out. People wasting water on superfluous things does not support the fact that we need to limit our water usage. It merely states that people are wasteful. Therefore, *A* is incorrect. Answer Choice *C* may be tempting, but it is not the correct one, as this article is not about reducing water usage in order to help those who don't have easy access to water, but about the fact that the planet is running out of drinking water. Choice *D* is incorrect because nowhere in the article does it state that only first world countries have access to drinking water.

95. C: The primary purpose is to present a problem (the planet is running out of water) with a solution (to reduce water waste), therefore the correct answer is *C*. Choice *A* is incorrect because the passage does not have a sequential timeline of events and is therefore not in chronological order. It may be

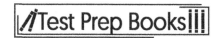

tempting to think the author compares and contrasts people who do not have access to drinking water to those who do, but that does not fit with the primary purpose of the article, which is to convince people to reduce their water usage. Thus, Choice *B* is incorrect. Choice *D* is incorrect because descriptions are not the primary content of this article. Remember that a descriptive writing style describes people, settings, or situations in great detail with many adjectives. While a descriptive writing voice may be used alongside a persuasive writing style, it is generally not the primary voice when trying to convince a reader to take a certain stance.

96. A: If the assertion is that the earth does not have enough drinking water, then having abundant water stores that are not being reported would certainly challenge this assertion. Choice *B* is incorrect because even if much of the water we drink does come from rain, that means the human population would be dependent on rain in order to survive, which would more support the assertion than challenge it. Because the primary purpose of the passage is not to help those who cannot get water, then Choice *C* is not the correct answer. Even if Choice *D* were true, it does not dismiss the other ways in which people are wasteful with water, and is also not the point.

97. B: Choice *B* is correct because the article uses a lot of emotionally charged language and also suggests what needs to be done with the information provided. The article does not contain elements of a narrative, which include plot, setting, characters, and themes. Not only does the article lack these things, but it does not follow a timeline, which is a key element of a narrative voice. Thus, Choice *A* is incorrect. Choice *C* is incorrect because the article uses information in order to be persuasive, but the purpose is not solely to inform on the issue. Choice *D* is incorrect because the article is not written in primarily descriptive language.

98. C: Choice *C* is correct because people who waste water on lawns in the desert, or run a half-full dishwasher, or fill their personal pools are not taking into account how much water they are using because they get an unlimited supply, therefore they are taking it for granted. Choice *A* is incorrect because it is explicitly stated within the text: "running dishwashers that are only half full." Choice *B* is also explicitly stated: "meanwhile people in Africa are dying of thirst." While Choice *D* is implicitly stated within the whole article, it is not implicitly stated within the sentence.

99. B: Choice *B* is correct because the author uses this example in order to show people, through emotional appeal, that they take water for granted, because they get water freely from their faucets, while millions of people have to endure great hardships to get drinking water. Choice *A* does not pertain directly to the main idea of the article, nor does it pertain to the author's purpose. The main idea is that people should reduce their water usage, and the author's purpose is to persuade the reader to do so. A person walking for miles in intense heat does not align with the main point. Choice *C* is incorrect because the selection never mentions that water is only available in first world countries. Choice *D* is the author's purpose for the entire passage, but not the purpose for mentioning the difficulty in getting water for some of the population.

100. A: The primary purpose and the main idea are essentially the same thing, and the main idea is that people should reduce their water usage because there is not a lot of available drinking water on Earth. Choice *B* is a *reason* that people should reduce their water usage, but it is not the main idea. Choice *C* is a demonstration of how people are not aware of the amount of water they use, but again, not the main idea. Choice *D* is a suggestion for reducing water usage, but still not the main idea.

101. A: The tone is incredulous. While contemplative is an option because of the inquisitive nature of the text, Choice *A* is correct because Frederick Douglass is astonished that he, a former slave, would be

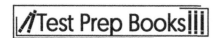

called upon to celebrate liberty that was not extended to him or to others of his race. Choice B is incorrect because Frederick Douglass is drawing contrasts between two groups of people rather than being inclusive. Choice C is incorrect because Frederick Douglass is expressing strong emotion, incredulity, rather than contemplation. Choice D is incorrect because Frederick Douglass is not nonchalant, nor accepting of the circumstances which he describes.

102. C: C: Choice C, contented, is the only word that has the opposite meaning of obdurate. Therefore, Choices A, B, and D are incorrect.

103. B: To address the hypocrisy of the Fourth of July holiday. While the speaker makes biblical references, it is not the main focus of the passage, thus eliminating Choice *A* as an answer. The passage also makes no mention of wealthy landowners and doesn't speak of any positive response to the historical events, so Choices *C* and *D* are not correct.

104. D: Choice D is the correct answer because it clearly references the disparity between slaves and free men in the United States. Choice A is incorrect because it demonstrates Frederick Douglass's knowledge of the Bible. Choice B is incorrect because it demonstrates his incredulity at his invitation to speak (referring back to question 37). Choice C is incorrect because Frederick Douglass is highlighting the terrible situation of slaves, but he is not highlighting the disparity between slaves and free men.

105. D: It is an example of hyperbole; the physical distance between Frederick Douglass and his audience was not, in fact, immeasurable. However, it clearly demonstrated the differences in the lives and situations of free men and slaves in the United States. Choice A is incorrect because assonance is the repetition of sounds and commonly occurs in poetry. Choice B is incorrect because parallelism refers to two statements that correlate, or parallel each other, in some manner.

106. C: Recognize the equivocation of the speaker and those that he represents. Choice C is correct because the speaker is clear about his intention and stance throughout the text; he does not equivocate, so this answer choice is the only one that biblical references do not help the reader to do. Choice A is incorrect because quotations from the Bible would have been common at the time, creating a common ground between Frederick Douglass and his audience. Choice B is incorrect because another group of people affected by slavery are being referenced, and Frederick Douglass is clearly drawing a connection between that group of people and American slaves. Choice D is incorrect because Frederick Douglass's speech is designed to appeal to the listener's sense of humanity and create an abhorrence for slavery.

107. D: The use of "I" could serve to have a "hedging" effect, allow the reader to connect with the author in a more personal way, and cause the reader to empathize more with the egrets. However, it doesn't distance the reader from the text, making Choice *D* the answer to this question.

108. C: The quote provides an example of a warden protecting one of the colonies. Choice *A* is incorrect because the speaker of the quote is a warden, not a hunter. Choice *B* is incorrect because the quote does not lighten the mood, but shows the danger of the situation between the wardens and the hunters. Choice *D* is incorrect because there is no humor found in the quote.

109. D: A *rookery* is a colony of breeding birds. Although *rookery* could mean Choice *A*, houses in a slum area, it does not make sense in this context. Choices *B* and *C* are both incorrect, as this is not a place for hunters to trade tools or for wardens to trade stories.

110. B: An important bird colony. The previous sentence is describing "twenty colonies" of birds, so what follows should be a bird colony. Choice *A* may be true, but we have no evidence of this in the text. Choice *C* does touch on the tension between the hunters and wardens, but there is no official "Bird Island Battle" mentioned in the text. Choice *D* does not exist in the text.

111. D: To demonstrate the success of the protective work of the Audubon Association. The text mentions several different times how and why the association has been successful and gives examples to back this fact. Choice *A* is incorrect because although the article, in some instances, calls certain people to act, it is not the purpose of the entire passage. There is no way to tell if Choices *B* and *C* are correct, as they are not mentioned in the text.

112. C: To have a better opportunity to hunt the birds. Choice *A* might be true in a general sense, but it is not relevant to the context of the text. Choice *B* is incorrect because the hunters are not studying lines of flight to help wardens, but to hunt birds. Choice *D* is incorrect because nothing in the text mentions that hunters are trying to build homes underneath lines of flight of birds for good luck.

113. B: A period of time. "Four score and seven years ago" is the equivalent of eighty-seven years, because the word "score" means "twenty." Choices *A* and *C* are incorrect because the context for describing a unit of measurement or a literary movement is lacking. Choice *D* is incorrect because although Lincoln's speech is a cornerstone in political rhetoric, the phrase "Four score and seven years ago" is better narrowed to a period of time.

114. D: Abraham Lincoln is the former president of the United States, so the correct answer is *D*, "The American Civil War." Though the U.S. was involved in World War I and II, Choices *A* and *C* are incorrect because a civil war specifically means citizens fighting within the same country. Choice *B* is incorrect, as "The War of Spanish Succession" involved Spain, Italy, Germany, and Holland, and not the United States.

115. A: The speech calls on the audience to consider the soldiers who died on the battlefield as ideas to perpetuate freedom so that their deaths would not be in vain. Choice *B* is incorrect because, although they are there to "dedicate a portion of that field," there is no mention in the text of an annual memorial service. Choice *C* is incorrect because there is no charged language in the text, only reverence for the dead. Choice *D* is incorrect because "forget[ting] the lives that were lost" is the opposite of what Lincoln is suggesting.

116. A: Choice A is correct because Lincoln's intention was to memorialize the soldiers who had fallen as a result of war as well as celebrate those who had put their lives in danger for the sake of their country. Choices B and C are incorrect because Lincoln's speech was supposed to foster a sense of pride among the members of the audience while connecting them to the soldiers' experiences. Choice D is incorrect because Lincoln does not a distinction between soldiers and civilians but rather pointing his audience toward the sacrifices made by the soldiers on the battlefield at Gettysburg.

117. C: The text mentions all of the listed properties of minerals except the instance of minerals being organically formed. Objects or substances must be naturally occurring, must be a homogeneous solid, and must have a definite chemical composition in order to be considered a mineral.

118. A: Choice *A* is the correct answer because geology is the study of earth related science. Choice *B* is incorrect because psychology is the study of the mind and behavior. Choice *C* is incorrect because biology is the study of life and living organisms. Choice *D* is incorrect because botany is the study of plants.

119. A: Choice *A* is the correct answer because the prefix "homo" means same. Choice *B* is incorrect because "differing in some areas" would be linked to the root word "hetero," meaning "different" or "other."

120. C: Choice *C* is the correct answer because *-logy* refers to the study of a particular subject matter.

Practice Test #3

English Language Skills

1. DIRECTIONS: Choose the sentence that demonstrates the first-person perspective.
   a. I am going to the store.
   b. Frank saw his sister over the weekend.
   c. They stopped by the delicatessen for lunch.
   d. You need to adjust your mirrors before driving.

2. DIRECTIONS: Choose the sentence that has the correct use of a contraction.
   a. Since he was lactose intolerant, he couldnt' drink milk.
   b. The dog was chasing it's tail.
   c. Raspberries arent my favorite fruit.
   d. She'd live to be ninety-five.

3. DIRECTIONS: Identify the introductory phrase in the following sentence:
   Feeling under the weather, Maggie considered taking a sick day from work.
   a. from work
   b. Feeling under the weather
   c. taking a sick day
   d. Maggie considered

4. DIRECTIONS: Which of the following words is an example of a subordinate conjunction?
   a. Over
   b. Rush
   c. Because
   d. The

5. DIRECTIONS: Choose the sentence that contains a relative pronoun.
   a. Ezekiel hoped to get a gift for Anne.
   b. The boy who ate too much candy developed a stomachache.
   c. The woman shared her story with the journalist.
   d. This color is my favorite.

6. DIRECTIONS: Which of the following sentences contains a dependent clause?
   a. Before the thunderstorm hit, my flowers were blooming vividly.
   b. John liked to eat Italian food.
   c. My siblings are Mark and Carol.
   d. She went to the store and bought rice, beans, and tomato sauce.

7. DIRECTIONS: Identify the subject in the following sentence:
   In Australia, venomous insects are common.

   a. Australia
   b. Insects
   c. Venomous
   d. Common

8. DIRECTIONS: Choose the sentence that demonstrates the future continuous verb tense.
   a. By 2:00 p.m., I will have eaten twice today.
   b. I'm cleaning the floor right now.
   c. Joanne will be attending college in the fall.
   d. The kids wanted to skate, but their parents didn't let them.

9. DIRECTIONS: Choose the sentence that does NOT contain a spelling error.
   a. The knight forgot his sword and sheild.
   b. She figured there was a write way to go about the task.
   c. Marlene was excited to apply for the cosmitology program.
   d. The teacher felt the principal would use fair judgment in deciding the boy's punishment.

10. DIRECTIONS: Which of the following is a sentence fragment?
    a. I wasn't happy.
    b. They found the treasure.
    c. She needs help.
    d. Because she told me to.

11. DIRECTIONS: Choose the sentence with an appositive noun phrase.
    a. My brother enjoys strawberry shortcake.
    b. In the game of tag, which they played for hours, the children had fun.
    c. My friend, a public school teacher, was applying to graduate school.
    d. Dorothy was afraid of lions, tigers, and bears.

12. Choose the preposition in the following sentence:
    I would like to buy the painting on the shelf.

    a. To
    b. On
    c. Like
    d. The

13. DIRECTIONS: Identify the part of speech in the underlined portion of the following sentence:
    When my family went to Yosemite National Park, the skies were crystal clear.

    a. Adjective
    b. Adverb
    c. Noun
    d. Conjunction

14. DIRECTIONS: Choose the sentence with the incorrect use of possession.
    a. My grandma's cookies are the best in town.
    b. Your drawings are better than hers.
    c. He felt that his boss' critiques were valid.
    d. The girls put their dolls away.

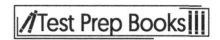

15. DIRECTIONS: Choose the sentence with an infinitive.
   a. The stock prices fluctuated wildly.
   b. Greg was winning the game of pool.
   c. Misha was, without a doubt, the strongest interview candidate.
   d. My son wants to learn Spanish by the end of the year.

16. DIRECTIONS: Choose the sentence with the incorrect spelling.
   a. I wasn't sure how the greasy food would affect my stomach.
   b. The bus was stationery until 9:00 a.m.
   c. Honesty was one of his strongest principles.
   d. Senators work in the Capitol Building.

17. DIRECTIONS: Choose the sentence with correct punctuation.
   a. John was worried about the car; it was making some odd noises.
   b. Bob ordered a Reuben sandwich. With mustard.
   c. I love the following scents, rose, lilac — and geranium.
   d. Laura was happy because: she passed her exam.

18. DIRECTIONS: Choose the sentence that demonstrates the present perfect verb tense.
   a. I will have worked at my company for fifteen years.
   b. I do not agree with how my son has been living.
   c. You're going to the doctor on Wednesday.
   d. The boys have seen the movie three times.

19. DIRECTIONS: Choose the option that corrects an error in the underlined portion of the sentence below. If no error exists, choose "No change is necessary."
   Batman, my favorite superhero, lives in Gotham City.
   a. my favorite superhero —
   b. my most favorite superhero,
   c. my favorite, superhero
   d. No change is necessary.

20. DIRECTIONS: Choose the sentence with correct comma usage.
   a. The wine tastes sour, and bitter.
   b. Steve, the plumber, called this morning.
   c. I named my horse Chestnut, after the color of his hair.
   d. My friend Joe ate his lunch, a burger, fries, and soda, early.

21. DIRECTIONS: Choose the option that corrects an error in the underlined portion of the sentence below. If no error exists, choose "No change is necessary."
   He started his day with a walk, eating a piece of toast, and read the newspaper.
   a. walking, eating piece of toast, and reading the newspaper.
   b. a walk, a piece of toast, and reading the newspaper.
   c. a walk, eating a piece of toast, and reading the newspaper.
   d. No change is necessary.

213

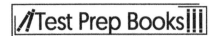
22. DIRECTIONS: Choose the sentence with a gerund phrase.
   a. Five months ago, Louise had surgery.
   b. I took a wrong turn at the fork in the road.
   c. My family's favorite summer pastime is sailing.
   d. Derek would like to see a concert.

23. DIRECTIONS: Choose the sentence that includes a present participle.
   a. I packed my climbing shoes.
   b. Yesterday, I ate beef fajita tacos.
   c. Ruth and Frank had been traveling for business.
   d. Can you pick up the kids from school tomorrow?

24. DIRECTIONS: Identify the part of speech in the following sentence:
   The financial analyst had strong feelings about the <u>proposed</u> budget.
   a. Verb
   b. Adjective
   c. Conjunction
   d. Article

25. DIRECTIONS: Choose the sentence that demonstrates the second-person perspective.
   a. I met my girlfriend in Illinois.
   b. Pistachio is my favorite ice cream flavor.
   c. How old are you?
   d. That man is walking three dogs.

26. DIRECTIONS: Choose the sentence with incorrect subject-verb agreement.
   a. Susan likes to go for runs early in the morning.
   b. My cat, like the animals out in the barn, are frightened of the storm.
   c. In my opinion, all of the magazine's articles are highly interesting.
   d. Either chair is fine for my living room.

27. DIRECTIONS: Choose the option that corrects an error in the underlined portion of the sentence below. If no error exists, choose "No change is necessary."
   I saw three animals at the aquarium: <u>fish, turtles, and sea lions</u>.
   a. fish and turtles and sea lions.
   b. fish, turtles, sea lions.
   c. fish, turtles — sea lions.
   d. No change is necessary

28. DIRECTIONS: Identify the part of speech in the underlined portion of the following sentence:
   My son wanted <u>an</u> action figure instead of a stuffed animal.
   a. Preposition
   b. Article
   c. Conjunction
   d. Adverb

29. DIRECTIONS: Identify the adjective clause in the following sentence:

This week, I saw the cat that had a missing eye again.
a. that had a missing eye
b. This week
c. I saw the cat
d. again

30. DIRECTIONS: Identify the predicate in the following sentence:

Let's go to sleep early tonight.
a. Let's
b. Early
c. Go
d. Tonight

31. DIRECTIONS: Choose the sentence with no spelling errors.
a. After it snowed, Eliza hoped their would be no school tomorrow.
b. I felt that the biography was an accurate portreiyal of the subject's life.
c. There are many customs in Britain that Americans do not understand.
d. Unfortunately, the doctor was sued for neglegence.

32. DIRECTIONS: Identify the type of verb in the underlined portion of the following sentence:

I am going on vacation to Peru this summer.
a. Helping
b. Linking
c. Action
d. Passive

33. DIRECTIONS: Identify the prepositional phrase in the following sentence:.

That coffee shop on the corner has excellent croissants every morning.
a. That coffee shop
b. on the corner
c. has excellent croissants
d. every morning

34. DIRECTIONS: Choose the sentence that demonstrates the third-person perspective.
a. Are you going to eat that?
b. I would not miss my favorite band in concert for anything!
c. Do you and your cousin want separate rooms at the hotel?
d. The cows in the field looked healthy and happy.

35. DIRECTIONS: Choose the sentence with correct capitalization.
a. The mailman would always bring mister Rogers's mail on time.
b. She moved to the City of Memphis, Tennessee, to go to college.
c. Did you know that Queen Elizabeth II has ruled the British monarchy for over seventy years?
d. The republic of the Congo is in western Africa.

215

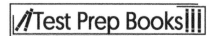
36. DIRECTIONS: Identify the noun phrase in the following sentence:

The tiny plane, which was old and rusty, did not look sturdy.
   a. The tiny plane
   b. which was
   c. old and rusty
   d. did not look sturdy

37. DIRECTIONS: Choose the option that corrects an error in the underlined portion of the sentence below. If no error exists, choose "No change is necessary."

She shouted, "The name of the restaurant is <u>The Olde Tavern."</u>
   a. The Olde Tavern".
   b. "The Olde Tavern."
   c. 'The Olde Tavern."
   d. No change is necessary

38. DIRECTIONS: Choose the sentence with correct use of an apostrophe.
   a. Were going to the beach this four'th of July.
   b. I forgot to return my book, so it's only a matter of time before I get a late fee.
   c. Martins friend's wanted to take him out for his birthday.
   d. Those hiking boots are Thomas'.

39. DIRECTIONS: Choose the sentence that demonstrates simple past tense.
   a. I sneezed because of the flowers.
   b. Mike had been taking a nap.
   c. The kids had finished playing video games.
   d. I was cleaning thoroughly before my parents' visit.

40. DIRECTIONS: Choose the run-on sentence.
   a. I normally prefer cherry pie over blueberry pie, but Martha's blueberry pie is an exception.
   b. I really wanted a dog but ended up getting a cat it looked lonely at the shelter and my sister fell in love with it.
   c. My mom, a bingo enthusiast, won five games on Tuesday night.
   d. If there is anything I can do, no matter how small, please let me know.

Mathematics

41. A school has 15 teachers and 20 teaching assistants. They have 200 students. What is the ratio of faculty to students?
   a. 3:20
   b. 4:17
   c. 3:2
   d. 7:40

216

42. Express the solution to the following problem in decimal form:

$$\frac{3}{5} \times \frac{7}{10} \div \frac{1}{2}$$

 a. 0.042
 b. 84%
 c. 0.84
 d. 0.42

43. Simplify the following fraction:

$$\frac{\frac{5}{7}}{\frac{9}{11}}$$

 a. $\frac{55}{63}$

 b. $\frac{7}{1,000}$

 c. $\frac{13}{15}$

 d. $\frac{5}{11}$

44. Bernard can make $80 per day. If he needs to make $300 and only works full days, how many days will this take?
 a. 2
 b. 3
 c. 4
 d. 5

45. $4\frac{1}{3} + 3\frac{3}{4} =$

 a. $6\frac{5}{12}$

 b. $8\frac{1}{12}$

 c. $8\frac{2}{3}$

 d. $7\frac{7}{12}$

46. Add and express in reduced form $\frac{5}{12} + \frac{4}{9}$.

 a. $\frac{9}{17}$

 b. $\frac{1}{3}$

 c. $\frac{31}{36}$

 d. $\frac{3}{5}$

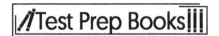

47. Express the following as a reduced mixed number: 54/15.
   a. 3 3/5
   b. 3 1/15
   c. 3 3/54
   d. 3 1/54

48. Express the following as an improper fraction: 8 3/7.
   a. 11/7
   b. 21/8
   c. 5/3
   d. 59/7

49. Express the following as an improper fraction: 11 5/8.
   a. 55/8
   b. 93/8
   c. 16/11
   d. 19/5

50. Round to the nearest tenth: 8.067
   a. 8.07
   b. 8.1
   c. 8.00
   d. 8.11

51. A nurse gives liquid medicine to their patient in the morning and in the afternoon. In the morning, the dose is $\frac{1}{2}$ ounce, and in the afternoon, the dose is $\frac{3}{4}$ ounce. If the nurse has 1 ounce at the beginning of the day, how much more will they need to give the complete dosage for the day?
   a. $\frac{1}{2}$ ounce
   b. $\frac{1}{4}$ ounce
   c. $\frac{3}{4}$ ounce
   d. 1 ounce

52. Convert 20% to a fraction in lowest terms.
   a. $\frac{20}{100}$
   b. $\frac{1}{20}$
   c. $\frac{1}{5}$
   d. $\frac{1}{2}$

53. Which of the following is not equivalent to the ratio of 20:44?
   a. $\frac{10}{22}$
   b. 5:11
   c. 44:20
   d. $0.\overline{45}$

218

54. Which of the following equations is true?

a. $\frac{300}{500} = 0.35$

b. $0.04 = .4\%$

c. $45.8 \div 0.2 = 22.9$

d. $\frac{1}{4} + \frac{1}{8} - \frac{1}{12} = \frac{7}{24}$

55. A lifeguard's salary during her first 30 days on the job is $15.00 an hour. Once she reaches 30 days, her salary increases by $0.75 an hour. What is the percent increase of her salary?

a. 5%

b. 95%

c. 75%

d. 15%

56. What is $\frac{4}{5} \div \frac{2}{3}$?

a. $\frac{8}{15}$

b. $\frac{1}{5}$

c. $\frac{6}{5}$

d. $\frac{2}{15}$

57. Candace purchases fencing that is 33 feet long. She already has fencing that is $\frac{1}{3}$ the length of her purchase. How many total *yards* of fencing does Candace have now?

a. 44

b. 14.7

c. 132

d. $33\frac{1}{3}$

58. How much simple interest is owed on $11,000 if borrowed for 2 years at 2.5%?

a. $550

b. $275

c. $55,000

d. $5,500

59. The foot of a ladder is placed 8 feet away from the side of a house. If the top of the ladder rests 6 feet up on the side of the building, how long is the ladder?

a. 7 ft

b. 8 ft

c. 9 ft

d. 10 ft

60. Which of the following is the heaviest quantity?

a. 75 g

b. 0.1 kg

c. 6,500 mg

d. 85,000 mg

61. Kaitlin's recipe for meatloaf calls for 3 pounds of ground beef and 1 pound of ground pork. How many ounces of meat does she need to buy at the store if she doubles the recipe?
    a. 8
    b. 64
    c. 128
    d. 0.5

62. How many inches are in one quarter of a mile?
    a. 15,840
    b. 1,320
    c. 4
    d. 1,584

63. What is the average rate of speed of 325 miles if that distance is traveled in 300 minutes?
    a. 650 mph
    b. 65 mph
    c. 1.08 mph
    d. 0.92 mph

64. Keith puts 8 gallons of gas in his car for a total cost of $27.20. How much would it cost to fill a 22-gallon tank?
    a. $70.40
    b. $22.00
    c. $3.40
    d. $74.80

65. If the surface area of a sphere is 324π square feet, calculate the radius of the sphere in inches.
    a. 9 inches
    b. 90 inches
    c. 108 inches
    d. 27 inches

66. Convert 4.15% to a decimal.
    a. 0.415
    b. 0.0415
    c. 4.15
    d. 0.00415

67. In a kennel, there are 4 cats for every 5 dogs. There are 81 total animals (dogs and cats) at the kennel. How many cats are there?
    a. 45
    b. 40
    c. 30
    d. 36

68. If $6x - 4 = 128$, then what does x equal?
    a. 20
    b. 22
    c. 124
    d. 12

69. If $0.25x + 15 = 14$, then what does x equal?
    a. -1
    b. -0.25
    c. -4
    d. 4

70. If $\frac{x}{3} + \frac{1}{2} = \frac{5}{6}$, then what does x equal?
    a. 1
    b. $\frac{1}{2}$
    c. 2
    d. $\frac{1}{6}$

71. What is the slope of the line containing the points (-5, 2) and (5, 4)?
    a. 5
    b. undefined
    c. $\frac{1}{5}$
    d. $-\frac{1}{5}$

72. Which of the following is largest?
    a. 0.45
    b. 0.096
    c. 0.3
    d. 0.313

73. At the beginning of the day, Xavier has 20 apples. At lunch, he meets his sister Emma and gives her half of his apples. After lunch, he stops by his neighbor Jim's house and gives him 6 of his apples. He then uses $\frac{3}{4}$ of his remaining apples to make an apple pie for dessert at dinner. At the end of the day, how many apples does Xavier have left?
    a. 4
    b. 6
    c. 2
    d. 1

74. An emergency department had 252 patients last week. This week, that number increased to 378. Express this increase as a percentage.
    a. 26%
    b. 50%
    c. 35%
    d. 12%

75. Mo needs to buy enough material to cover the walls around the stage for a theater performance. If he needs 79 feet of wall covering, what is the minimum number of yards of material he should purchase if the material is sold only by whole yards?

    a. 23 yards

    b. 25 yards

    c. 26 yards

    d. 27 yards

76. A couple buys a house for $150,000. They sell it for $165,000. By what percentage did the house's value increase?

    a. 10%

    b. 13%

    c. 15%

    d. 17%

77. If Danny takes 48 minutes to walk 3 miles, how long should it take him to walk 5 miles maintaining the same speed?

    a. 32 min

    b. 64 min

    c. 80 min

    d. 96 min

78. A solution needs 5 ml of saline for every 8 ml of medicine given. How much saline is needed for 45 ml of medicine?

    a. $\frac{225}{8}$ ml

    b. 72 ml

    c. 28 ml

    d. $\frac{45}{8}$ ml

79. What unit of volume is used to describe the following 3-dimensional shape?

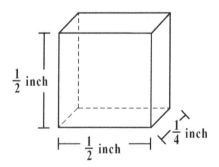

    a. Square inches

    b. Inches

    c. Cubic inches

    d. Squares

80. Which common denominator would be used in order to evaluate $\frac{2}{3} + \frac{4}{5}$?

   a. 15

   b. 3

   c. 5

   d. 10

Reading Comprehension

Questions 81–94 are based on the following two passages:

Passage 1

Shakespeare and His Plays

People who argue that William Shakespeare is not responsible for the plays attributed to his name are known as anti-Stratfordians (from the name of Shakespeare's birthplace, Stratford-upon-Avon). The most common anti-Stratfordian claim is that William Shakespeare simply was not educated enough or from a high enough social class to have written plays overflowing with references to such a wide range of subjects like history, the classics, religion, and international culture. William Shakespeare was the son of a glove-maker, he only had a basic grade school education, and he never set foot outside of England—so how could he have produced plays of such sophistication and imagination? How could he have written in such detail about historical figures and events, or about different cultures and locations around Europe? According to anti-Stratfordians, the depth of knowledge contained in Shakespeare's plays suggests a well-traveled writer from a wealthy background with a university education, not a countryside writer like Shakespeare. But in fact, there is not much substance to such speculation, and most anti-Stratfordian arguments can be refuted with a little background about Shakespeare's time and upbringing.

First of all, those who doubt Shakespeare's authorship often point to his common birth and brief education as stumbling blocks to his writerly genius. Although it is true that Shakespeare did not come from a noble class, his father was a very *successful* glove-maker and his mother was from a very wealthy land-owning family—so while Shakespeare may have had a country upbringing, he was certainly from a well-off family and would have been educated accordingly. Also, even though he did not attend university, grade school education in Shakespeare's time was actually quite rigorous and exposed students to classic drama through writers like Seneca and Ovid. It is not unreasonable to believe that Shakespeare received a very solid foundation in poetry and literature from his early schooling.

Next, anti-Stratfordians tend to question how Shakespeare could write so extensively about countries and cultures he had never visited before (for instance, several of his most famous works like *Romeo and Juliet* and *The Merchant of Venice* were set in Italy, on the opposite side of Europe!). But again, this criticism does not hold up under scrutiny. For one thing, Shakespeare was living in London, a bustling metropolis of international trade, the most populous city in England, and a political and cultural hub of Europe. In the daily crowds of people, Shakespeare would certainly have been able to meet travelers from other countries and hear firsthand accounts of life in their home country. And, in addition to the influx of information from world travelers, this was also the age of the printing press, a jump in technology that made it possible to print and circulate books much more easily than in the past. This also allowed for a freer flow

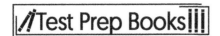

Practice Test #3 | Reading Comprehension

of information across different countries, allowing people to read about life and ideas from throughout Europe. One needn't travel the continent in order to learn and write about its culture.

Passage 2

The following passage is from The Shakespeare Problem Restated *by G.G. Greenwood*

Now there is very good authority for saying, and I think the truth is so, that at least two of the plays published among the works of Shakespeare are not his at all; that at least three others contain very little, if any, of his writing; and that of the remainder, many contain long passages that are non-Shakespearean. But when we have submitted them all the crucible of criticism we have a magnificent residuum of the purest gold. Here is the true Shakespeare; here is the great magician who, by a wave of his wand, could transmute brass into gold, or make dry bones live and move and have immortal being. Who was this great magician—this mighty dramatist who was "not of an age, but for all time"? Who was the writer of *Venus* and *Lucrece* and the *Sonnets* and *Lear* and *Hamlet*? Was it William Shakespeare of Stratford, the Player? So it is generally believed, and that hypothesis I had accepted in unquestioning faith till my love of the works naturally led me to an examination of the life of the supposed author of them. Then I found that as I read my faith melted away "into thin air." It was not, certainly, that I had (nor have I now) any wish to disbelieve. I was, and I am, altogether willing to accept the Player as the immortal poet if only my reason would allow me to do so. Why not? . . . But the question of authorship is, nevertheless, a most fascinating one. If it be true, as the Rev. Leonard Bacon wrote that "The great world does not care sixpence who wrote *Hamlet*," the great world must, at the same time, be a very small world, and many of us must be content to be outside it. Having given, then, the best attention I was able to give to the question, and more time, I fear, than I ought to have devoted to it, I was brought to the conclusion, as many others have been, that the man who is, truly enough, designated by Messrs. Garnett and Gosse as a "Stratford rustic" is not the true Shakespeare. . .

That Shakespeare the "Stratford rustic and London actor" should have acquired this learning, this culture, and this polish; that *he* should have travelled into foreign lands, studied the life and topography of foreign cities, and the manners and customs of all sorts and conditions of men; that *he* should have written some half-dozen dramas . . . besides qualifying himself as a professional actor; that *he* should have done all this and a good deal more between 1587 and 1592 is a supposition so wild that it can only be entertained by those who are prepared to accept it as a miracle. "And miracles do not happen!"

81. Which sentence contains the author's thesis in the first passage?
a. People who argue that William Shakespeare is not responsible for the plays attributed to his name are known as anti-Stratfordians.
b. But in fact, there is not much substance to such speculation, and most anti-Stratfordian arguments can be refuted with a little background about Shakespeare's time and upbringing.
c. It is not unreasonable to believe that Shakespeare received a very solid foundation in poetry and literature from his early schooling.
d. Next, anti-Stratfordians tend to question how Shakespeare could write so extensively about countries and cultures he had never visited before.

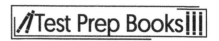

82. In the first paragraph in Passage 1, "How could he have written in such detail about historical figures and events, or about different cultures and locations around Europe?" is an example of which of the following?
    a. Hyperbole
    b. Onomatopoeia
    c. Rhetorical question
    d. Appeal to authority

83. In Passage 1, how does the author respond to the claim that Shakespeare was not well-educated because he did not attend university?
    a. By insisting upon Shakespeare's natural genius.
    b. By explaining grade school curriculum in Shakespeare's time.
    c. By comparing Shakespeare with other uneducated writers of his time.
    d. By pointing out that Shakespeare's wealthy parents probably paid for private tutors.

84. In Passage 1, the word *bustling* in the third paragraph most nearly means which of the following?
    a. Busy
    b. Foreign
    c. Expensive
    d. Undeveloped

85. In passage 2, the following sentence is an example of what?

"Here is the true Shakespeare; here is the great magician who, by a wave of his wand, could transmute brass into gold, or make dry bones live and move and have immortal being."

    a. Personification
    b. Metaphor
    c. Simile
    d. Allusion

86. In passage 2, the author's attitude toward Stratfordians can be described as which of the following?
    a. Accepting and forgiving
    b. Uncaring and neutral
    c. Uplifting and admiring
    d. Disbelieving and critical

87. What is the relationship between these two sentences from Passage 2?

Sentence 1: So, it is generally believed, and that hypothesis I had accepted in unquestioning faith till my love of the works naturally led me to an examination of the life of the supposed author of them.

Sentence 2: Then I found that as I read my faith melted away "into thin air."

    a. Sentence 2 explains the main idea in Sentence 1.
    b. Sentence 2 continues the definition begun in Sentence 1.
    c. Sentence 2 analyzes the comment in Sentence 1.
    d. Sentence 2 is a contrast to the idea in Sentence 1.

225

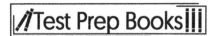

88. The writing style of Passage 1 could be best described as what?
    a. Expository
    b. Persuasive
    c. Narrative
    d. Descriptive

89. In passage 2, the word *topography* in the second paragraph most nearly means which of the following?
    a. Climate features of an area.
    b. Agriculture specific to place.
    c. Shape and features of the Earth.
    d. Aspects of humans within society.

90. The authors of the passages differ in their opinion of Shakespeare in that the author of Passage 2
    a. Believes that Shakespeare the actor did not write the plays.
    b. Believes that Shakespeare the playwright did not in act in the plays.
    c. Believes that Shakespeare was both the actor and the playwright.
    d. Believes that Shakespeare was neither the actor nor the playwright.

91. Which of the following would the two authors be most likely to disagree over?
    a. Readers of Shakespeare's plays should not care whether or not the "country Shakespeare" wrote the plays or not; the fact that they exist is reason enough for readers to be grateful.
    b. A person born into a lower socioeconomic class is not capable of writing plays with universal themes that creates new ways to use the English language.
    c. That a country education is not sufficient enough to have written the greatest plays in Western Civilization.
    d. That in order to write about the topography and civilization of a place, one must have travelled there and mingled with the people.

92. The author of Passage 1 believes that Shakespeare the actor *was* Shakespeare the writer because of which of the following?
    a. New evidence cites that Shakespeare did indeed travel a great bit between the years 1587 and 1592, suggesting that the playwright did have sufficient experience to write the great plays.
    b. There is sufficient evidence from Shakespeare's peers that proves that Shakespeare wrote the poems and plays that his name was signed to.
    c. An individual with Shakespeare's socioeconomic status and country education would be too limited in knowledge to write such brilliant plays.
    d. A country education and socioeconomic status do not deflect true genius if the individual is willing to absorb the textual and cultural knowledge surrounding them.

93. Which one of the following most accurately shows the relationship between the two passages?
    a. Passage 1 is written in concession with Passage 2.
    b. Passage 1 is written in opposition to Passage 2.
    c. Passage 1 is neutral to the stance of Passage 2.
    d. Passage 1 uses direct quotation from Passage 2 for contradiction.

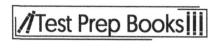

94. The last phrase in this sentence in Passage 1 is considered what?

    William Shakespeare was the son of a glove-maker, he only had a basic grade school education, and he never set foot outside of England—so how could he have produced plays of such sophistication and imagination?

    a. Rhetorical question
    b. Literary allusion
    c. Hyperbole
    d. Symbolism

Questions 95–100 are based upon the following passage:

This excerpt is adapted from *The Life-Story of Insects,* by Geo H. Carpenter.

Insects as a whole are preeminently creatures of the land and the air. This is shown not only by the possession of wings by a vast majority of the class, but by the mode of breathing to which reference has already been made, a system of branching air-tubes carrying atmospheric air with its combustion-supporting oxygen to all the insect's tissues. The air gains access to these tubes through a number of paired air-holes or spiracles, arranged segmentally in series.

It is of great interest to find that, nevertheless, a number of insects spend much of their time under water. This is true of not a few in the perfect winged state, as for example aquatic beetles and water-bugs ('boatmen' and 'scorpions') which have some way of protecting their spiracles when submerged, and, possessing usually the power of flight, can pass on occasion from pond or stream to upper air. But it is advisable in connection with our present subject to dwell especially on some insects that remain continually under water till they are ready to undergo their final moult and attain the winged state, which they pass entirely in the air. The preparatory instars of such insects are aquatic; the adult instar is aerial. All may-flies, dragon-flies, and caddis-flies, many beetles and two-winged flies, and a few moths thus divide their life-story between the water and the air. For the present we confine attention to the Stone-flies, the May-flies, and the Dragon-flies, three well-known orders of insects respectively called by systematists the Plecoptera, the Ephemeroptera and the Odonata.

In the case of many insects that have aquatic larvae, the latter are provided with some arrangement for enabling them to reach atmospheric air through the surface-film of the water. But the larva of a stone-fly, a dragon-fly, or a may-fly is adapted more completely than these for aquatic life; it can, by means of gills of some kind, breathe the air dissolved in water.

95. Which statement best details the central idea in this passage?
    a. It introduces certain insects that transition from water to air.
    b. It delves into entomology, especially where gills are concerned.
    c. It defines what constitutes as insects' breathing.
    d. It invites readers to have a hand in the preservation of insects.

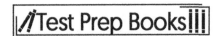

96. Which definition most closely relates to the usage of the word *moult* in the passage?
    a. An adventure of sorts, especially underwater
    b. Mating act between two insects
    c. The act of shedding part or all of the outer shell
    d. Death of an organism that ends in a revival of life

97. What is the purpose of the first paragraph in relation to the second paragraph?
    a. The first paragraph serves as a cause, and the second paragraph serves as an effect.
    b. The first paragraph serves as a contrast to the second.
    c. The first paragraph is a description for the argument in the second paragraph.
    d. The first and second paragraphs are merely presented in a sequence.

98. What does the following sentence most nearly mean?
    The preparatory instars of such insects are aquatic; the adult instar is aerial.

    a. The volume of water is necessary to prep the insect for transition rather than the volume of the air.
    b. The abdomen of the insect is designed like a star in the water as well as the air.
    c. The stage of preparation in between molting is acted out in the water, while the last stage is in the air.
    d. These insects breathe first in the water through gills, yet continue to use the same organs to breathe in the air.

99. Which of the statements reflect information that one could reasonably infer based on the author's tone?
    a. The author's tone is persuasive and attempts to call the audience to action.
    b. The author's tone is passionate due to excitement over the subject and personal narrative.
    c. The author's tone is informative and exhibits interest in the subject of the study.
    d. The author's tone is somber, depicting some anger at the state of insect larvae.

100. Which statement best describes stoneflies, mayflies, and dragonflies?
    a. They are creatures of the land and the air.
    b. They have a way of protecting their spiracles when submerged.
    c. Their larvae can breathe the air dissolved in water through gills of some kind.
    d. The preparatory instars of these insects are aerial.

Questions 101–106 are based on the following passage:

When researchers and engineers undertake a large-scale scientific project, they may end up making discoveries and developing technologies that have far wider uses than originally intended. This is especially true in NASA, one of the most influential and innovative scientific organizations in America. NASA spinoff technology refers to innovations originally developed for NASA space projects that are now used in a wide range of different commercial fields. Many consumers are unaware that products they are buying are based on NASA research! Spinoff technology proves that it is worthwhile to invest in science research because it could enrich people's lives in unexpected ways.

The first spinoff technology worth mentioning is baby food. In space, where astronauts have limited access to fresh food and fewer options about their daily meals, malnutrition is a serious

228

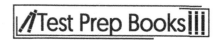

concern. Consequently, NASA researchers were looking for ways to enhance the nutritional value of astronauts' food. Scientists found that a certain type of algae could be added to food, improving the food's neurological benefits. When experts in the commercial food industry learned of this algae's potential to boost brain health, they were quick to begin their own research. The nutritional substance from algae then developed into a product called life's DHA, which can be found in over 90% of infant food sold in America.

Another intriguing example of a spinoff technology can be found in fashion. People who are always dropping their sunglasses may have invested in a pair of sunglasses with scratch resistant lenses—that is, it's impossible to scratch the glass, even if the glasses are dropped on an abrasive surface. This innovation is incredibly advantageous for people who are clumsy, but most shoppers don't know that this technology was originally developed by NASA. Scientists first created scratch resistant glass to help protect costly and crucial equipment from getting scratched in space, especially the helmet visors in space suits. However, sunglasses companies later realized that this technology could be profitable for their products, and they licensed the technology from NASA.

101. What is the main purpose of this article?
   a. To advise consumers to do more research before making a purchase
   b. To persuade readers to support NASA research
   c. To tell a narrative about the history of space technology
   d. To define and describe instances of spinoff technology

102. What is the organizational structure of this article?
   a. A general definition followed by more specific examples
   b. A general opinion followed by supporting arguments
   c. An important moment in history followed by chronological details
   d. A popular misconception followed by counterevidence

103. Why did NASA scientists research algae?
   a. They already knew algae was healthy for babies.
   b. They were interested in how to grow food in space.
   c. They were looking for ways to add health benefits to food.
   d. They hoped to use it to protect expensive research equipment.

104. What does the word "neurological" mean in the second paragraph?
   a. Related to the body
   b. Related to the brain
   c. Related to vitamins
   d. Related to technology

105. Why does the author mention space suit helmets?
   a. To give an example of astronaut fashion
   b. To explain where sunglasses got their shape
   c. To explain how astronauts protect their eyes
   d. To give an example of valuable space equipment

229

106. Which statement would the author probably NOT agree with?
   a. Consumers don't always know the history of the products they are buying.
   b. Sometimes new innovations have unexpected applications.
   c. It is difficult to make money from scientific research.
   d. Space equipment is often very expensive.

Questions 107–111 are based on the following passage:

As long ago as 1860 it was the proper thing to be born at home. At present, so I am told, the high gods of medicine have decreed that the first cries of the young shall be uttered upon the anesthetic air of a hospital, preferably a fashionable one. So young Mr. and Mrs. Roger Button were fifty years ahead of style when they decided, one day in the summer of 1860, that their first baby should be born in a hospital. Whether this anachronism had any bearing upon the astonishing history I am about to set down will never be known.

I shall tell you what occurred, and let you judge for yourself.

The Roger Buttons held an enviable position, both social and financial, in ante-bellum Baltimore. They were related to the This Family and the That Family, which, as every Southerner knew, entitled them to membership in that enormous peerage which largely populated the Confederacy. This was their first experience with the charming old custom of having babies— Mr. Button was naturally nervous. He hoped it would be a boy so that he could be sent to Yale College in Connecticut, at which institution Mr. Button himself had been known for four years by the somewhat obvious nickname of "Cuff."

On the September morning <u>consecrated</u> to the enormous event he arose nervously at six o'clock, dressed himself, adjusted an impeccable stock, and hurried forth through the streets of Baltimore to the hospital, to determine whether the darkness of the night had borne in new life upon its bosom.

When he was approximately a hundred yards from the Maryland Private Hospital for Ladies and Gentlemen he saw Doctor Keene, the family physician, descending the front steps, rubbing his hands together with a washing movement—as all doctors are required to do by the unwritten ethics of their profession.

Mr. Roger Button, the president of Roger Button & Co., Wholesale Hardware, began to run toward Doctor Keene with much less dignity than was expected from a Southern gentleman of that picturesque period. "Doctor Keene!" he called. "Oh, Doctor Keene!"

The doctor heard him, faced around, and stood waiting, a curious expression settling on his harsh, medicinal face as Mr. Button drew near.

"What happened?" demanded Mr. Button, as he came up in a gasping rush. "What was it? How is she? A boy? Who is it? What—"

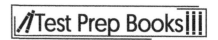

"Talk sense!" said Doctor Keene sharply. He appeared somewhat irritated.

"Is the child born?" begged Mr. Button.

Doctor Keene frowned. "Why, yes, I suppose so—after a fashion." Again he threw a curious glance at Mr. Button.

The Curious Case of Benjamin Button, F.S. Fitzgerald, 1922

107. What major event is about to happen in this story?
   a. Mr. Button is about to go to a funeral.
   b. Mr. Button's wife is about to have a baby.
   c. Mr. Button is getting ready to go to the doctor's office.
   d. Mr. Button is about to go shopping for new clothes.

108. What kind of tone does the above passage have?
   a. Nervous and Excited
   b. Sad and Angry
   c. Shameful and Confused
   d. Grateful and Joyous

109. What is the meaning of the word "consecrated" in paragraph 4?
   a. Numbed
   b. Chained
   c. Dedicated
   d. Moved

110. What does the author mean to do by adding the following statement?

"rubbing his hands together with a washing movement—as all doctors are required to do by the unwritten ethics of their profession."

   a. Suggesting that Mr. Button is tired of the doctor.
   b. Trying to explain the detail of the doctor's profession.
   c. Hinting to readers that the doctor is an unethical man.
   d. Giving readers a visual picture of what the doctor is doing.

111. Which of the following best describes the development of this passage?
   a. It starts in the middle of a narrative in order to transition smoothly to a conclusion.
   b. It is a chronological narrative from beginning to end.
   c. The sequence of events is backwards—we go from future events to past events.
   d. To introduce the setting of the story and its characters

Questions 112-116 are based on the following passage:

Dana Gioia argues in his article that poetry is dying, now little more than a limited art form confined to academic and college settings. Of course, poetry remains healthy in the academic setting, but the idea of poetry being limited to this academic subculture is a stretch. New technology and social networking alone have contributed to poets and other writers' work being shared across the world. YouTube has emerged to be a major

231

asset to poets, allowing live performances to be streamed to billions of users. Even now, poetry continues to grow and voice topics that are relevant to the culture of our time. Poetry is not in the spotlight as it may have been in earlier times, but it's still a relevant art form that continues to expand in scope and appeal.

Furthermore, Gioia's argument does not account for live performances of poetry. Not everyone has taken a poetry class or enrolled in university—but most everyone is online. The Internet is a perfect launching point to get all creative work out there. An example of this was the performance of Buddy Wakefield's *Hurling Crowbirds at Mockingbars*. Wakefield is a well-known poet who has published several collections of contemporary poetry. One of my favorite works by Wakefield is *Crowbirds*, specifically his performance at New York University in 2009. Although his reading was a campus event, views of his performance online number in the thousands. His poetry attracted people outside of the university setting.

Naturally, the poem's popularity can be attributed both to Wakefield's performance and the quality of his writing. *Crowbirds* touches on themes of core human concepts such as faith, personal loss, and growth. These are not ideas that only poets or students of literature understand, but all human beings: "You acted like I was hurling crowbirds at mockingbars / and abandoned me for not making sense. / Evidently, I don't experience things as rationally as you do" (Wakefield 15-17). Wakefield weaves together a complex description of the perplexed and hurt emotions of the speaker undergoing a separation from a romantic interest. The line "You acted like I was hurling crowbirds at mockingbars" conjures up an image of someone confused, seemingly out of their mind . . . or in the case of the speaker, passionately trying to grasp at a relationship that is fading. The speaker is looking back and finding the words that described how he wasn't making sense. This poem is particularly human and gripping in its message, but the entire effect of the poem is enhanced through the physical performance.

At its core, poetry is about addressing issues/ideas in the world. Part of this is also addressing the perspectives that are exiguously considered. Although the platform may look different, poetry continues to have a steady audience due to the emotional connection the poet shares with the audience.

112. Which one of the following best explains how the passage is organized?
   a. The author begins with a long definition of the main topic, and then proceeds to prove how that definition has changed over the course of modernity.
   b. The author presents a puzzling phenomenon and uses the rest of the passage to showcase personal experiences in order to explain it.
   c. The author contrasts two different viewpoints, then builds a case showing preference for one over the other.
   d. The passage is an analysis of another theory that the author has no stake in.

113. The author of the passage would likely agree most with which of the following?
   a. Buddy Wakefield is a genius and is considered at the forefront of modern poetry.
   b. Poetry is not irrelevant; it is an art form that adapts to the changing time while containing its core elements.
   c. Spoken word is the zenith of poetic forms and the premier style of poetry in this decade.
   d. Poetry is on the verge of vanishing from our cultural consciousness.

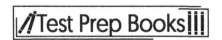

114. Which one of the following words, if substituted for the word *exiguously* in the last paragraph, would LEAST change the meaning of the sentence?

    a. Indolently

    b. Inaudibly

    c. Interminably

    d. Infrequently

115. Which of the following is most closely analogous to the author's opinion of Buddy Wakefield's performance in relation to modern poetry?

    a. Someone's refusal to accept that the Higgs Boson will validate the Standard Model.

    b. An individual's belief that soccer will lose popularity within the next fifty years.

    c. A professor's opinion that poetry contains the language of the heart, while fiction contains the language of the mind.

    d. A student's insistence that psychoanalysis is a subset of modern psychology.

116. What is the primary purpose of the passage?

    a. To educate readers on the development of poetry and describe the historical implications of poetry in media.

    b. To disprove Dana Gioia's stance that poetry is becoming irrelevant and is only appreciated in academia.

    c. To inform readers of the brilliance of Buddy Wakefield and to introduce them to other poets that have influenced contemporary poetry.

    d. To prove that Gioia's article does have some truth to it and to shed light on its relevance to modern poetry.

Questions 117-120 are based on the following passage:

Smoking tobacco products is terribly destructive. A single cigarette contains over 4,000 chemicals, including 43 known carcinogens and 400 deadly toxins. Some of the most dangerous ingredients include tar, carbon monoxide, formaldehyde, ammonia, arsenic, and DDT. Smoking can cause numerous types of cancer including throat, mouth, nasal cavity, esophageal, gastric, pancreatic, renal, bladder, and cervical cancer.

Cigarettes contain a drug called nicotine, one of the most addictive substances known to man. Addiction is defined as a compulsion to seek the substance despite negative consequences. According to the National Institute of Drug Abuse, nearly 35 million smokers expressed a desire to quit smoking in 2015; however, more than 85 percent of those who struggle with addiction will not achieve their goal. Almost all smokers regret picking up that first cigarette. You would be wise to learn from their mistake if you have not yet started smoking.

According to the U.S. Department of Health and Human Services, 16 million people in the United States presently suffer from a smoking-related condition and nearly nine million suffer from a serious smoking-related illness. According to the Centers for Disease Control and Prevention (CDC), tobacco products cause nearly six million deaths per year. This number is projected to rise to over eight million deaths by 2030. Smokers, on average, die ten years earlier than their nonsmoking peers.

In the United States, local, state, and federal governments typically tax tobacco products, which leads to high prices. Nicotine users who struggle with addiction sometimes pay more for a pack of cigarettes than for a few gallons of gas. Additionally, smokers tend to stink. The smell of smoke is all-consuming and creates a pervasive nastiness. Smokers also risk staining their teeth and fingers with yellow residue from the tar.

Smoking is deadly, expensive, and socially unappealing. Clearly, smoking is not worth the risks.

117. Which of the following best describes the passage?
    a. Narrative
    b. Persuasive
    c. Expository
    d. Technical

118. Which of the following statements most accurately summarizes the passage?
    a. Tobacco is less healthy than many alternatives.
    b. Tobacco is deadly, expensive, and socially unappealing, and smokers would be much better off kicking the addiction.
    c. In the United States, local, state, and federal governments typically tax tobacco products, which leads to high prices.
    d. Tobacco products shorten smokers' lives by ten years and kill more than six million people per year.

119. The author would be most likely to agree with which of the following statements?
    a. Smokers should only quit cold turkey and avoid all nicotine cessation devices.
    b. Other substances are more addictive than tobacco.
    c. Smokers should quit for whatever reason that gets them to stop smoking.
    d. People who want to continue smoking should advocate for a reduction in tobacco product taxes.

120. Which of the following represents an opinion statement on the part of the author?
    a. According to the Centers for Disease Control and Prevention (CDC), tobacco products cause nearly six million deaths per year.
    b. Nicotine users who struggle with addiction sometimes pay more for a pack of cigarettes than a few gallons of gas.
    c. They also risk staining their teeth and fingers with yellow residue from the tar.
    d. Additionally, smokers tend to stink. The smell of smoke is all-consuming and creates a pervasive nastiness.

Essay

Read the two topics presented below. Select one of the topics to write your essay. Prepare an essay of about 300 to 600 words on the essay you choose.

Topic 1

Over the past decade, e-reader devices have become popular due to their convenience and on-the-go functionality. Many readers now prefer to build a digital library of books that they can access at any time on an e-reader. Others argue that they have a better experience reading a physical book rather than a digital one, and they enjoy building a physical collection of books in their home. Take a side on the issue and argue whether or not you prefer e-readers or physical books. Use specific examples to support your argument.

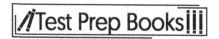

Topic 2

With the rise of streaming services, new movies may get simultaneously released on digital platforms and in movie theaters. However, some production companies will only release the movie in theaters first, delaying the digital streaming release or not providing one at all. People against digital releases argue that they can take away from the excitement of a traditional movie release. Those in favor digital releases endorse them as an opportunity for companies to provide flexible entertainment options for their customers. Take a side on the issue and argue whether or not new movies should be released on digital platforms or in theaters only. Use specific examples to support your argument.

Answer Explanations #3

English Language Skills

1. A: Choice *A* is correct because the speaker is talking about themselves, so the sentence correctly uses first-person perspective as indicated by the word *I*. Choice *B* is incorrect because it uses third-person perspective to describe the subject, *Frank*. Choice *C* is incorrect because it uses third-person perspective to describe the subject, *they*. Choice *D* is incorrect because it uses second-person perspective, as indicated by the use of *you/your*.

2. D: Choice *D* is correct because *she'd* is the correct contraction to replace the phrase *she would*. Choice *A* is incorrect because *couldn't* is the correct contraction for *could not*. Choice *B* is incorrect because *it's* is a contraction for the phrase *it is*, rather than the possessive pronoun *its*. Choice *D* is incorrect because an apostrophe is missing in the word *aren't*.

3. B: Choice *B* is correct because the introductory phrase gives context to the clause, *Maggie considered taking a sick day at work*. Choices *A*, *C*, and *D* are incorrect because they are components of the main clause and do not introduce it.

4. C: Choice *C* is correct because the purpose of a subordinate conjunction is to introduce a subordinate clause (a clause that cannot stand alone as a sentence). The subordinate conjunction *because* always introduces a clause that will provide context to the main clause of a sentence. Choice *A* is incorrect because the word *over* is a preposition. Choice *B* is incorrect because the word *rush* can function as either a noun, a verb, or an adjective depending on the sentence. Choice *D* is incorrect because the word *the* is an article.

5. B: Choice *B* is correct because the relative pronoun *who* provides context in the relative adjective clause, *the boy who ate too much*. Choices *A*, *C*, and *D* are incorrect because they do not contain any relative pronouns. *Her* in Choice *C* is a personal pronoun, not a relative one.

6. A: Choice *A* is correct because the dependent clause, *before the thunderstorm hit*, complements the main independent clause, *my flowers were blooming vividly*. Choices *B*, *C*, and *D* are incorrect because they are all independent clauses.

7. B: Choice *B* is correct because the word *insects* is the subject of the sentence. Choice *A* is incorrect because the word *Australia* is part of a prepositional phrase that is describing the main clause. Choice *C* is incorrect because the word *venomous* is an adjective. Choice *D* is incorrect because the word *common* is part of the predicate and is describing the subject.

8. C: Choice *C* is correct because the phrase *will be attending* fulfills the future continuous verb tense function of specifying an action that will take place and continue in the future. Choice *A* is incorrect because it demonstrates future perfect verb tense. Choice *B* is incorrect because it demonstrates present continuous verb tense. Choice *D* is incorrect because it demonstrates simple past tense.

9. D: Choice *D* is correct because the sentence contains no spelling errors. Choice *A* is incorrect because the word *shield* is spelled wrong. Choice *B* is incorrect because the word *right* is spelled wrong. Choice *C* is incorrect because the word *cosmetology* is spelled wrong.

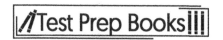

10. D: Choice *D* is correct because the subordinate clause, *because she told me to*, cannot stand alone as a sentence. Choices *A*, *B*, and *C* are incorrect because they are all independent clauses that can stand alone as sentences.

11. C: Choice *C* is correct because the sentence contains the appositive noun phrase, *a public school teacher*, which provides additional context to the sentence. Choices *A*, *B*, and *D* are incorrect because they do not contain appositive noun phrases.

12. B: Choice *B* is correct because the word *on* is a preposition. Choice *A* is incorrect because the word *to* is functioning as part of an infinitive verb phrase. Choice *C* is incorrect because the word *like* is a verb. Choice *D* is incorrect because the word *the* is an article.

13. A: Choice *A* is correct because *crystal-clear* is a compound adjective describing the noun *skies*. Choices *B*, *C*, and *D* are incorrect identifications of the part of speech.

14. C: Choice *C* is correct because the word *boss'* is the incorrect possessive form in the context of the sentence. One boss is giving critiques, so the possessive form *boss's* should be used. Choices *A*, *B*, and *D* are incorrect because they all follow correct rules of possession.

15. D: Choice *D* is correct because infinitive verb forms include a verb preceded by the word *to*. The sentence contains the infinitive verb phrase, *to learn*. Choices *A*, *B*, and *C* are incorrect because they do not contain any infinitive verbs.

16. B: Choice *B* is correct because it contains the incorrect spelling for the word *stationary*. When referring to something that is not moving, the spelling is *stationary*; when referring to writing materials like notecards and envelopes, the spelling is *stationery*. Choices *A*, *C*, and *D* are incorrect because they all have correct spelling.

17. A: Choice *A* is correct because the semicolon correctly joins the two independent clauses in the sentence. Choice *B* is incorrect because the phrase *with mustard* cannot stand alone as a sentence, so it should not be preceded by a period. Choice *C* is incorrect because a colon should be used to separate the main clause from the list of scents, and an em dash should not be used in a list. The sentence can be corrected to: "I love the following scents: rose, lilac, and geranium." Choice *D* is incorrect because the conjunction *because* is being used to introduce the second clause, so a colon is not necessary.

18. D: Choice *D* is correct because the verb phrase *have seen* demonstrates the present perfect tense. Choice *A* is incorrect because the verb phrase *will have worked* demonstrates the future perfect tense. Choice *B* is incorrect because the verb phrase *do not agree* demonstrates simple present tense, and the verb phrase *has been living* demonstrates present perfect continuous tense. Choice *C* is incorrect because the verb *going* demonstrates present continuous tense.

19. D: Choice *D* is correct because the appositive phrase *my favorite superhero* is correctly set off from the main clause using commas. Choices *A* and *C* are incorrect because they contain incorrect punctuation. Choice *B* is incorrect because the adjective *favorite* is a superlative, so adding the word *most* to modify it is unnecessary.

20. B: Choice *B* is correct because the appositive phrase *the plumber* is correctly set off with commas to add context to the subject, *Steve*. Choice *A* is incorrect because the two adjectives, *sour* and *bitter*, are already joined by the coordinating conjunction *and*, so a comma is not necessary. Choice *C* is incorrect because the essential appositive noun, *Chestnut*, gives meaning to the sentence, so it should not be set off with a comma. Choice *D* is incorrect because the list complicates the structure of the sentence, so em dashes can be used instead of commas to separate the list from the main clause: "My friend Joe ate his lunch — a burger, fries, and soda — early."

21. A: Choice *A* is correct because it demonstrates parallel structure in the list *walking, eating a piece of toast, and reading the newspaper*. Each item in the list is presented in the form of a verb ending in *-ing*. Choices *B, C,* and *D* are incorrect because the lists are not parallel; they either include inconsistent verb tenses or a mixture of noun and verb phrases.

22. C: Choice *C* is correct because the word *sailing* is a verbal acting as a noun in the gerund phrase, *is sailing*. Choices *A, B,* and *D* are incorrect because they do not contain any gerunds.

23. A: Choice *A* is correct because the word *climbing* is a verbal acting as an adjective, making it a present participle. Choices *B, C,* and *D* are incorrect because they do not contain any present participles.

24. B: Choice *B* is correct because the word *proposed* is acting as an adjective to modify the noun *budget*. Choices *A, C,* and *D* are incorrect identifications of the part of speech.

25. C: Choice *C* is correct because the speaker is using the pronoun *you* to directly address the listener/reader, so the sentence is demonstrating second-person perspective. Choices *A* and *B* are incorrect because they demonstrate first-person perspective. Choice *D* is incorrect because it demonstrates third-person perspective.

26. B: Choice *B* is the right answer because the main subject of the sentence is a singular cat, so the use of the verb *are* is incorrect and should be corrected to *is*. Choices *A, C,* and *D* are not the right answers because they all exhibit correct subject-verb agreement.

27. D: Choice *D* is correct because the underlined portion of the sentence demonstrates a correct use of a colon to link two independent clauses, and the list demonstrates correct comma usage. Choice *A* is incorrect because the word *and* should not be used to link all items in a list instead of commas. Choice *B* is incorrect because the word *and* is needed to link the final item in the list. Choice *C* is incorrect because the list is incorrectly punctuated with an em dash.

28. B: Choice *B* is correct because the word *an* is an article that provides context to the noun *action figure*. Choices *A, C,* and *D* are incorrect identifications of the part of speech.

29. A: Choice *A* is correct because the adjective clause *that had a missing eye* is a dependent clause that adds to the main clause, *I saw the cat*. Choice *B* is incorrect because *this week* is an introductory adjective phrase, which cannot stand alone as a clause because it lacks a verb. Choice *C* is incorrect because *I saw the cat* is the main independent clause of the sentence. Choice *D* is incorrect because the word *again* is an adverb describing the main verb, *saw*.

30. C: Choice *C* is correct because *go* is the main verb of the sentence and functions as the predicate. Choice *A* is incorrect because the contraction *let's* identifies the main subject of the sentence, *us*. Choice *B* is incorrect because the word *early* is an adverb describing the word *go*. Choice *D* is incorrect because the word *tonight* is also an adverb.

31. C: Choice *C* is correct because it contains no spelling errors. Choice *A* is incorrect because the word *there* is spelled incorrectly. Choice *B* is incorrect because the word *portrayal* is spelled incorrectly. Choice *D* is incorrect because the word *negligence* is spelled incorrectly.

238

32. A: Choice *A* is correct because the word *am* is a form of the verb *to be* that is helping to express the main verb, *going*. Choices *B*, *C*, and *D* do not identify the correct type of verb.

33. B: Choice *B* is correct because the prepositional phrase *on the corner* uses the preposition *on* and adds context to the main subject, the coffee shop. Choice *A* is incorrect because *that coffee shop* is the noun phrase that identifies the main subject. Choice *C* is incorrect because *has excellent croissants* is an adjective clause that describes the coffee shop. Choice *D* is incorrect because *every morning* is a noun phrase providing additional quantifying context to the adjective clause.

34. D: Choice *D* is correct because the sentence utilizes third-person *they/them* perspective. Choices *A* and *C* are incorrect because they use second-person *you/your* perspective. Choice *B* is incorrect because it uses first-person *I/my* perspective.

35. C: Choice *C* is correct because the main subject, *Queen Elizabeth II*, and the nationality, *British*, are correctly capitalized. Choice *A* is incorrect because *Mister Rodgers* is a proper noun and should be capitalized. Choice *B* is incorrect because *city of Memphis* is not a proper noun, so the word *city* should not be capitalized. Choice *D* is incorrect because *The Republic of the Congo* is a proper noun, so it should follow proper capitalization rules.

36. A: Choice *A* is correct because *the tiny plane* is the noun phrase that identifies the subject of the sentence. Choices *B* and *C* are incorrect because they are both part of the non-defining adjective clause, *which was old and rusty*. Choice *D* is incorrect because *did not look sturdy* is an adjective clause describing the main subject, *the tiny plane*.

37. D: Choice *D* is correct because the sentence is correct as is. Choices *A*, *B*, and *C* are incorrect because they do not follow correct punctuation for quotations.

38. B: Choice *B* is correct because the word *it's* is a contraction for *it is* and correctly uses an apostrophe. Choice *A* is incorrect because there should not be an apostrophe in *fourth*, but there should be one in *we're* to form the contraction for *we are*. Choice *C* is incorrect because there should not be an apostrophe in the word *friends*, but there should be one in *Martin's* since the sentence specifies possession. Choice *D* is incorrect because *Thomas's* has the incorrect use of an apostrophe for possession.

39. A: Choice *A* is correct because the verb *sneezed* indicates simple past tense. Choice *B* is incorrect because it demonstrates past perfect continuous tense. Choice *C* is incorrect because it demonstrates past perfect tense. Choice *D* is incorrect because it demonstrates past continuous tense.

40. B: Choice *B* is correct because the sentence contains multiple independent and dependent clauses that should be separated using punctuation. The sentence could be corrected to: "I really wanted a dog, but I ended up getting a cat. It looked lonely at the shelter, and my sister fell in love with it." Choices *A*, *C*, and *D* are incorrect because they all utilize correct punctuation to separate the independent and dependent clauses.

Mathematics

41. D: The total faculty is $15 + 20 = 35$. So, the ratio is 35:200. Then, divide both of these numbers by 5, since 5 is a common factor to both, with a result of 7:40.

239

42. C: The first step in solving this problem is expressing the result in fraction form. Separate this problem first by solving the division operation of the last two fractions. When dividing one fraction by another, invert or flip the second fraction and then multiply the numerator and denominator.

$$\frac{7}{10} \times \frac{2}{1} = \frac{14}{10}$$

Next, multiply the first fraction with this value:

$$\frac{3}{5} \times \frac{14}{10} = \frac{42}{50}$$

In this instance, you can find the decimal form by converting the fraction into $\frac{x}{100}$, where x is the number from which the final decimal is found. Multiply both the numerator and denominator by 2 to get the fraction as an expression of $\frac{x}{100}$.

$$\frac{42}{50} \times \frac{2}{2} = \frac{84}{100}$$

In decimal form, this would be expressed as 0.84.

43. A: First simplify the larger fraction by separating it into two. When dividing one fraction by another, remember to *invert* the second fraction and multiply the two as follows:

$$\frac{5}{7} \times \frac{11}{9}$$

The resulting fraction $\frac{55}{63}$ cannot be simplified further, so this is the answer to the problem.

44. C: The number of days can be found by taking the total amount Bernard needs to make and dividing it by the amount he earns per day:

$$\frac{300}{80} = \frac{30}{8} = \frac{15}{4} = 3.75$$

But Bernard is only working full days, so he will need to work 4 days, since 3 days is not a sufficient amount of time.

45. B:

$$4\frac{1}{3} + 3\frac{3}{4}$$

$$4 + 3 + \frac{1}{3} + \frac{3}{4}$$

$$7 + \frac{1}{3} + \frac{3}{4}$$

Adding the fractions gives:

$$\frac{1}{3} + \frac{3}{4}$$

$$\frac{4}{12} + \frac{9}{12}$$

$$\frac{13}{12} = 1 + \frac{1}{12}$$

Thus:

$$7 + \frac{1}{3} + \frac{3}{4} = 7 + 1 + \frac{1}{12}$$

$$8\frac{1}{12}$$

46. C: $\frac{31}{36}$

Set up the problem and find a common denominator for both fractions.

$$\frac{5}{12} + \frac{4}{9}$$

Multiply each fraction across by 1 to convert to a common denominator.

$$\frac{5}{12} \times \frac{3}{3} + \frac{4}{9} \times \frac{4}{4}$$

Once over the same denominator, add across the top. The total is over the common denominator.

$$\frac{15 + 16}{36} = \frac{31}{36}$$

47. A: $3\frac{3}{5}$. Divide 54 by 15:

$$\begin{array}{r} 3 \\ 15\overline{)54} \\ -45 \\ \hline 9 \end{array}$$

The result is $3\frac{9}{15}$. Reduce the remainder for the final answer, $3\frac{3}{5}$.

48. D: 59/7

The original number was 8 3/7. Multiply the denominator by the whole number portion. Add the numerator and put the total over the original denominator.

$$\frac{(8 \times 7) + 3}{7} = \frac{59}{7}$$

49. B: 93/8

The original number was 11 5/8. Multiply the denominator by the whole number portion. Add the numerator and put the total over the original denominator.

$$\frac{(8 \times 11) + 5}{8} = \frac{93}{8}$$

50. B: 8.1

To round 8.067 to the nearest tenths, use the digit in the hundredths.

6 in the hundredths is greater than 5, so round up in the tenths.

8.0̲67

0 becomes a 1.

8.1

51. B: $\frac{1}{4}$ ounce. First, calculate the total that the nurse needs for the day:

$$\frac{1}{2} + \frac{3}{4} = \frac{2}{4} + \frac{3}{4} = \frac{5}{4}$$

If the nurse starts out with 1 ounce, they will need $\frac{1}{4}$ ounce additional for the day:

$$\frac{5}{4} - 1 = \frac{5}{4} - \frac{4}{4} = \frac{1}{4}$$

52: C: $\frac{1}{5}$. Recall that a percentage means "per 100." Therefore, drop the percentage sign and write 20 over 100 in a fraction: $\frac{20}{100}$. This is not in lowest terms because both the numerator and denominator have a common factor of 20. Dividing a 20 out of both the numerator and the denominator results in the fraction $\frac{1}{5}$.

53. C: 44:20. 20:44 can be written as a fraction as $\frac{20}{44}$, which is equivalent to $\frac{10}{22}$ and $\frac{5}{11}$. The second fraction can be written in ratio form as 5:11. Therefore, Choices A and B are the same as 20:44. $\frac{5}{11}$ can be converted to a decimal by the division $5 \div 11$, which is equal to the repeating decimal $0.\overline{45}$. Therefore, Choice D is also equivalent to 20:44. 44:20 is equal to the fraction $\frac{44}{20}$, which is not equivalent to the other options; therefore, Choice C is correct.

54. D: $\frac{1}{4} + \frac{1}{8} - \frac{1}{12} = \frac{7}{24}$. Choice A is incorrect because $\frac{300}{500} = 0.6$. Choice B is incorrect because $0.04 = 4\%$. Choice C is incorrect because:

$$45.8 \div 0.2 = 229$$

Finally, Choice D is correct because:

$$\frac{1}{4} + \frac{1}{8} - \frac{1}{12} = \frac{6}{24} + \frac{3}{24} - \frac{2}{24} = \frac{7}{24}$$

55. A: 5%. The change in salary is equal to the increase of $0.75. Dividing this amount by her starting salary, $\frac{0.75}{15} = 0.05$ is obtained. This amount is equivalent to 5%. Therefore, her salary increased by 5%.

56. C: $\frac{6}{5}$. To divide a fraction by a fraction, multiply the first fraction by the reciprocal of the second and then reduce. Therefore, the answer is:

$$\frac{4}{5} \div \frac{2}{3} = \frac{4}{5} \times \frac{3}{2} = \frac{12}{10} = \frac{6}{5}$$

57. B: 14.7. Candace purchase 33 feet of fencing. She already had $\frac{1}{3}(33) = 11$ feet of fencing. Therefore, she now has 44 feet of fencing. To convert feet to yards, use the conversion rate of 3 ft $=$ 1 yd. Therefore, divide 44 by 3 to obtain 14.7 yards, rounded to one decimal point.

58. A: $550. The formula for simple interest is $I = prt$, where I is the interest, p is the principal, t is the time in years and r is the interest rate, written as a decimal. In this case, the principal is $11,000, the time is 2, and the interest rate is 0.025. Therefore:

$$I = 11000(2)(0.025) = \$550$$

59. D: 10 ft. The ladder forms a right triangle with a building. The ladder is the hypotenuse, and the given lengths are the other two sides of the triangle. From the Pythagorean Theorem, we have $a^2 + b^2 = c^2$. In this case:

$$8^2 + 6^2 = 64 + 36 = 100$$

Therefore, $c^2 = 100$ and $c = \sqrt{100} = 10$. Therefore, the ladder is 10 ft long.

60. B: 0.1 kg. The answer can be found by converting all of the values to grams and selecting the largest. Use the conversions 1 g = 1000 mg and 1 kg $=$ 1000 g, to get 0.1 kg $=$ 100 g (multiplied by 1,000), 6500 mg $=$ 6.5 g (divided by 1,000), and 85,000 mg $=$ 85 g (divided by 1,000). Therefore, the largest value is 0.1 kg $=$ 100 g.

61. C: If Kaitlin doubles her recipe, she needs 8 pounds of meat. Because one pound is equal to 16 ounces, she needs $8(16) = 128$ total ounces of meat.

62. A: 15,840. First, use the conversion that 1 mi $=$ 5,280 ft. Therefore, one quarter of a mile (or 0.25%) is equal to $0.25(5280) = 1,320$ ft. Because 1 foot is equal to 12 inches, 1,320 ft is equivalent to:

$$1320(12) = 15,840 \text{ ft}$$

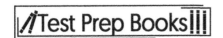

63. B: 65 mph. Because 60 miles is equal to one hour, dividing 300 by 60 results in a time of 5 hours. Then, using the distance formula $d = rt$, where d is the total distance traveled, r is the rate, and t is time, the problem gives $325 = r \cdot 5$. Dividing both sides by 5 results in the average rate of speed of 65 mph.

64. D: $74.80. A proportion can be set up to solve this problem. Let x represent the cost to fill up a 22-gallon tank. Then, $\frac{8}{27.20} = \frac{22}{x}$. Cross multiplication results in $8x = 598.4$. Dividing both sides by 8 gives the result of $x = 74.8$. Therefore, it would cost $74.80 to fill up the 22-gallon tank.

Another way to solve the problem would be to figure out the price per gallon and then multiplying that by 22 gallons:

$$\$27.20 \div 8 \text{ gallons} = \$3.40 \text{ per gallon}$$

$$\$3.40 \times 22 \text{ gallons} = \$74.80$$

65. C: 108 inches. The surface area of a sphere is equal to $4\pi r^2$, where r is the radius. In this case, $4\pi r^2 = 324\pi$. Dividing both sides by 4π results in the equation $r^2 = 81$. Taking the square root shows that the radius is 9 ft long. Multiply 9 by 12 to convert feet to inches. Therefore, the radius is 108 inches long.

66. B: 0.0415. To convert a percentage to a decimal, move the decimal two places to the right and drop the % symbol. Even though 4.15% already has a decimal, this step still needs to be completed. Moving the decimal point two units to the left involves adding a zero in front of the 4. Therefore, the answer is 0.0415.

67. D: 36. If there are 4 cats for every 5 dogs, that means that for every 9 animals, 4 of them are cats. A proportion can be set up to solve this problem. Let x be the total number of cats in the kennel. Then, $\frac{4}{9} = \frac{x}{81}$. Cross multiplying results in $324 = 9x$, and dividing each side by 9 results in $x = 36$. Therefore, there are 36 cats in the kennel.

68. B: 22. To solve this equation, first add 4 to both sides, which results in $6x = 132$. Then, divide both sides by 6 to obtain $x = 22$.

69. C: -4. First, subtract 15 off both sides of the equation to obtain $0.25x = -1$. Then, divide both sides by the decimal 0.25 to obtain:

$$x = -\frac{1}{0.25} = -4$$

70. A: 1. First, subtract $\frac{1}{2}$ from both sides. However, because there is a denominator of 6 on the right, $\frac{1}{2}$ should be converted to $\frac{3}{6}$ first. Therefore, the equation is $\frac{1}{3}x = \frac{5}{6} - \frac{3}{6}$, which results in $\frac{x}{3} = \frac{2}{6}$. This is a proportion which can be solved by cross multiplication. Dividing $6x = 6$ by 6 on both sides results in $x = 1$.

71. C: $\frac{1}{5}$. The slope of the line containing two points is the change in y over the change in x, or:

$$m = \frac{y_2 - y_1}{x_2 - x_1}$$

In this case, the slope is:

$$\frac{4-2}{5-(-5)} = \frac{2}{5+5} = \frac{2}{10} = \frac{1}{5}$$

72. A: Figure out which is largest by looking at the first non-zero digits. Choice *B*'s first non-zero digit is in the hundredths place. The other three all have non-zero digits in the tenths place, so it must be *A*, *C*, or *D*. Of these, *A* has the largest first non-zero digit.

73. D: This problem can be solved using basic arithmetic. Xavier starts with 20 apples, then gives his sister half, so 20 divided by 2.

$$\frac{20}{2} = 10$$

He then gives his neighbor 6, so 6 is subtracted from 10.

$$10 - 6 = 4$$

Lastly, he uses $\frac{3}{4}$ of his apples to make an apple pie, so to find remaining apples, the first step is to subtract $\frac{3}{4}$ from one and then multiply the difference by 4.

$$\left(1 - \frac{3}{4}\right) \times 4 = ?$$

$$\left(\frac{4}{4} - \frac{3}{4}\right) \times 4 = ?$$

$$\left(\frac{1}{4}\right) \times 4 = 1$$

74. B: The first step is to calculate the difference between the larger value and the smaller value.

$$378 - 252 = 126$$

To calculate this difference as a percentage of the original value, and thus calculate the percentage *increase*, 126 is divided by 252, then this result is multiplied by 100 to find the percentage = 50%.

75. D: In order to solve this problem, the number of feet in a yard must be established. There are 3 feet in every yard. The equation to calculate the minimum number of yards is $79 \div 3 = 26\frac{1}{3}$.

If the material is sold only by whole yards, then Mo would need to round up to the next whole yard in order to cover the extra $\frac{1}{3}$ yard. Therefore, the answer is 27 yards. None of the other choices meets the minimum whole yard requirement.

76. A: The value went up by $165,000 – $150,000 = $15,000. Out of $150,000, this is $\frac{15,000}{150,000} = \frac{1}{10}$. Convert this to having a denominator of 100, the result is $\frac{10}{100}$ or 10%.

77. C: 80 min. To solve the problem, a proportion is written consisting of ratios comparing distance and time. One way to set up the proportion is:

$$\frac{3}{48} = \frac{5}{x} \left(\frac{distance}{time} = \frac{distance}{time} \right) \text{ where } x \text{ represents the unknown value of time}$$

To solve a proportion, the ratios are cross-multiplied:

$$(3)(x) = (5)(48) \rightarrow 3x = 240$$

The equation is solved by isolating the variable, or dividing by 3 on both sides, to produce $x = 80$.

78. A: Every 8 ml of medicine requires 5 ml. The 45 ml first needs to be split into portions of 8 ml. This results in $\frac{45}{8}$ portions. Each portion requires 5 ml. Therefore:

$$\frac{45}{8} \times 5 = 45 \times \frac{5}{8} = \frac{225}{8} \text{ ml is necessary}$$

79. C: Volume of this 3-dimensional figure is calculated using length x width x height. Each measure of length is in inches. Therefore, the answer would be labeled in cubic inches.

80. A: A common denominator must be found. The least common denominator is 15 because it has both 5 and 3 as factors. The fractions must be rewritten using 15 as the denominator.

Reading Comprehension

81. B: But in fact, there is not much substance to such speculation, and most anti-Stratfordian arguments can be refuted with a little background about Shakespeare's time and upbringing. The thesis is a statement that contains the author's topic and main idea. The main purpose of this article is to use historical evidence to provide counterarguments to anti-Stratfordians. Choice A is simply a definition; Choice C is a supporting detail, not a main idea; and Choice D represents an idea of anti-Stratfordians, not the author's opinion.

82. C: Rhetorical question. This requires readers to be familiar with different types of rhetorical devices. A rhetorical question is a question that is asked not to obtain an answer but to encourage readers to consider an issue more deeply.

83. B: By explaining grade school curriculum in Shakespeare's time. This question asks readers to refer to the organizational structure of the article and demonstrate understanding of how the author provides details to support the argument. This particular detail can be found in the second paragraph: "even though he did not attend university, grade school education in Shakespeare's time was actually quite rigorous."

84. A: Busy. This is a vocabulary question that can be answered using context clues. Other sentences in the paragraph describe London as "the most populous city in England" filled with "crowds of people," giving an image of a busy city full of people. Choice B is incorrect because London was in Shakespeare's home country, not a foreign one. Choice C is not mentioned in the passage. Choice D is not a good answer choice because the passage describes how London was a popular and important city, probably not an undeveloped one.

85. B: This sentence is an example of a metaphor. Metaphors make a comparison between two things, usually saying that one thing *is* another thing. Here, the author is saying that Shakespeare *is* "the great magician." Choice *A*, personification, is when an inanimate object is given human characteristics, so this is incorrect. Choice *C*, simile, is making a comparison between two things using *like* or *as*, so this is incorrect. Choice *D*, allusion, is an indirect reference to a place, person, or event that happened in the past, so this is also incorrect.

86. D: Remember from the first passage that anti-Stratfordians are those who believe that Shakespeare *did not* write the plays, so Stratfordians are people who believe that Shakespeare *did* write the plays. The author of Passage 2 is disbelieving and critical of the Stratfordian point of view. We see this especially in the second paragraph, where the author states it is a supposition "so wild that it can only be entertained by those who are prepared to accept it as a miracle." All of the other answer choices are incorrect.

87. D: Sentence 2 is a contrast to the idea in Sentence 1. In the first sentence, the author states that they, at one time, believed that Shakespeare was the author of his plays. The second sentence is a contrast to that statement by saying the author no longer believes that the author of the plays is Shakespeare. The other answer choices are incorrect.

88. B: This writing style is best described as persuasive. The author is trying to persuade the audience, with evidence, that Shakespeare actually wrote his own dramas. Choice *A*, expository writing, means to inform or explain. Expository writing usually does not set out to persuade the audience of something, only to inform them, so this choice is incorrect. Choice *C*, narrative writing, is used to tell a story, so this is incorrect. Choice *D*, descriptive writing, uses all five senses to paint a picture for the reader, so this choice is also incorrect.

89. C: Topography is the shape and features of the Earth. The author is implying here that whoever wrote Shakespeare's plays studied the physical features of foreign cities. Choices *A, B,* and *D* are incorrect. Choice *A* is simply known as climate. Choice *B* would just be considered the "agriculture of a particular area." Choice *D*, aspects of humans within society, would be known as *anthropology.*

90. A: The author of Passage 2 believes that Shakespeare the actor did not write the plays. We see this at the end of the first paragraph where the author contends that the "'Stratford rustic' is not the true Shakespeare." The author does believe that Shakespeare was an actor, as the author calls this Shakespeare a "Player" throughout the text, so Choices *B* and *D* are incorrect. Choice *C* is incorrect, as the author does not believe that Shakespeare wrote the plays.

91. D: That in order to write about the topography and civilization of a place, one must have travelled there and mingled with the people. We are clear the two authors would disagree over this sentiment. The author of Passage 1 says that "[o]ne needn't travel the continent in order to learn and write about its culture." The author of Passage 2 says "that *he* should have travelled into foreign lands, studied the life and topography of foreign cities" is an assertion that the one who wrote the plays *must have* travelled into foreign lands and studied the life and topography of foreign cities. Choice *A* is something the author of Passage 2 quotes, but we can assume both the authors *do care* whether or not Shakespeare wrote the plays. Choices *B and C* are close. However, the author of Passage 2 does not mention the country education, so we do not know their opinion on Choice *C*. The author does hint that the socioeconomic status of the "rustic" actor would be a limitation to Shakespeare's abilities. However, the author of Passage 2 is most straightforward about Choice *D*.

247

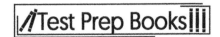 **Answer Explanations #3 | Reading Comprehension**

92. D: This is the argument that the author voices in the second paragraph of Passage 2. A country education and socioeconomic status do not deflect true genius if the individual is willing to absorb the textual and cultural knowledge surrounding them. Choice A is incorrect; there is no "new evidence" mentioned in the first passage about Shakespeare having travelled. Choice B is incorrect; there is no evidence from Shakespeare's peers that he wrote the plays. Choice C is incorrect; this is the author's belief in Passage 2, not Passage 1.

93. B: Passage 1 is written in opposition to Passage 2. We can see the author of Passage 1 stating that it's likely that Shakespeare wrote his own plays. The author of Passage 2 says that it is unlikely that Shakespeare wrote his own plays. This makes Choices A and C incorrect. Choice D is incorrect because we have no direct quotation in Passage 1 that comes directly from Passage 2, only general concepts.

94. A: The last phrase is an example of a rhetorical question. Rhetorical questions are asked in order to make a dramatic effect or point rather than to receive an actual answer. Choice B, literary allusion, are indirect references to some historical event, person, or object. Choice C, hyperbole, is an exaggeration of something, so this is incorrect. Choice D, symbolism, is used to represent an idea or quality of something, like how a rose symbolizes love in western culture.

95. A: It introduces certain insects that transition from water to air. Choice B is incorrect because although the passage talks about gills, it is not the central idea of the passage. Choices C and D are incorrect because the passage does not "define" or "invite," but only serves as an introduction to stoneflies, dragonflies, and mayflies and their transition from water to air.

96. C: The act of shedding part or all of the outer shell. Choices A, B, and D are incorrect.

97. B: The first paragraph serves as a contrast to the second. Notice how the first paragraph goes into detail describing how insects are able to breathe air. The second paragraph acts as a contrast to the first by stating "[i]t is of great interest to find that, nevertheless, a number of insects spend much of their time under water." Watch for transition words such as "nevertheless" to help find what type of passage you're dealing with.

98. C: The stage of preparation in between molting is acted out in the water, while the last stage is in the air. Choices A, B, and D are all incorrect. *Instars* is the phase between two periods of molting, and the text explains when these transitions occur.

99. C: The author's tone is informative and exhibits interest in the subject of the study. Overall, the author presents us with information on the subject. One moment where personal interest is depicted is when the author states, "It is of great interest to find that, nevertheless, a number of insects spend much of their time under water."

100. C: Their larva can breathe the air dissolved in water through gills of some kind. This is stated in the last paragraph. Choice A is incorrect because the text mentions this in a general way at the beginning of the passage concerning "insects as a whole." Choice B is incorrect because this is stated of beetles and water-bugs, and not the insects in question. Choice D is incorrect because this is the opposite of what the text says of instars.

101. D: To define and describe instances of spinoff technology. This is an example of a purpose question—*why* did the author write this? The article contains facts, definitions, and other objective information without telling a story or arguing an opinion. In this case, the purpose of the article is to

248

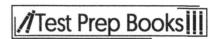

inform the reader. The only answer choice that is related to giving information is answer Choice *D*: to define and describe.

102. A: A general definition followed by more specific examples. This organization question asks readers to analyze the structure of the essay. The topic of the essay is about spinoff technology; the first paragraph gives a general definition of the concept, while the following two paragraphs offer more detailed examples to help illustrate this idea.

103. C: They were looking for ways to add health benefits to food. This reading comprehension question can be answered based on the second paragraph—scientists were concerned about astronauts' nutrition and began researching useful nutritional supplements. Choice *A* in particular is not true because it reverses the order of discovery (first NASA identified algae for astronaut use, and then it was further developed for use in baby food).

104. B: Related to the brain. This vocabulary question could be answered based on the reader's prior knowledge; but even for readers who have never encountered the word "neurological" before, the passage does provide context clues. The very next sentence talks about "this algae's potential to boost brain health," which is a paraphrase of "neurological benefits." From this context, readers should be able to infer that "neurological" is related to the brain.

105. D: To give an example of valuable space equipment. This purpose question requires readers to understand the relevance of the given detail. In this case, the author mentions "costly and crucial equipment" before mentioning space suit visors, which are given as an example of something that is very valuable. Choice *A* is not correct because fashion is only related to sunglasses, not to NASA equipment. Choice *B* can be eliminated because it is simply not mentioned in the passage. While Choice *C* seems like it could be a true statement, it is also not relevant to what is being explained by the author.

106. C: It is difficult to make money from scientific research. The article gives several examples of how businesses have been able to capitalize on NASA research, so it is unlikely that the author would agree with this statement. Evidence for the other answer choices can be found in the article. In Choice *A*, the author mentions that "many consumers are unaware that products they are buying are based on NASA research." Choice *B* is a general definition of spinoff technology. Choice *D* is mentioned in the final paragraph.

107. B: Mr. Button's wife is about to have a baby. The passage begins by giving the reader information about traditional birthing situations. Then, we are told that Mr. and Mrs. Button decide to go against tradition to have their baby in a hospital. The next few passages are dedicated to letting the reader know how Mr. Button dresses and goes to the hospital to welcome his new baby. There is a doctor in this excerpt, as Choice *C* indicates, and Mr. Button does put on clothes, as Choice *D* indicates. However, Mr. Button is not going to the doctor's office nor is he about to go shopping for new clothes.

108. A: The tone of the above passage is nervous and excited. We are told in the fourth paragraph that Mr. Button "arose nervously." We also see him running without caution to the doctor to find out about his wife and baby—this indicates his excitement. We also see him stuttering in a nervous yet excited fashion as he asks the doctor if it's a boy or girl. Though the doctor may seem a bit abrupt at the end, indicating a bit of anger or shame, neither of these choices is the overwhelming tone of the entire passage. Despite the circumstances, joy and gratitude are not the main tone in the passage.

109. C: Dedicated. Mr. Button is dedicated to the task before him. Choice *A*, numbed, Choice *B*, chained, and Choice *D*, moved, all could grammatically fit in the sentence. However, they are not synonyms with *consecrated* like Choice *C* is.

110. D: Giving readers a visual picture of what the doctor is doing. The author describes a visual image—the doctor rubbing his hands together—first and foremost. The author may be trying to make a comment about the profession; however, the author does not "explain the detail of the doctor's profession" as Choice *B* suggests.

111. D: To introduce the setting of the story and its characters. We know we are being introduced to the setting because we are given the year in the very first paragraph along with the season: "one day in the summer of 1860." This is a classic structure of an introduction of the setting. We are also getting a long explanation of Mr. Button, what his work is, who is related to him, and what his life is like in the third paragraph.

112. C: The author contrasts two different viewpoints, then builds a case showing preference for one over the other. Choice *A* is incorrect because the introduction does not contain an impartial definition, but rather, an opinion. Choice *B* is incorrect. There is no puzzling phenomenon given, as the author doesn't mention any peculiar cause or effect that is in question regarding poetry. Choice *D* does contain another's viewpoint at the beginning of the passage; however, to say that the author has no stake in this argument is incorrect; the author uses personal experiences to build their case.

113. B: Choice *B* accurately describes the author's argument in the text: that poetry is not irrelevant. While the author does praise, and even value, Buddy Wakefield as a poet, the author never heralds him as a genius. Eliminate Choice *A*, as it is an exaggeration. Not only is Choice *C* an exaggerated statement, but the author never mentions spoken word poetry in the text. Choice *D* is incorrect because this statement contradicts the writer's argument.

114. D: *Exiguously* means not occurring often, or occurring rarely, so Choice *D* would LEAST change the meaning of the sentence. Choice *A*, *indolently*, means unhurriedly, or slow, and does not fit the context of the sentence. Choice *B*, *inaudibly*, means quietly or silently. Choice *C*, *interminably*, means endlessly, or all the time, and is the opposite of the word *exiguously*.

115. D: A student's insistence that psychoanalysis is a subset of modern psychology is the most analogous option. The author of the passage tries to insist that performance poetry is a subset of modern poetry, and therefore, tries to prove that modern poetry is not "dying," but thriving on social media for the masses. Choice *A* is incorrect, as the author is not refusing any kind of validation. Choice *B* is incorrect; the author's insistence is that poetry will *not* lose popularity. Choice *C* mimics the topic but compares two different genres, while the author does no comparison in this passage.

116. B: The author's purpose is to disprove Gioia's article claiming that poetry is a dying art form that only survives in academic settings. In order to prove his argument, the author educates the reader about new developments in poetry (Choice *A*) and describes the brilliance of a specific modern poet (Choice *C*), but these serve as examples of a growing poetry trend that counters Gioia's argument. Choice *D* is incorrect because it contradicts the author's argument.

117. B: Narrative, Choice *A*, means a written account of connected events. Think of narrative writing as a story. Choice *C*, expository writing, generally seeks to explain or describe some phenomena, whereas Choice *D*, technical writing, includes directions, instructions, and/or explanations. This passage is

250

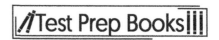

persuasive writing, which hopes to change someone's beliefs based on an appeal to reason or emotion. The author is aiming to convince the reader that smoking is terrible. They use health, price, and beauty in their argument against smoking, so Choice *B*, persuasive, is the correct answer.

118. B: The author is opposed to tobacco. He cites disease and deaths associated with smoking. He points to the monetary expense and aesthetic costs. Choice *A* is wrong because alternatives to smoking are not addressed in the passage. Choice *C* is wrong because it does not summarize the passage but rather is just a premise. Choice *D* is wrong because, while these statistics are a premise in the argument, they do not represent a summary of the piece. Choice *B* is the correct answer because it states the three critiques offered against tobacco and expresses the author's conclusion.

119. C: We are looking for something the author would agree with, so it should be anti-smoking or an argument in favor of quitting smoking. Choice *A* is wrong because the author does not speak against means of cessation. Choice *B* is wrong because the author does not reference other substances but does speak of how addictive nicotine, a drug in tobacco, is. Choice *D* is wrong because the author would not encourage reducing taxes to encourage a reduction of smoking costs, thereby helping smokers to continue the habit. Choice *C* is correct because the author is attempting to persuade smokers to quit smoking.

120. D: Here, we are looking for an opinion of the author's rather than a fact or statistic. Choice *A* is wrong because quoting statistics from the Centers of Disease Control and Prevention is stating facts, not opinions. Choice *B* is wrong because it expresses the fact that cigarettes sometimes cost more than a few gallons of gas. It would be an opinion if the author said that cigarettes were not affordable. Choice *C* is incorrect because yellow stains are a known possible adverse effect of smoking. Choice *D* is correct as an opinion because smell is subjective. Some people might like the smell of smoke, they might not have working olfactory senses, and/or some people might not find the smell of smoke akin to "pervasive nastiness," so this is the expression of an opinion. Thus, Choice *D* is the correct answer.

Dear FTCE General Knowledge Test Taker,

We would like to start by thanking you for purchasing this study guide for your FTCE General Knowledge exam. We hope that we exceeded your expectations.

Our goal in creating this study guide was to cover all of the topics that you will see on the test. We also strove to make our practice questions as similar as possible to what you will encounter on test day. With that being said, if you found something that you feel was not up to your standards, please send us an email and let us know.

We would also like to let you know about another book in our catalog that may interest you.

FTCE Elementary Education

This can be found on Amazon: amazon.com/dp/1628457074

FTCE Reading

amazon.com/dp/1637757131

We have study guides in a wide variety of fields. If the one you are looking for isn't listed above, then try searching for it on Amazon or send us an email.

Thanks Again and Happy Testing!
Product Development Team
info@studyguideteam.com

FREE Test Taking Tips Video/DVD Offer

To better serve you, we created videos covering test taking tips that we want to give you for FREE. **These videos cover world-class tips that will help you succeed on your test.**

We just ask that you send us feedback about this product. Please let us know what you thought about it—whether good, bad, or indifferent.

To get your **FREE videos**, you can use the QR code below or email freevideos@studyguideteam.com with "Free Videos" in the subject line and the following information in the body of the email:

   a. The title of your product

   b. Your product rating on a scale of 1-5, with 5 being the highest

   c. Your feedback about the product

If you have any questions or concerns, please don't hesitate to contact us at info@studyguideteam.com.

Thank you!

Made in United States
Orlando, FL
23 September 2024

51892830R00143